6019

**Power Without
Responsibility**

POWER WITHOUT
RESPONSIBILITY

How Congress Abuses the
People Through Delegation

David Schoenbrod

Yale University Press
New Haven and London

Published with assistance from the Louis Stern
Memorial Fund.

Designed by James J. Johnson.
Set in Aster Roman type by Marathon Typography
Service, Durham, North Carolina.
Printed in the United States of America by Edwards
Brothers, Inc., Ann Arbor, Michigan.

Library of Congress Cataloging-in-Publication Data

Schoenbrod, David.
    Power without responsibility : how Congress
abuses the people through delegation / David
Schoenbrod.
        p.   cm.
    Includes bibliographical references and index.
    ISBN 0-300-05363-0
    1. Delegated legislation—United States.
2. Administrative procedure—United States.
3. United States. Congress—Powers and duties.
I. Title.
KF5411.S36   1993
342.73′066—dc20
[347.30266]   93-13260

A catalogue record for this book is available from
the British Library.

10 9 8 7 6 5 4 3 2 1

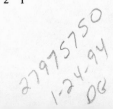

To Frank Campbell
Kind teacher, kind friend

Contents

10. The Constitution Prohibits
    Delegation   155

11. Why the Courts Should Stop
    Delegation (and Nobody Else
    Can)   165

12. How the Courts Should Define
    Unconstitutional Delegation   180

Part VI   **Conclusion**

13. America Is No Exception   195

    Notes   199
    Index   256

Preface

I have come to believe that Congress
and the president, rather than the unelected officials in the federal agencies,
should make the laws—that is, the rules
that govern us.

Opposition to delegation of the power
to make law is generally assumed to
reflect insensitivity to the public's need
for protection. This is because the last
dispute in which delegation was at the
center stage of national politics pitted a
"conservative" Supreme Court against a
"liberal" president (Franklin Roosevelt)
and because the pervasive use of delegation since then makes regulation without delegation seem impossible. However,
my own opposition to delegation grows
out of my previous efforts to make regulation work, and my proposal would produce regulation that is more effective yet
less burdensome. As a student during the
1960s, I spent my summers working for
that perfect apostle of the New Deal,
Hubert Humphrey, and aspired someday
to sit in Congress or run an agency that,
in the New Deal mold, would make laws.
By the 1970s, like much of my generation, I had come to distrust agencies, and
served as one of the leaders of the Natural Resources Defense Council, a nonprofit corporation that pressured agencies to make laws that would fulfill the
promises of environmental statutes. That
experience made me see statutes that del-

egate as a way for politicians to play to the grandstand rather than to make the hard choices needed to protect the public. It started me wondering whether the public really benefits from delegation. Seeking an answer to that question, I became a legal scholar.

I now believe that delegation has produced a regulatory system so cumbersome that it cannot provide the protection that people do need, so large that it needlessly stifles the economy, and so complex that it keeps voters from knowing whom to hold accountable for the consequences. I will show how regulation without delegation can work.

Opposition to delegation also generally is assumed to reflect a belief that the legislative branch of government is more trustworthy than the executive. But my opposition to delegation stems from distrust of both legislative and executive officials. Precisely because of this distrust I want legislators and the president to make law only by taking publicly recorded positions, as they must when they enact or sign statutes, rather than by pressuring agencies in private, as they do after they delegate.

Acknowledgments

Because this book draws upon diverse disciplines and occupational experiences and treads upon the divisions between diverse ideologies, I sought the help of a similarly diverse and accordingly large group of people. Albert K. Butzel, John Hart Ely, Samuel Estreicher, Morris P. Fiorina, Stanley Gilbert, Michael S. Greve, Allen S. Hammond IV, Alon Harel, Oliver A. Houck, John P. Keith, William P. La Piana, Jethro K. Lieberman, Alan Loeb, William T. Mayton, Henry P. Monaghan, James A. Moody, Michael J. Perry, Edward A. Purcell, Jr., Victor G. Rosenblum, Ross Sandler, Jan F. Selby, Gene R. Shreve, Michael B. W. Sinclair, Nadine Strossen, and Harry H. Wellington read all or part of the evolving manuscript. From all, I got thoughtful suggestions as well as moral support. From some, I also got disagreement, but that too proved valuable by sharpening my focus on the points of contention. Some of these readers, together with Robert H. Bork, James F. Simon, and G. Edward White, helped launch this book by suggesting improvements in my proposal to publishers and foundations. I also got valuable feedback from making presentations to the law faculties at the University of Indiana–Bloomington, New York Law School, and Tulane University. James A. Moody graciously provided massive quantities of documents and information on the navel orange marketing order. Since this book builds upon the articles that I published over the years in various scholarly journals, my debt to those who helped me with them, and particularly to William E. Nelson, continues. Most of all, I was blessed to have for the entirety of this project a research assistant as astute, reflective, and thorough as Deborah Paulus, New York Law School class of 1993.

Yale University Press gave me not only a book contract but also the sagacious support of editors John S. Covell and Cynthia Wells. New York Law School, the Carthage Foundation and the Smith-Richardson Foundation jointly provided eighteen months of financial support that allowed me to devote full time to this book. Without that freedom from distractions, writing a book of this scope would have been a protracted agony rather than the joy that it was. Cheryl Keller and Richard Larry of the foundations' staffs gave me sound advice, as well as encouragement. William R. Mills and other members of the library staff at New York Law School guided me to a wide variety of sources. Kitty Montañez-Reyes, Dorthea Perry, Lisa M. Primus, and other administrative staff at the law school lightened my burden at important points. James T. McClymonds, New York Law School class of 1993, significantly eased the final manuscript preparation.

My thanks to each of you.

Introduction

PART I

The Nub of the Argument

As a good government is an empire of laws, the first question is, how shall the laws be made?

—JOHN ADAMS, 1776

We the People of the United States . . . do ordain and establish this Constitution of the United States.

ARTICLE I

Section 1. All legislative Powers herein granted shall be vested in a Congress . . .

—*Constitution of the United States*, 1787

THE FIRST ARTICLE OF THE CONSTITUTION answers John Adams' "first question" by empowering Congress, acting subject to the president's veto power, to make law by enacting statutes. For at least the first two-thirds of the Supreme Court's history, it said that Article I bars Congress and the president from handing on to others their power to make law. But in the late 1930s the Court adopted a new understanding of the Constitution that permits Congress and the president to enact statutes that broadly empower federal agencies or departments to issue regulations and other decrees that state the law. Congress and the president now delegate lawmaking power wholesale.[1] When the lawmakers we elect have others make the law, the people lose.

CHAPTER 1

The People Lose Oranges

The works of the roots of the vines, of the trees, must be destroyed to keep up the price, and this is the saddest, bitterest thing of all. Carloads of oranges dumped on the ground. The people came for miles to take the fruit, but this could not be. How would they buy oranges at twenty cents a dozen if they could drive out and pick them up? And men with hoses squirt kerosene on the oranges, and they are angry at the crime, angry at the people who have come to take the fruit.

—JOHN STEINBECK, *The Grapes of Wrath*, 1939

Along the "Famoso Drag Strip," oranges are piled in hillocks more than eight feet high, expanses of bright, round fruit stamped with the Sunkist label and left to rot in the sun. Rivers of orange juice wind off the pavement and soak into the soil. The smell is alternatively sweet and putrid at the site of this tremendous orange dump made necessary by a raft of regulations governing agriculture.

—DOUG FOSTER, 1981

In 1933 Congress and the president enacted a statute that delegated to the secretary of agriculture the power to make laws, called "agricultural marketing orders," that limit how much each grower of an agricultural product may ship. One such law led to Sunkist's oranges being fed to cattle rather than people. That law illustrates how delegation shields Congress and the president from blame for harming their constituents.[2]

The agricultural marketing order for California and Arizona navel oranges seeks to increase the price we pay for these oranges by restricting the amount that growers may supply. The orange "growers"—many of whom are actually tax-shelter partnerships or other absentee investors—sell their fruit through handlers, who ordinarily pick, pack, and ship the oranges. The order provides that the secretary may limit the total quantity of oranges to be shipped each week for domestic consumption as fresh fruit and shall apportion that total among handlers based upon the relative sizes of their growers' crops. The secretary did so from 1933 to 1992 with brief interruptions. The quotas usually prevented the sale in the domestic fresh fruit market of about one-third of the crop. Some of that fruit was exported. Most, however, was processed for juice and other products, fed to cattle, or left to rot in dumps or orchards. By diverting oranges from the market for fresh fruit, the quotas increased growers' revenues at the expense of consumers because the price in the fresh fruit market is more sensitive to the quantity supplied than is the price in the processing market.[3]

But the quotas *did not* increase the long-term profits of most orange growers. Restricting the supply of California and Arizona navel oranges could work to increase their price only so much because consumers could buy oranges from Florida and Texas growers, who have successfully avoided marketing orders that limit their sales, or could switch to other sorts of fruit. A more important reason is that higher orange prices induced some California and Arizona growers to plant more orange trees. As the orange harvest increased, the quotas had to divert a larger share away from the fresh fruit market to keep prices from falling. So both growers who increased production and those who did not had to either sell more of their crop for processing or let it rot. The increase in the supply delivered for processing drove the price down so far that growers often were paid *less* than the cost to them of having the fruit picked, without any compensation for the cost of growing it. According to the Department of Justice, "operating a losing business (navel oranges for processing) [had] become the price of admission for entering the business of selling fresh navel oranges," and the marketing order "[did] not increase long-run grower returns." In other words, the extra money that the order extracted from consumers did not go into the growers' pockets but instead was wasted on producing extra, unwanted oranges. Nonetheless, just as the quotas had increased profits at first, abandoning them might at first cut growers' profits, until lower prices lead to a decrease in production. Fearing such an effect, growers of most crops do not want and do not have marketing orders that limit supply.[4]

While the growers might have suffered temporary losses had the quotas been eliminated, with the order in force consumers suffered losses that were "perennial and increasing." Back in 1940, Sunkist's president had warned citrus growers that, without quotas, only those who produced "the best quality fruit" at "the lowest cost" would thrive. As it happened, consumers paid a higher price for fewer oranges of worse quality under the marketing order. Some of the oranges taken off our plates were used for purposes of much less value to us; others were exported at prices domestic consumers subsidized. Meanwhile, the reduced supply of domestic fruit led to increased fruit imports. Consumers got worse fruit because growers were prevented from selling oranges at their peak and because the artificially inflated price growers received for a part of their crop reduced their incentive to improve quality.[5]

Sunkist, the dominant marketer and processor of California and Arizona citrus fruit, was the chief beneficiary of the quotas and has fought hard to retain them. Although structured as a growers' cooperative (Sunkist Growers, Inc.), Sunkist resembles a Fortune 500 corporation more than a grange group. Sunkist not only markets the fruit packed for its members by handlers affiliated with it, but also manufactures orange juice and hundreds of other citrus products. Sales through thirty-one offices in the United States and Canada and four overseas subsidiaries totalled $956 million in 1991. It is, in its own words, "the largest fresh produce shipper in the United States," "the most diversified citrus processing and marketing operation in the world," and "among the largest landowners in California."[6]

Benefits to Sunkist, it should be noted, are not tantamount to benefits to all orange growers. Sunkist's management, like that of a for-profit corporation with many stockholders, has considerable power to put its own interests ahead of those of its many grower-members. Sunkist's glossy annual reports disclose nothing to its members about how much top management is paid individually or collectively. Also, almost half the growers have opted out of Sunkist membership.[7]

Sunkist gains from the quotas in many ways. First, without them, it stands to lose members and affiliated handlers. With them, however, Sunkist controls the sales even of the growers and handlers who refuse to sell through it because Sunkist dominates the administration of the order, as will be discussed in Chapter 3. Second, Sunkist can buy the oranges needed to supply its processing plants for far less than the cost of growing them. Third, the quotas give a competitive advantage to Sunkist and some of the larger unaffiliated handlers that ally themselves with Sunkist in the order's administration. The weekly quotas imposed on all handlers are set to accommodate Sunkist's own sales plans. The quotas also impose extra production costs on the smaller, unaffiliated handlers that compete with Sunkist. Finally, some independent handlers and growers believe that Sunkist, through its influence over the order's enforcement, lets its affiliated handlers violate the quotas.[8]

Sunkist and the Department of Agriculture have argued that the quotas benefit everyone, but their arguments have attracted scant independent support in recent decades. (I respond to the merits of their arguments later.) According to a 1981 study by economists in the Department of Agriculture itself, "consumers are taxed more than producers are subsidized." Important segments within the orange industry oppose the quotas. These include most of the independent handlers. They account for almost half the crop. In addition, important elements within Sunkist's own membership oppose the quotas. Since the early 1970s, the orange quotas have been opposed actively by such powerful governmental bodies as the Department of Justice, President Reagan's Council of Economic Advisors, the Small Business Administration, the Federal Trade Commission, the Office of Management and Budget, President Ford's Cost of Living Council, and President Bush's Council on Competitiveness. The quotas have been criticized in scathing editorials in the *New York Times*, the *Wall Street Journal*, and the leading California newspapers and has been attacked by the Consumers Union, Public Voice for Food and Health Policy, and various libertarian groups. The secretary of agriculture suspended the quotas in February 1992, after opposition to the order increased within the orange industry, but reinstated them in October 1992. He again suspended the quotas in December 1992, simultaneously observing that he retained the power under the marketing order to reinstate them again. At Sunkist's behest, a judge temporarily enjoined the suspension. He then refused to continue the injunction, observing that information that had to be given to the court was "hidden from me by plaintiffs" and added, "I have never had such a blatantly clear suggestion to the court that wasn't in accordance with the record." Meanwhile, legislators likely to have influence with the Clinton administration, such as Senators-elect Dianne Feinstein and Barbara Boxer of California and Senator Patrick Leahy urged the Department of Agriculture to keep the quotas in place. Additional marketing orders continue to restrict the supplies of nectarines, milk, and other foods at a reported cost to a four-person family of $500 per year.[9]

The question is, how did Sunkist get a democratically elected government to keep in force for so long a law that seemed to benefit so few at the expense of so many? Part of the reason is that the benefits conferred by the orange quotas were concentrated largely on one body, Sunkist, while the costs imposed were diffused among consumers and the many small companies in the citrus industry. Everyone harmed by the quotas had a stake much smaller than Sunkist's; Sunkist's preeminent interest warranted its devoting money and energy to make powerful political connections in Congress and the White House. Like many large corporations, Sunkist employs Washington counsel with close connections to influential legislators. Sunkist also employs lobbyists. Its former lobbyist, James Lake, alternated work for Sunkist with stints as press secretary for the 1980 Reagan election campaign, communications director and press secretary for the 1984 Reagan reelection campaign, and communications advisor for the 1988 Bush campaign. Lake was described by House Democratic Whip Tony L. Coelho of California as "one of my closest personal friends." The Sunkist political action committee—although far smaller than the political action committees of various corporations, unions, and other agricultural interests—makes substantial contributions to an ideologically diverse array of candidates from both parties. Sunkist's chairman, Ralph Bodine, gave more than $100,000 to the Republican National Committee in 1988, plus $51,300 to the Democratic Party. Still, Sunkist's political action committee generally gave no more than $5,000 a year to any one legislator, which is hardly enough, even when supplemented by gifts through other channels, to get a legislator to take a politically risky action.[10]

Delegation helps to explain how Sunkist got its way. With delegation, Sunkist could get the law it wanted without legislators or the president having to do anything that would provide effective ammunition to a political opponent. The statute that delegates to the secretary the power to issue marketing orders lets the secretary decide whether to limit supplies of any particular crop from any particular growing region and, if so, by how much. In making those decisions, the secretary must seek to maintain "orderly" markets, increase farmers' income, prevent unreasonable price increases for consumers, and protect the public interest.[11] Delegation allows our elected lawmakers to disclaim any responsibility for harm done to consumers for three reasons: because the wording of the statute reflects concern for consumers, because the statute took its present form long before the current legislators took office, and because the secretary in effect makes the law. The public is unlikely to know of the marketing order's existence, as it comes from deep within the bowels of the bureaucracy rather than from Congress. In contrast, for Sunkist to see enacted a law that restricts competition without using delegation, legislators would have to vote for and the president would have to sign a statute that limits the supply of navel oranges to consumers. They would need to amend the statute frequently to take account of changing market and crop conditions. Our elected lawmakers could not deny direct responsibility for raising the price of oranges. They conceivably might still enact such a statute, but they would have to risk political vulnerability.

With delegation, the elected lawmakers who receive contributions from Sunkist work actively on its behalf, but they do so behind the scenes, in ways that Chapter 3 will detail, rather than by casting votes on the floor of Congress or by signing bills. So they still make law, but not in the publicly accountable way that the Constitution contemplated.

Delegation, Like Budget Deficits, Hides Costs

Delegation can shield our elected lawmakers from blame for harming the public not only when a regulatory program, such as the navel orange marketing order, serves no legitimate public purpose, but also when a regulatory program should serve an important public purpose. Then the consequences of delegation for the public can be even greater because lawmakers can use delegation to escape blame both for failing to achieve that purpose and for imposing unnecessary costs.

Understanding how such pervasive consequences flow from a seemingly technical change in the lawmaking process requires defining the fine but fundamental difference between a statute that makes law and one that delegates. According to the *Oxford English Dictionary*, a law is "a rule of conduct imposed by authority"; therefore, a statute makes law when it states a rule of conduct. For example, a statute that prohibits power plants from emitting pollution above a certain rate or that prohibits orange growers from shipping more than a certain proportion of their crop makes law, because the statute itself defines what conduct is illegal. In contrast, a statute delegates when it empowers an agency to state the rules governing such emissions or shipments, even if the statute instructs the agency in some detail about what goals to achieve or what procedures to follow in making the rules.

Even though all statutory laws require some interpretation,[12] statutes that state laws differ in a critical way from statutes that delegate. In making laws, Congress has to allocate both rights and duties in the very course of stating what conduct it prohibits, and so must make manifest the benefits and costs of regulation. When Congress delegates, it tends to do only half its job—to distribute rights without imposing the commensurate duties. So it promises clean air without restricting polluters and higher incomes for farmers without increasing the price of groceries. In striking poses popular to each and every constituency, Congress ducks the key conflicts. Those conflicts, however, will inevitably surface when the agency tries to translate the popular abstractions of the statutory goals—such as "clean" air or "orderly" agricultural markets—into rules of conduct.

Congress and the president delegate for much the same reason that they continue to run budget deficits. With deficit spending, they can claim credit for the benefits of their expenditures yet escape blame for the costs. The public must pay ultimately of course, but through taxes levied at some future time by some other officials. The point is not that deficits always have bad economic consequences, but that they have the political consequence of allowing officials to duck responsibility for costs.

Likewise, delegation allows legislators to claim credit for the benefits which a regulatory statute promises yet escape the blame for the burdens it will impose, because they do not issue the laws needed to achieve those benefits. The public inevitably must suffer regulatory burdens to realize regulatory benefits, but the laws will come from an agency that legislators can then criticize for imposing excessive burdens on their constituents. Just as deficit spending allows legislators to appear to deliver money to some people without taking it from others, delegation allows them to appear to deliver regulatory benefits without imposing regulatory costs. It provides "a handy set of mirrors—so useful in Washington—by which a politician can appear to kiss both sides of the apple."[13]

Politicians understand that delegation helps them to avoid blame. For example, in 1988 legislators used delegation to try to give themselves a 50-percent pay raise without losing votes in the next election. They enacted a statute that delegated to a commission the power to set pay for themselves and other top officials whose pay they linked to their own. Under the statute, if the commission grants a pay increase, another statute passed before (but not after) the increase goes into effect could cancel it.[14] When the commission recommended the 50-percent increase, some legislators introduced bills to cancel it. But that action was part of a plan in which the congressional leadership would prevent a vote on the bills until it was too late to stop the increase. Legislators could then tell their constituents that they would have voted against the increase if given a chance. Thus they could get the pay raise and also credit for opposing it. However, the size of the increase, in an atmosphere of antipathy to Congress, provoked such a storm of protest and publicity that the public came to see through the charade. Embarrassed, the House leadership conducted a secret ballot among members to determine whether to hold a roll-call vote on the pay increase. Fifty-seven percent of the members who responded opposed a roll call, although 95 percent of the House members surveyed by the Public Citizen group claimed that they had supported it. After public opposition to the pay increase rose to an extraordinary 88 percent, Congress passed a bill to cancel it.

The pay raise controversy illustrates the willingness of Congress to use delegation to manipulate voters' perceptions of its activities. In this instance the manipulation failed—indeed backfired—because the public came to see it for what it was. Yet such manipulation is usually successful because routine government action is neither so readily understood nor so pregnant with symbolic value as the pay raise was, and so eludes the sustained attention of the press and the public.

So far, I have suggested that delegation as well as budget deficits help lawmakers escape blame for the direct costs of federal regulation, such as the higher grocery prices caused by marketing orders. Both budget deficits and delegation also impose important indirect costs on the public. Budget deficits require interest payments on the new debt, increase inflation, and raise interest rates. Delegation has indirect costs of even greater consequence, as illustrated by the environmental statutes that I tried to make work in my own career.

In those statutes, Congress and the president generally did not resolve the key conflicts between business and environmental groups but instead promised to satisfy each side and instructed the Environmental Protection Agency (EPA) to make the laws accordingly. Subsequently, when EPA attempted to issue a law that industry did not like, legislators—sometimes even those who took the strongest environmental positions on the floor of Congress—would tell EPA to back off. And, on the other hand, should EPA fail to satisfy environmentalists, legislators—sometimes even those with close ties to industry—would strike environmentalist poses. To camouflage the statute's lack of substance, our elected lawmakers had included all the decisions on procedures that any constituent might want—for example, the agency shall issue a law to protect the public from pollutant x by deadline y, but not before preparing an analysis of the impact on industry z— although they knew that the agency could never come close to discharging these duties with the time, resources, and political power given to it.[15]

This experience, which I detail in a later chapter, illustrates the profound indirect costs of delegation:

- It undercuts the government's capacity to resolve disputes through compromise by allowing the only officials with authoritative power to impose compromises to instead claim to be all things to all interests.
- It allows disputes to be prolonged and keeps standards of conduct murky, because pressure from legislators and the complicated procedures imposed upon agencies turn lawmaking into an excruciatingly slow process. Agencies typically report that they have issued only a small fraction of the laws that their longstanding statutory mandates require.[16] Competing interests devote large sums of money and many of their best minds to this seemingly interminable process. Meanwhile, those potentially subject to regulation have no reliable way to plan their activities, as they do not know what the law eventually will be. The public is unprotected during these struggles: a statute that delegates provides no law until an agency makes one.

In the very act of allowing our elected lawmakers to shape laws that make themselves look like heroes, delegation renders them less responsible to the people and less responsive to their interests.

The Case for Delegation

Many people think, as I once did, that delegation is necessary and desirable.[17] Defenders of delegation argue that it is consistent with democracy: elected lawmakers make the fundamental policy choices when they delegate and then can supervise the agencies making law and repeal undesirable laws. They also maintain that delegation produces more sensible laws by transferring lawmaking from elected officials, who are beholden to concentrated interests, to experts, who can base their decisions solely upon a cool appraisal of the public interest. Even if agencies are subject to political pressures, defenders continue, agency procedures require their officials to consider the arguments of all interests, and their laws are subject to judicial review. Statutes that delegate, these writers observe, often give agencies irrational instructions, which suggests that laws made without delegation would similarly be irrational. Defenders of delegation also argue that Congress and the president lack the time to undertake the great quantity of work that agencies do. Moreover, our government's reliance on delegation has grown so much over the past sixty years that ending delegation now is impossible.

Why We Should Reconsider Delegation

The United States embraced delegation during the Great Depression, the direst peacetime emergency in our history. In those desperate times, many Americans believed the New Deal proponents of delegation who promised that transferring power from Congress to agencies would truly produce a less political and more helpful sort of government, one not dominated by concentrated interests. But, as the Sunkist story suggests and later chapters will show, the promise is unfulfilled. Agency heads are usually not apolitical and, indeed, concentrated interests often prevail more easily in an agency than they can in Congress. Effective participation in agency lawmaking usually requires expensive legal representation as well as close connections to members of Congress who will pressure the agency on one's behalf. The agency itself is often closely linked with the industry it regulates. Not only large corporations, but also labor unions, cause-based groups, and other cohesive minority interests sometimes can use delegation to triumph over the interests of the larger part of the general public, which lacks the organization, finances, and know-how to participate as effectively in the administrative process.

The failure of delegation to make government work as its New Deal supporters hoped did not become apparent until long after the delegation debate had exited from political center stage. The Great Depression, World War II, and the Korean War had sustained a sense of emergency that made reforms that might reduce the efficacy of federal agencies unthinkable. By the 1970s, when scholars began to understand more clearly how delegation really works, it was already so deeply embedded in the structure of government that it seemed like part of the landscape. Stopping delegation at that point would have produced the most dramatic change in government since the Civil War, and reliance upon it has increased markedly since then. And, although scholars of law, political science, and other disciplines have now produced a huge literature describing how lawmaking really works in agencies and in Congress, they generally have not used this information to rethink whether Congress should delegate. Delegation has become an assumption rather than a choice.[18]

Why should we end, or at least severely curtail, delegation? Because delegation undercuts democracy, undoes the Constitution's most comprehensive protection of liberty, and ultimately makes government less effective in achieving the popular purposes of regulatory statutes.

Democracy

We can refuse to reelect legislators who make laws we dislike. Delegation shortcircuits this democratic option by allowing our elected lawmakers to hide behind unelected agency officials.

When this concern was raised in the 1940s, the Supreme Court wrongly dismissed it with the argument that Congress and the president still are responsible for the laws made under delegation because they specify the fundamental policy choices in statutes and leave to the agencies only the more technical questions appropriate for resolution by experts.[19] This argument assumes that Congress and the president make the hard choices, but in fact, as I have argued, they often delegate precisely in order to avoid the hard choices. The Supreme Court also relies upon the power of Congress to repeal agency laws, but that capacity does little to soften the blow delegation inflicts against democratic accountability. Legislators usually hold no vote on whether to let an agency law stand, so they need offend neither those constituents who support nor those who oppose the law in question. Yet they can actively please both groups by doing casework on their behalf; casework, unlike roll-call voting, is not of public record.

Delegation thus allows members of Congress to function as ministers rather than legislators; they express popular aspirations and tend to their flocks rather than make hard choices. With delegation members can escape being ejected from office except upon grounds that would oust a minister from the pulpit—scandal. In those exceptional cases when incumbent legislators do lose elections, their defeat is far more likely to be caused by some escapade or chicanery than by how they shaped the law.[20]

Liberty

Liberty means, according to those who wrote the Constitution, the right to be left alone except when government must intervene for a public purpose. Liberty is infringed when government uses its coercive power for a private as opposed to a public purpose. The Framers understood, however, that no readily applicable principle distinguishes a private from a public purpose. Therefore, instead of writing into the Constitution a direct prohibition of regulation for private purposes, they sought to discourage such regulation by making it difficult to enact laws that lacked broad public support. To this end, they required that, to become law, bills receive a majority in the House and Senate and approval by the president or, should the president veto a bill, two-thirds majorities in the House and Senate. Modern analysis shows that there was something to the Framers' theory: the differing constituencies and terms of office of the two houses of Congress and the president mean that broader support is needed to get a bill through Congress than through a unicameral legislature.

To illustrate how delegation jeopardizes liberty, consider that delegation was essential to obtain the law prohibiting federally funded family planning organizations from discussing abortion with their clients. In 1970 Congress delegated to the secretary of health and human services broad authority to make laws governing such organizations. The agency laws adopted shortly thereafter forbade the use of federal funds to pay for abortions but not to support organizations that gave advice about abortion. "Pro-life" forces lobbied the Reagan administration to amend the laws to forbid discussion of abortion, which it did in its waning days, almost twenty years after the statute was enacted.[21]

"Pro-choice" groups argued to the Supreme Court that the amended law violated their constitutional rights to free speech and privacy, but secured the votes of only three justices.[22] As the case suggests, the constitutional rights enumerated in the Bill of Rights limit governmental power only in quite specialized ways. Indeed, even in periods when liberal Democrats have appointed most of the federal judges, courts have held only infrequently that federal laws violated the Bill of Rights. Because the Bill of Rights often is not applicable or is not applied to laws that nevertheless jeopardize liberty, the legislative process established by the Constitution plays a vital role in defending liberty.

Delegation negates that defense. If Congress had not delegated the power to make abortion laws, the pro-life groups would have had to convince majorities in the House and Senate, as well as the Reagan administration, to amend the laws. The absence of demonstrated majority support in the legislature was irrelevant, the Supreme Court decided; the secretary had authority to prohibit abortion counseling because the relevant statute did not *prohibit* him from doing so. On this argument, since Congress had delegated its authority back in 1970, the only way for the pro-choice forces to block a law against abortion counseling was to amend the delegating statute. At that point, however, they would have encountered the procedural obstacles to enacting statutes that the Constitution uses to protect liberty. Pro-choice groups could not have mustered the supermajorities needed to overcome a presidential veto, although pro-life groups could not have gotten majorities behind their position in the House and Senate.[23] Delegation made all the difference. Delegation thus turns on its head the protection of liberty built into the legislative process.

Delegation negates the protection of liberty afforded by the legislative process not just in the case of abortion counseling but throughout the entire gamut of federal regulation, as the constraints placed on Sunkist's competitors illustrate.

Protection of the Public

The public needs protection from a wide variety of evils, and Congress cannot make all the necessary decisions, but Congress would not have to assume *judicial* or *executive* power to stop delegating *legislative* power. Congress would have to take back one kind of agency function: making the law—that is, the rules of private conduct. It would not have to make rules concerning, for instance, the management of the budget and other public property or the exercise of the powers granted the president in Article II of the Constitution. It would not have to take over such agency functions as making decisions about the *enforcement* of the rules of private conduct (for example, interpreting the laws, exercising prosecutorial discretion), organizing agency operations (for example, assigning tasks to the staff), running the agency (for example, hiring employees, buying equipment), and making recommendations to Congress (for example, proposing changes in laws).

The one thing Congress could not do is delegate the power to enact the law. Elected officials would have to take that responsibility. And even then, Congress could call upon agencies to draft proposed laws. Indeed, the New Deal's leading theoretician of the administrative process, James Landis, concluded that agencies would have a better chance of breaking the stalemates that often prevent them from protecting the public if they could act as "the technical agent in the initiation of rules of conduct, yet at the same time . . . have [the elected lawmakers] share in the responsibility for their adoption."[24]

My definition of delegation distinguishes statutes that require law-making from those that require interpretation of the law (a distinction elaborated in Chapter 12). A statute that says "Do not emit more than x pounds of pollutant y" does not delegate, because it lays down a rule. However, a statute that says "Do not emit unreasonable amounts of pollution" does delegate, unless somehow our customs give the word *unreasonable* a clear meaning in this context.

Legislated laws could be quite general. For example, one section of the 1990 Clean Air Act tells EPA to base emissions limitations for many categories of sources on the levels achieved by the cleanest 12 percent of the plants in each category.[25] Through this general formula, Congress established a rule of conduct applicable to many pollutants from many kinds of sources by stating the criterion separating permissible and impermissible conduct.

On the other hand, legislated laws need not be as seemingly mechanistic as a numerical limit on pollution. Title VII, for example, prohibits employment decisions based upon race, color, religion, sex, or national origin except when based upon bona fide occupational qualifications. This provision has required extensive interpretation and these interpretations are subject to debate.[26] Nonetheless, concepts such as *discrimination* (in the sense of equality of opportunity) and *bona fide occupational qualification*, unlike terms such as *public interest*, need not be interpreted as a general invitation for courts or the Equal Employment Opportunity Commission to make policy. Such a statute presents hard cases but makes many more cases easy.

Enacting laws, even laws that present difficult issues of interpretation, forces legislators to take political responsibility for imposing regulatory costs and benefits. In contrast, delegation allows Congress to stay silent about what the agency will prohibit, so it severs the link between the legislator's vote and the law, upon which depend both democratic accountability and the safeguards of liberty provided by Article I.

Congress can make sufficient time to enact the laws needed to protect the public. Legislators now spend more time soliciting campaign contributions and campaigning for reelection than legislating. When they do legislate, they often decide at great length technical issues which they properly could leave to other branches of government (the micromanagement in the annual budget is one example), yet they delegate important questions of broad policy.

Nor would protecting the public require Congress to enact a body of laws as massive and complex as that which the present federal regulatory apparatus cranks out. Academic experts from across a broad ideological spectrum believe that Congress would have served the public better by relying, in various instances, on the marketplace, the states, or some relatively simple forms of federal intervention rather than on the detailed laws that it requires agencies to issue. For example, instead of regulating the energy efficiency of appliances, as it now does, the federal government could rely upon consumers' own interest in choosing products that are energy efficient and less expensive to operate. The government could continue to require manufacturers to supply the information consumers need about the energy efficiency of competing products. If the reason for regulation is that the price that consumers now pay for energy fails to reflect the environmental costs of energy use, the federal government could tax energy use.

The current choice of direct, complicated regulation is bad for the people. Manufacturers know better than regulators which products most readily can be made more energy efficient, and consumers know better than regulators how much energy efficiency is worth to them. For example, a consumer who plans to use an air conditioner only a few days a year might prefer to avoid the higher initial cost of an efficient model. What is more, promoting energy conservation through regulation creates the risk that large manufacturers can hijack regulatory power for the selfish purpose of imposing costs on smaller competitors, at their expense and that of consumers.[27]

Legislators, however, have a personal stake in preferring complex federal laws promulgated by agencies. Leaving the problem to the market or the states denies them the opportunity to take credit for the solution and to do casework for the regulated interests in return for favors from them. Intervening through a congressionally imposed tax would require them to take the blame for the cost of the solution.[28] Most consumers do not understand that the present approach increases product prices.

Congress continues to enlarge the power of federal agencies, given that it is the agencies rather than the lawmakers that receive the primary blame for the direct and indirect costs of regulation. Delegation thus broadens the federal government's regulatory jurisdiction over our lives, even while it reduces government's capacity both to protect us from the harms about which we care the most and to effect compromises and therefore resolve disputes about what the law should be.

The Importance of Delegation in Perspective

Many problems other than delegation plague the governance of our nation. These problems include voter apathy, the tendency of many interest groups to insist parochially on what they see as their rights rather than to seek compromise,[29] the power of concentrated interests, the ineffectuality of laws aimed at preventing campaign contributions from functioning as bribes, stalemates about policy choices, the willingness of members of Congress to mortgage the future by incurring massive budget deficits, the creation of equally massive unfunded federal insurance liabilities, and the neglect of our publicly owned infrastructure and its consequent deterioration. Veteran observers of the political scene also note that controversies now get settled less often through electoral choices than by "revelation, investigation, and prosecution," while elections often are about false ideological choices.[30]

Some of these problems are so deeply rooted in human nature that they cannot be eliminated; the elimination of others would require reforms quite different from ending delegation. Still, delegation exacerbates most of these problems: It helps to shield elected lawmakers from blame for harming the public at the behest of the interests that have given them campaign contributions. Because by means of delegation politicians promise every interest group that it will get its way, groups are encouraged to insist on what they then see as their "rights" rather than to compromise. Meanwhile, responsibility for resolving the dispute has been shifted onto an agency, which often has less real power to impose a solution than Congress does. Instead of taking positions on real disputes, legislators are free to talk about "values" and "goals," which helps to explain why elections revolve around false ideological choices. The inevitable failure of agencies to deliver all that Congress has promised also helps set the stage for "revelation, investigation, prosecution."[31]

I also believe that delegation contributes to voter apathy. The most important reason for voters to pay attention to public affairs and to vote is not self-interest—because any one vote hardly ever makes a difference—but the civic duty that we all owe to each other to keep tabs on the officials upon whom we have conferred power. The satisfaction that fulfilling our civic duty should confer turns into depression when those officials elude our control. According to contemporary surveys, many citizens "[believe that] the present political system [is] impervious to public direction" and "do not believe that they are living in a democracy."[32] Delegation helps to explain why so many people feel this way. Undelegated lawmaking requires our elected representatives to stand up and be counted, sometimes in dramatic confrontations. With delegation, lawmaking even on the most controversial subjects becomes, for most of us, an incomprehensible bore. And, by allowing lawmakers to give us ideological self-portraits rather than hard information on where they are prepared to stand, delegation helps them fool us and allows them to mortgage the nation's future to prolong their own time in power.

Who Should Decide Whether to Delegate?

Congress and the president are unlikely to stop or reduce delegation of their own accord. Like deficit spending, delegation is a course of least political resistance.

It is the Supreme Court that should take the lead in bringing delegation to an end. Although the Constitution does not prohibit deficit spending, it does prohibit the delegation of legislative power. Yet, since the New Deal, the Court has left the decision of whether to delegate largely up to Congress and the president, in part out of a belief that legislators' concern for their own power will keep Congress from delegating too much. This belief is simplistic. Legislators enhance their power by delegating: they retain the ability to influence events by pressuring agencies, while they shed responsibility for the exercise of power by avoiding public votes on hard choices.

The Supreme Court should declare unconstitutional all delegation of legislative power or, if the Court thinks that effective government requires some delegation, it should permit only delegation of uncontroversial details. The Court has the means, as I will show, to require a gradual transition away from delegation in a way that is practical and consistent with its judicial role.

Defenders of delegation argue that it is a question of policy that appointed justices should leave to elected officials. But because the Constitution was designed to protect the people from their elected officials, those elected officials should not be trusted with the power to decide when to violate it, particularly when the violation jeopardizes democracy and liberty. Stopping such violations is the Supreme Court's job.

Defenders of delegation advance a series of other arguments for why the Court should let Congress and the president delegate. They claim that the Constitution can be interpreted as allowing delegation. Even if the Constitution was intended to prohibit delegation, they add, subsequent judicial decisions allowing delegation preclude courts in our time from supporting this original meaning. And even if the Constitution can now be interpreted as forbidding delegation, the courts still should not take up the issue because the people can vote lawmakers who delegate out of office and because trying to stop delegation would provoke stiff resistance from Congress and the president. Further, the courts lack a clear test of improper delegation so that, in deciding which statutes to strike down, they would exercise the very legislative power that supposedly cannot be delegated. Each of these arguments gets serious consideration in the final part of the book, but none of them justifies the Supreme Court's allowing delegation.

Although the Supreme Court should take the lead, the people must also play a role. When the Court last frontally challenged delegation, in 1935, President Roosevelt mounted an attack upon it that forced it to back down. The attack succeeded partly because the people were panicked about the Depression, had idealized how agencies would use delegated power, and had lost sight of why the Constitution responded as it did to the question, "How shall the laws be made?" This prime question deserves reconsideration during this era marked more by skepticism about government than panic about the future.

Evolving Ideas of Delegation

PART II

The Vain Search for Virtuous Lawmakers

A LOOK AT AMERICAN HISTORY SHOWS THAT our current methods of making law are neither as natural nor as inevitable as our habitual use of them makes them seem. Each was a product of its time, and what worked in 1787, or 1935, may not work today. The constant factor is that Americans usually have sought lawmaking processes that are democratically accountable, that safeguard liberty, and that allow the government to protect the public effectively. I agree that these are the right goals and will analyze delegation in light of them.

Thanks, probably, to the dramatic confrontation between President Franklin D. Roosevelt and the Supreme Court, we wrongly tend to think of opposition to delegation as peculiar to regulated businesses or, as Justice Thurgood Marshall did, to conservatives such as the Supreme Court justices who sought to block the New Deal. Historically, however, big businesses have often pushed delegation, liberals have often opposed it, and important jurists have believed that delegation is unconstitutional.

In trying to prevent lawmakers from using for their own private advantage the public power with which they are entrusted, Americans have often changed lawmaking and regulative procedures.

Each time, we hoped that lawmaking was entrusted to those who would put the public's interest ahead of their own. Each time, we were disillusioned. Nonetheless we again adopted a new lawmaking method, hoping all over again that it would produce virtuous lawmakers. I proceed on the premise that public officials—whether elected, appointed, or anointed—are unlikely to be more virtuous than the rest of us.

From the King to the Constitution

The yearning for leaders with extraordinary virtue is ancient. Pharaohs, caesars, and kings have claimed to be gods, or to have been given the right to rule by a god, and have explained that their "divine right" to office carried with it a divine duty to rule unselfishly. But, in fact, of course, they often ruled selfishly. In modern times, this led the British, for example, to force their kings to share power, especially the power to regulate and tax. By the time of the American Revolution, the British monarchy had evolved into a parliamentary system in which the nobility represented in the House of Lords and the people represented in the House of Commons took the lead in lawmaking.

The parliamentary system also promised to yield virtuous lawmakers. Members of the houses of Parliament were supposed to represent their entire class throughout the commonwealth, rather than just their own interests or those of their constituents. On this premise Britains believed that the American colonies did not need actual representation in Parliament, as they had "virtual" representation through every member of the House of Commons. The colonists, however, eventually concluded that the king and Parliament had failed to uphold this promise of virtue, thereby violating the colonists' rights as English subjects. They rejected virtual representation and, ultimately, rule from London.[1]

Although they had seen that their former countrymen lacked virtue, the rebels relied upon their own "public virtue" in establishing their first state governments. The state constitutions gave most lawmaking power to legislators who, it was hoped, would "have no interest of their own to seek" but rather would pursue "but one interest, the good of the people at large." But, in addition to advancing their own interests, the legislators also unjustly harmed minorities at the behest of majorities which wanted statutes that, for instance, cancelled debts, debased currency, took property, or restricted unpopular religions and speech.[2]

Such experience forced Americans to see that, like their former colonial rulers, they themselves and those whom they elected might lack virtue. By 1787, James Madison maintained that one could count upon the virtue of only a portion of the population—the group that some termed the "natural aristocracy," by which was meant "an *aristocracy* of experience, and of the best understandings." George Washington, perhaps more realistic, doubted his own capacity for the self-denial motivated solely by brotherly love (virtue) and aspired instead to self-denial motivated by a desire for the respect of others (honor). More pessimistic still was John Adams. Before the Revolution he had believed that "public Virtue is the only Foundation of Republics" and that the war would "inspire Us with many Virtues." Yet by the 1780s Adams came to think that Americans "never merited the Character of very exalted Virtue" and that "we cannot alter the nature of men." A similar rude awakening about human nature made some patriots wonder whether, despite winning a war to free themselves from a king, they should now bend their knees and beg someone to become their king, just as the British had after deposing James II in the Glorious Revolution.[3]

To avoid that fate or worse, the delegates who assembled in 1787 in Philadelphia to draft a new constitution set out to answer three demands. The first was the demand of the people that the national government be made accountable to them. The second was the Federalists' demand for a government better able to meet national needs than that created by the Articles of Confederation, which barely had sufficed to win the Revolutionary War. The third demand, of both the Federalists and the Antifederalists, was that the new constitution protect individual liberty from the people's lack of virtue.[4]

The word *liberty* had shifted in meaning because of the unhappy experience with state governments. Before the Revolution it had meant the people's freedom from oppression by unaccountable leaders, but it came to mean each individual's freedom from oppression by the people themselves. Liberty was now the right to be left alone except when government had to coerce citizens to protect the public interest. If some interest group managed to use government's coercive power for its private ends, liberty would be denied. James Madison defined an interest group—then termed a *faction*—as "a number of citizens, whether amounting to a majority or minority of the whole, who are united and actuated by some common impulse of passion, or of interest, adverse to the rights of other citizens, or to the permanent and aggregate interests of the community."[5]

It is easy to deplore selfishness but hard to define it. As Madison himself acknowledged, people can act selfishly despite good intentions because of the natural tendency to confuse one's own interest with the public interest.[6] Thus an attempt to protect liberty by including a provision in the Constitution forbidding the use of governmental power for selfish purposes would give great power to those charged with applying the provision but would not solve the problem.

The Constitution, as Madison and others explained in *The Federalist Papers*, attempts to reconcile majority rule, an effective national government, and liberty through three strategies. First, the Framers tried to design methods of selecting officials that would place the virtuous few in the White House and Congress, and so filter the passions of the public "through the medium of a chosen body of citizens, whose wisdom may best discern the true interest of their country, and whose patriotism and love of justice, will be least likely to sacrifice it to temporary or partial considerations" (*Federalist* No. 10, at 62). They provided that an electoral college would elect the president and that state legislatures would elect senators. Voters still would choose representatives by direct election, but congressional districts were made large to deter factious candidates. Unfortunately, these selection procedures often failed to produce virtuous leaders, as Madison later seemed to acknowledge. In any event, the Twelfth Amendment to the Constitution, ratified in 1804, curtailed the discretion of the electoral college, and the Seventeenth Amendment, ratified in 1913, put the election of senators directly in the hands of voters.[7]

The second strategy anticipated that, as Madison put it, "enlightened statesmen will not always be at the helm" (*Federalist* No. 10, at 60). The solution was to structure the government to pit interest groups against each other. The nation would include "so many separate descriptions of citizens, as will render an unjust combination of a majority of the whole, very improbable, if not impracticable" (*Federalist* No. 51, at 351 [J. Madison]), and the legislative body would be large enough to ensure that representatives of these diverse interests would be present and tend to neutralize each other.[8] This strategy has a degree of plausibility. The belief that a larger group is more likely to see diverse sides of an issue is probably the genesis of such traditional structures as the jury and the corporate board of directors. Moreover, an interest such as a religious sect bent on imposing its faith on others was more likely to be in the majority at the state rather than the national level. This second measure reduces but does not eliminate the threat to liberty because, as Madison himself acknowledged, minority interests can combine to form a party that pursues an agenda harmful to those outside the party.

The Constitution's third strategy to reconcile democracy with liberty was to allocate power among elected officials in a way that makes it more difficult to use public power to oppress individuals. Article I of the Constitution vests the power to make law in the houses of Congress and the president, Article II vests the power to enforce law in the president, and Article III vests the power to adjudicate in the courts. This separation of powers means that those who enact a given law must worry that it may later be enforced against everyone to whom its terms apply, friend and foe alike.

The Constitution not only *separates* the power to make law from the power to enforce it and judge cases under it but also *shares* the power to make law among the House, the Senate, and the president. Each of the three entities who make the law under Article I controls a separate switch. Each switch must be turned on before a new law can take effect, with the exception that supermajorities of the House and the Senate may legislate after the president vetoes a bill. Article I structures lawmaking in this baroque way, rather than placing it entirely in a unicameral legislature, in order to frustrate special interests, including self-aggrandizing legislators. The House, Senate, and president each represent the people, but they are not clones of each other. Each is elected for different tenures based upon different apportionments of voting power, which means that public support sufficient to produce success in one forum will not necessarily produce success in the others. The Article I legislative process in effect requires a supermajority to legislate. As a result, it would be far harder for an interest group to succeed than in a unicameral legislature, and easier for a minority of lawmakers to block an attempt to hurt their constituents.

This system of separated and shared powers would make it possible, the Framers hoped, "even for bad men to act for the public good." Moreover, in frustrating interest groups, the legislative process would make representation more than a one-way street: the representative not only would tell the central government what local interests want but also would tell local interests why the central government cannot fulfill their every wish. Madison further hoped that conflict would persuade local interests to put their claims in a broader perspective and help them to become more reasonable, if not virtuous.[9]

Critics of the proposed constitution objected that, unlike many state constitutions, it contained no bill of rights. Alexander Hamilton argued that no specific enumeration of rights was necessary, as the constitution's system of separated and shared powers and the limits on national power would be "in every rational sense, and to every useful purpose, A BILL OF RIGHTS" (Federalist No. 84, at 581). Hamilton's position was flawed. A sufficiently large majority may well succeed in getting oppressive legislation by the House, Senate, and president. The supporters of the Constitution decided to oblige those who demanded a bill of rights by having Congress propose a series of amendments to the Constitution for ratification by the states.[10]

This Bill of Rights, as finally ratified, defines certain aspects of liberty, such as freedom of religion, upon which government may not intrude. But the Bill of Rights was not intended to replace separated and shared powers as a protection of liberty. The Framers thought of the separated and shared powers in the Constitution and the enumerated liberties in the Bill of Rights as complementary ways to protect individuals from government, and so would have viewed separation of powers as no less a right than the enumerated ones. The Framers cited with approval a provision of the Massachusetts Constitution of 1780 that required separation of powers as necessary to "a government of laws and not of men" (Federalist No. 47, at 327–28 [J. Madison]).[11]

Disputes about delegation quickly arose under the new Constitution. For example, in the Alien Act of 1798, Congress allowed the president to deport "dangerous" aliens in peacetime. Although no one brought a delegation challenge against this statute, it was "vigorously and contemporaneously attacked as unconstitutional."[12] As another example, Britain and France, then at war, each authorized the seizing of ships that traded with its enemy. In response Congress enacted a statute in 1810 providing that if the president found either of the two countries had revoked the decree authorizing the seizure of American ships and its opponent failed within three months to do the same, the president must bar trade with that country. President James Madison subsequently found that France had revoked its decree but Britain had not, and he barred trade with Britain. His action was challenged on the ground that the statute unconstitutionally delegated legislative power. In *Cargo of the Brig Aurora v. United States*, the Supreme Court's first ruling in a delegation case, the Court reasoned from the premise that Congress may not delegate its legislative power. The Court decided, however, that the statute did not delegate legislative power. The president, it held, was not making a law by banning trade with Britain but rather was executing a law made by Congress. In other words, the Court found, correctly, that the statute enacted a law for the President to interpret and apply through deciding whether the factual preconditions for the statute's ban on trade existed.[13] The Court might have reached the same result by holding that the statute sanctioned the exercise of independent executive powers regarding war and foreign affairs.

Before the Civil War, Congress enacted relatively few regulatory statutes. Since few delegation cases reached the Supreme Court, it had little occasion or need to define improper delegation.[14] On balance, however, early legislative practice seemed to accord with the theory of the Constitution—variously known as the *delegation doctrine* or the *nondelegation doctrine*—that Congress rather than administrators shall make the law. According to de Tocqueville, writing in 1835, "the nation participates in the making of its laws by the choice of its legislators, and in the execution of them by the choice of agents of the executive government; it may also be said to govern itself, so feeble and so restricted is the share left to the administrators, so little do the authorities forget their popular origins and the power from which they emanate."[15]

From Bureaucracy to Delegation

Republican reformers of the late nineteenth century and the Progressives of the early twentieth century helped to launch American bureaucracy. Yet, the Republican reformers at least saw themselves as staunch defenders of the Constitution. These Republicans sounded like the Framers. They described the Civil War at its outset as an "ordeal" that would reverse "the decay and degeneracy of national virtue." They wanted to "bring back that better era of the republic in which, when men consecrated themselves to the public service, they utterly abnegated all selfish purposes."[16] After 1865, the Republican reformers recognized that despite the war, powerful officials, including some in their own party, used their public powers for tyrannical purposes. They feared that, unrestrained by virtue, the wrong sort of majority would use the vast power of government to wreck society by changing the existing social order too rapidly.[17]

Establishing a bureaucracy was part of the Republican reformers' effort to protect individual liberty, and society in general, from elected officials. The "spoils" system of public employment would be replaced with a merit-based civil service. The reformers, like the Framers, wanted a "natural aristocracy" to make the decisions, but they argued that the merit needed to wield public power came from scientific training. For the reformers, science—not as a body of knowledge but as method of analysis—could settle any issue, not just questions of observable fact. They tried to develop and teach a "scientific morality" that would resolve all policy conflicts through the systematic assembling and analysis of information, and a "science of justice" that would use parallel methods to resolve all common-law conflicts. They failed to see that mimicry of the methods of hard science could take one only so far, since uncertainty in matters of fact and, more fundamentally, questions of values often mean that there is no right answer.[18]

The Republican reformers also embraced the separation of powers as a means to prevent the abuse of power.[19] However, they sought to fragment power still more finely by creating separate bureaus for different problems and, within each bureau, establishing set procedures that would further restrict officials' autonomy.

But, although the Republican reformers (sometimes known as "political mugwumps") revered the Constitution's design, other proponents of bureaucracy, including a group known as "economic mugwumps," scorned that design. For the economic mugwumps, the checks and balances built into the Constitution to protect liberty and ensure democratic accountability were impediments for expert administrators aiming to create a truly efficient government. From this perspective, Woodrow Wilson, during his academic career, proposed amending the Constitution to facilitate bureaucratic administration. Believing that unelected administrators could make better public policy because they responded to science rather than politics, the economic mugwumps wanted to insulate administrators from the political arena by appointing them to independent commissions—sometimes known as "independent agencies"—on which they would serve fixed terms.[20]

The conflict between the reformers' ideal of scientific government and the Constitution's prohibition on the delegation of legislative power did not become widely apparent until well after 1900, by which time the Progressives were the leading proponents of reform based upon expert administration. As Robert Wiebe states: "Arriving around 1900 and gaining momentum after 1910, the bureaucratic orientation did not reach its peak of success until the nineteen twenties. Partly because its climax lay in the future, partly because its ideas lent themselves to piecemeal adoption, the bureaucratic revolution came rather quietly, almost surreptitiously, in the years before the First World War, with very few clear-voiced champions."[21]

Early statutes setting up agencies at the national level were read not to grant the power to make law.[22] Following a long debate over the national regulation of railroads, in 1887 Congress created by statute the first major federal administrative agency, the Interstate Commerce Commission (ICC). The Supreme Court ruled that the statute, the Interstate Commerce Act, stated the law itself, by incorporating the common law. The job of the ICC, an independent agency, was to help the courts apply the law by discovering violations and making preliminary findings of fact. The courts, rather than the agency, would have the last word in interpreting the law. Although the common law that provided the basis for the statutory laws was ambiguous, the reformers generally did not view the act as either unacceptably ambiguous or as delegating because, for them, legal science provided the right way to interpret the common law.[23] In retrospect, however, the act failed to demarcate sufficiently what was prohibited, thus delegating legislative power to the courts.

Overall, during the nineteenth century, the federal government did not consciously create strong, lawmaking agencies.[24] In 1890 Congress enacted a statute that removed duties on certain agricultural imports, but provided that the duties be reimposed on imports from countries which the president found to have imposed "reciprocally unequal and unreasonable" duties on our exports. In *Field v. Clark*, decided in 1892, the Supreme Court announced that "Congress cannot delegate legislative power to the President" but upheld the statute on the doubtful basis that the president had only to find a fact under a statute, as in *Brig Aurora*. In *Brig Aurora*, the president indeed had to find a fact: Had the British or French rescinded their policies of raiding our ships? But in the later example there was no fact for the president to find. Although the statute called for the president to determine whether the tariffs of the exporting country and the United States were "reciprocally unequal," and inequality can be a fact in some contexts—as in deciding whether two ships are of equal length—there is no ready way to compare the tariff structure of the United States with that of another country that imports a much different mix of goods than we do. Instead, the president had to determine if the other country was charging reasonable tariffs, which is not a question of fact. The statute's appeal to equality, although it was of no practical help in determining what conduct was required—added to the Republican reformers' inflated notions of the capacity of science to settle controversies —seemed to blind the Court to the truth that the statute required the president to dictate the law rather than to find facts.[25]

The Court nonetheless might have reached the right result for the wrong reason. From a broad view of the president's powers to conduct foreign relations under Article II, the president was exercising executive power in representing us against foreign powers, rather than exercising a legislative power in the form of laying down a law to govern our relationships at home. The Court sounded this theme at length but in the end relied upon its conclusion that the president had only to find a fact.[26] The justices' reliance on a wrong reason led to trouble in subsequent cases.

Many of the same themes were repeated during the early decades of the twentieth century, when Progressivism flourished. Some political leaders (such as presidents Theodore Roosevelt and Woodrow Wilson) favored strong agencies, while others (such as President William Howard Taft) sounded Madisonian principles of separation of powers. As Congress created more agencies, the Court generally continued to interpret the statutes that created them as giving agencies only the power to enforce legislated laws grounded in the common law.[27]

The Supreme Court did strike down some statutes on the ground that they delegated legislative power. In 1921, *United States v. L. Cohen Grocery Co.* struck down a statute that made it a crime to charge "unjust or unreasonable" prices for "any necessaries." The trial court quashed an indictment against Cohen Grocery Company for charging excessive prices for sugar in part because "Congress alone has power to define crimes against the United States. This power cannot be delegated either to the courts or to the juries of this country." The Supreme Court agreed that the statute "delegate[d] legislative power, in the very teeth of the settled significance . . . of the Constitution." Neither the concept of law as scientific nor the popular trust in scientific policymaking by experts obscured the lawmaking role that this statute gave to courts. After all, the statute created a crime outside the common-law tradition, and the juries that would make pricing policy were not experts.[28]

Two other cases—*Knickerbocker Ice Co. v. Stewart*, decided in 1920, and *Washington v. W. C. Dawson*, decided in 1924—struck down statutes that instructed federal courts to apply state workers' compensation statutes in admiralty cases. The Court reasoned that, since Article III of the Constitution gave federal courts exclusive jurisdiction over admiralty cases, Congress must enact the law itself if it wished statutory law to apply in those cases. Given that dubious premise, it was easy to conclude that Congress had delegated its power to state legislatures.[29]

With *J.W. Hampton, Jr., & Co. v. United States*, decided in 1928, the Court took a giant step toward explicitly allowing Congress to delegate. Congress had authorized the president to impose protectionist tariffs of up to 50 percent when he found this necessary to "equalize . . . differences in costs of production in the United States and the principal competing country." The Court upheld this statute, citing *Field v. Clark*, but the rationale that the president had only to find facts under a law made even less sense in *Hampton & Co.* The president cannot weigh the equality of the costs of production in foreign and domestic industries without first having decided such broad policy questions as the appropriate levels of wages and profits in the domestic industry. The opinion in *Hampton & Co.* made less appeal than *Field v. Clark* to the special powers of the president in foreign affairs, and rightly so, because the president's decision turned on whether domestic industries earned enough money, rather than on whether foreign governments charged excessive tariffs.[30]

Perhaps because the Court in *Hampton & Co.* found it difficult to conclude that the statute met the test it had applied in many previous delegation cases—had Congress stated the law?—it framed the test in new terms. The question was, had Congress stated an "intelligible principle?" If this had meant that Congress must state an intelligible principle of what private conduct was prohibited, then the new test would have been the same as the old. But, as the case's facts make clear, the Court meant that Congress had done enough if it stated an "intelligible principle" concerning the goals that should move the president when he stated the law. The Court further stated, "In determining what [Congress] may do in seeking assistance from another branch, the extent and character of that assistance must be fixed according to common sense and the inherent necessities of the governmental co-ordination."[31] Since "the inherent necessities of the governmental co-ordination" is the sort of policy matter on which courts defer to Congress, *Hampton & Co.* implicitly allowed Congress to delegate.

The ideal that elected lawmakers should make the law still had popular appeal. President-elect Hoover said he wanted to repeal the statute upheld in *Hampton* because it delegated legislative power:

> The American people will never consent to delegating authority over the tariff to any commission, whether non-partisan or bi-partisan. Our people have a right to express themselves at the ballot upon so vital a question as this.
>
> There is only one commission to which delegation of that authority can be made. That is the great commission of their own choosing, the Congress of the United States and the President. It is the only commission which can be held responsible to the electorate.[32]

An editorial in the *Constitutional Review* said the statute was "the most dangerous advance in bureaucratic government ever attempted in America."[33]

Although *Hampton & Co.* had blessed delegation in all but name, four years later the Supreme Court professed it an obvious principle that Congress may not delegate legislative power. In 1933, the following year, the Court acknowledged that the statute in *Hampton & Co.* delegated legislative power, but in a "permissible"—that is, minor —way. The Court had stated for the first time that Congress could delegate legislative power.[34]

The Republican reformers' pretensions had, in sum, started the Court down a path that ended in the unmistakable delegation of legislative power. At the same time, the Supreme Court said that it honored the separation of powers because the "intelligible principle" test required that Congress make all the major policy decisions. The Court also could have believed that judicial review would protect liberty from overly aggressive agencies because judges at that time still reversed regulations which they thought served no public purpose.[35]

Delegation from the New Deal to the Present

The Early New Deal

A combination of forces turned covert and limited delegation into overt and massive administrative lawmaking in the New Deal period. New Dealers did not share the Framers' and the Republican reformers' concept of Article I of the Constitution as a protection of liberty. Influential historians in the period leading up to the New Deal instead described the obstacles Article I places in the way of enacting statutes as a ploy to keep the rich on top.[36] While other historians several decades later discredited this class-warfare theory of Article I, its dominance for a generation partially erased our recognition that separation of powers, as well as the Bill of Rights, serves to protect liberty. So Felix Frankfurter and James Landis, both architects of the New Deal, could assert that the delegation doctrine is a "jejune abstraction[]."[37] The New Deal era also brought criticism of democracy. Pointing out that voters are often uninformed, irrational, prejudiced, and gullible —and their representatives self-serving—some argued that appointed experts rather than elected legislators should make law. Landis maintained, however, that the administrative process was consistent with liberty and was democratically accountable.[38]

New Dealers could also point to a tradition of delegation. Prominent New Dealers were proponents of "legal realism," which argued that law is not a science that produces right answers.[39] Legal realists could easily conclude that statutes that tell an agency or courts to apply the common law delegate the power to make the law. Yet the New Dealers clung to the other part of the Republican reformers' and Progressives' scientific pretension, "scientific morality," which held that social science could produce a right answer to questions of policy. However, they wanted all agencies to be firmly under the president's control. Although a proposal to convert existing independent agencies into structures whose heads would serve at the pleasure of the president did not succeed, many new delegations were to agencies with that form.[40]

In his first inaugural address, Franklin Roosevelt compared the impact of the ongoing economic depression to a foreign invasion, arguing that Congress should grant him sweeping powers to fight it.[41] Shortly after taking office in 1933, he got Congress to pass two statutes designed to raise depressed prices. The Agricultural Adjustment Act

(AAA) sought to increase agricultural prices through several techniques, one of which was the marketing orders discussed in Chapter 1.[42] The other statute, the National Industrial Recovery Act (NIRA), sought to increase nonagricultural prices, principally by authorizing the president to issue industrial codes that could regulate all aspects of the industries they covered.[43] Because the AAA and the NIRA gave the president and his appointees the power to regulate almost every aspect of agriculture and industry without any meaningful restraint, the statutes delegated almost all congressional power over commerce.

These statutes departed from tradition in many ways. They gave short shrift to the Framers' concerns for democracy and liberty and the Republican reformers' concerns to fragment concentrations of power and slow the pace of change. Instead, they handed a few officials concentrated power to move rapidly toward a "New Deal." As James Whitman puts it, "To supporters and critics alike, [the NIRA] . . . seemed akin to the 'corporativism' of Italian Fascism." *Fortune* magazine approvingly declared, "The Corporative State is to Mussolini what the New Deal is to Roosevelt." The NIRA in fact did not delegate the ultimate authority to private cartels but rather to the president. Benito Mussolini, whom Roosevelt referred to in 1933 as that "admirable Italian gentleman" remarked upon hearing of the NIRA, "Ecco un ditatore!" ("Behold a dictator!") This massive delegation of legislative power to President Roosevelt took place in the same year that the German Reichstag delegated all its power to Adolph Hitler. While the New Deal, Italian Fascism, and German Nazism differed in the most fundamental ways, the similarities do help explain why, according to a Gallup poll, close to a majority of the American public in 1936 thought that the New Deal could well turn into a dictatorship.[44]

Big business welcomed the NIRA as a means of propping up prices at the expense of less well organized or powerful interests, such as consumers and small businesses. For instance, Standard Oil and other large petroleum companies saw the NIRA as the fulfillment of their long-term desire to raise prices undeterred by annoying competition from upstart crude oil producers.[45] The NIRA gave business and labor the lead role in proposing the laws that would apply to their industry. Consumers had little say. Although the president was supposed to protect the broad public interest, his appointees at the National Recovery Administration (NRA) generally promulgated the laws that the industry proposed. The result was laws that transferred wealth from buyers to sellers by restricting supply, operating much like the price-fixing cartels that the antitrust laws make illegal. One observer quipped that the major beneficiaries of the production quotas in the Atlantic mackerel industry code were the mackerel.[46]

In 1935 a unanimous Supreme Court struck down the industrial code provisions of the NIRA in *A.L.A. Schechter Poultry Corp. v. United States*. In a separate opinion, Justice Benjamin Cardozo called the code provisions "delegation running riot."[47] After the decision came down, Justice Brandeis told a top Roosevelt advisor, "This is the end of this business of centralization, and I want you to go back and tell the President that we are not going to let this government centralize everything. It's come to an end. As for your young men, you call them together and tell them to get out of Washington—tell them to go home, back to the States. That is where they must do their work."[48]

In another 1935 case, *Panama Refining Company v. Ryan*, the Court, with Justice Cardozo as a sole dissenter, struck down another NIRA provision that delegated to the president the power to prohibit the interstate shipment of oil produced in violation of state laws limiting oil production.[49] The statute vaguely indicated the goals that the president should consider in deciding whether to do so; it left the president with broad discretion in making the federal law, but no more than did the statute upheld in *Hampton & Co*. Some justices seemed motivated by policy disagreements with the New Deal as much as by constitutional principles.

The Later New Deal

Congress continued to delegate, but not in such bold strokes. Although the NIRA had delegated power over all aspects of industry, statutes enacted after *Schechter* and *Panama Refining* delegated authority over particular industries or particular aspects of industrial policy, such as labor relations. The NIRA had told the president to advance the public interest in whatever way he saw fit; the new statutes prescribed in general terms the goals that the delegates should pursue and the kinds of laws they could issue. For example, Congress amended the AAA to say that marketing orders could regulate crops in certain specified ways, such as limiting the quantity that each grower ships; at the same time it left the secretary of agriculture with broad discretion over whether and how to set those limits.[50] Although Congress did delegate broadly, it did not abdicate its power. It could still influence or override agency decisions, as later discussion will show. Congress also included in some delegations provisions that authorized one or both legislative houses to veto agency actions. The question was, would the Court find that delegations less broad than the NIRA violated the Constitution?

From *Schechter, Panama Refining,* and other decisions striking down New Deal legislation, President Franklin Roosevelt concluded that he needed to change the Court. Decrying the Court's interference with his efforts to deal with the Great Depression, he proposed legislation enlarging the size of the Court, so that he could appoint additional justices—the so-called Court-packing plan. He lost the battle for this legislation but won the war. Some justices retired and were replaced, and others bowed to the political pressure by voting differently in subsequent cases.[51] Although the Court never explicitly reversed its 1935 decisions and it continued to articulate essentially the same verbal formulae defining the scope of permissible delegation—indeed, *Schechter* and *Panama Refining* theoretically are good law today—it never again struck down a New Deal statute on delegation grounds. In 1939, for example, the Court upheld the broad delegation authorizing the secretary of agriculture to issue agricultural marketing orders.[52] The Supreme Court also made clear that judges could no longer strike down agency regulations just because they disagreed with the agency's contention that the regulations served a public interest.[53]

The Depression, which had made delegation seem so necessary, did not end until World War II created another emergency that seemed to make delegation necessary. The Court upheld wartime statutes regulating prices and profit against delegation challenges primarily on the fiction that the statutes provided standards, not on the theory that they authorized the president to exercise executive war powers.[54] Grounds for the latter approach could have been found in *Field v. Clark.* These World War II delegation cases supplied the basis for upholding expansive delegations after the war.[55]

After the New Deal

All subsequent administrations down to the present continued to embrace delegation. In particular, President Kennedy repeatedly sounded the themes of virtue and expertise through which New Dealers had justified delegation. He promised to bring "the best and the brightest" into his administration and described their job as applying expertise in the public interest. In his address at the 1962 Yale commencement exercises, he said:

> You must participate . . . in the solution of the problems that pour upon us, requiring the most sophisticated and technical judgment. . . . The central domestic problems of our time . . . relate not to basic clashes of philosophy or ideology, but to ways and means of reaching common goals—to research for sophisticated solutions to complex and obstinate issues. . . . What is at stake in our economic decisions today is not some grand warfare of rival ideologies which will sweep the country with passion but the practical management of a modern economy.[56]

Many people at that time believed that "public officials, given the correct information and sufficient authority, would do the right thing."[57]

The postwar Congress faced no judicial limit on its ability to delegate lawmaking to federal officials so long as the statutes passed said something about the goals that the agency laws should seek to attain. The Court upheld broad delegations in long-regulated fields on the rationale that agencies are guided by prior experience and precedents, and upheld broad delegations in virgin areas of regulation on the rationale that it is impracticable to require Congress to set precise standards when it has no experience in regulating these areas.[58] The Court argued that delegation is consistent with the constitutional goals both of democracy, because Congress oversees the agencies, and of liberty, because the courts can review contentions that an agency has acted arbitrarily.[59]

Indeed, a leading commentator advised attorneys in 1958 that claims against delegation were considered so farfetched that making them would discredit their other claims.[60] But 1958 also brought a case, *Kent v. Dulles*, that reflected concern about the impact of delegation upon liberty. The statute at issue seemingly granted broad discretion to the secretary of state to deny passports. Kent alleged that the secretary unconstitutionally had refused to issue him a passport because of his political views. In supporting him, the Court did not hold that the secretary had infringed his civil rights or that the statute delegated unconstitutionally; instead, the Court strained to interpret the statute as not delegating broad power to deny passports. The Court stated that when "activities or enjoyment, natural and often necessary to the well-being of an American citizen, such as travel, are involved, we will construe narrowly all delegated powers that curtail or dilute them."[61] This formula seemed to distinguish *Kent v. Dulles* from the cases upholding statutes that delegate the power to regulate businesses. Yet such a distinction is double-talk, as the "activities or enjoyment" described include working, carrying on a profession, or operating a business—precisely the subjects of the regulatory statutes in which the Court typically had allowed delegation.[62] Commentators have generally understood the more stringent approach of *Kent v. Dulles* to apply to statutes involving "protected freedoms" as opposed to statutes that regulate property.[63] But the Constitution's requirement that laws come from the Article I legislative process was designed to protect liberty in general, not just those aspects of liberty singled out in the Bill of Rights.

In some subsequent cases with civil liberties overtones, the Court followed the lead of *Kent v. Dulles* in affording citizens the protection of the legislative process. The Court also has held that state or federal statutes delegating broad discretion to regulate or punish speech or religion violate the First Amendment.[64] In addition, under the rubric of *void for vagueness* it has regularly struck down statutes that fail to define crimes clearly, on the basis that the legislature—rather than the police, judges, and juries—should state what constitutes a crime.[65] Under the rubric of *due process* it also construed the civil service laws to deny the Civil Service Commission the power to issue a law excluding resident aliens from many federal jobs.[66] The Court reasoned that since Congress had allowed the aliens to reside in the United States, it would be wrong for it to allow a lower level of government to remove one of the advantages of such residency, eligibility for federal employment. The Court acted as if attaching the rubrics *void for vagueness* and *due process* to these cases, rather than the rubric *delegation*, somehow explained why delegation was a problem in these cases but not in others.[67]

Beginning in the 1960s and 1970s, distrust of delegation emerged in contexts other than "protected freedoms." In the 1963 case of *Arizona v. California*, justices Douglas, Harlan, and Stewart dissented from a Court decision construing a statute to give the secretary of the interior discretion to allocate water among three states. They argued that the statute, as so construed, "raise[d] . . . the gravest constitutional doubts" because it provided no standards to guide the exercise of administrative discretion and so would result in a political decision made by an official who was not elected.[68] The Vietnam War, urban riots, civil rights protests, the first Earth Day, and Watergate set the stage for questioning the Republican reformer–New Deal–New Frontier claim that the public should trust experts to protect the public interest. Scholars discredited the principle of scientific morality that expertise could settle policy disputes and showed that agency experts are not insulated from political pressure in making laws and may, indeed, be captured by concentrated interests. Ralph Nader and his followers portrayed government regulators as ineffective or corrupt. Administrative law scholars pointed out that leaving a politically charged issue to an agency often results in regulatory gridlock. Some liberal judges, scholars, and lawyers attacked delegation.[69]

In response, starting in the 1970s, Congress changed how it delegated rather than stopping delegation. It gave agencies detailed instructions about the procedures that they should follow and the goals that they should seek to attain in lawmaking. Such instructions were supposed to allow courts reviewing agency action, "to see that important legislative purposes, heralded in the halls of Congress, are not lost or misdirected in the vast hallways of the federal bureaucracy." In other words, legislators conveniently misdiagnosed the problem with delegation as the executive's failure to execute rather than their own failure to legislate.[70] I will refer to the older style of delegation, in which the agency has broad discretion over the goals and procedures of lawmaking, as *broad delegation* and the newer style, in which that discretion is narrowed, as *narrow delegation*.

While Congress changed the way it delegated, the Supreme Court groped toward a new approach to delegation. In 1974 a majority invoked the delegation doctrine in a business regulation case—as opposed to a "protected freedoms" case—for the first time in almost forty years. *National Cable Television Association v. United States* dealt with a statute that seemingly gave federal agencies the power to tax those they regulated in order to cover the cost of regulation. The Court used concerns about delegation to justify construing the statute as not delegating the power to impose a tax.[71]

Then in 1980 *Industrial Union Department, AFL-CIO v. American Petroleum Institute* overturned a business regulation promulgated under the Occupational Safety and Health Act.[72] Congress had enacted legislation that authorized an agency to make laws governing safety and health in workplaces but had not agreed about whether the agency must find that the risk its law averts is significant relative to the cost of complying with the law. A five-justice majority struck down a law that the agency had issued without finding that the risk was significant. Four of them reached this result by interpreting the act to deny the power to protect health at any price; they reasoned that this approach would avoid any doubt that Congress had delegated too broadly. The fifth, Justice Rehnquist, voted to declare the act unconstitutional, a position with which Chief Justice Burger agreed in a subsequent case.[73] Neither *National Cablevision* nor *American Petroleum Institute* decided whether Congress could have delegated more broadly if it had clearly stated its intention to do so. Nonetheless, these two decisions gave concerns about delegation more respect than they had received in forty years.

In 1983 *Immigration and Naturalization Service v. Chadha* struck down a statute on what amounted to delegation grounds. The Court held that the statute unconstitutionally delegated legislative power because it allowed one house of Congress to veto the attorney general's decisions in immigration cases. At the time, such legislative veto provisions appeared in some two hundred statutes. *Chadha* stated that all these provisions were unconstitutional because they delegated legislative power to one or both houses of Congress acting without the president. To distinguish these delegations from delegations to agencies, the Court said that agencies do not exercise legislative power when they make laws because in that situation Congress lays down "standards" and courts ensure that agencies do not exceed them. This argument rested upon the false premise that the intelligible principle test guarantees congressional standards that truly control the agencies. So the Court failed to explain why a statute properly can delegate legislative power to an agency but not to a house of Congress.[74]

From *Kent v. Dulles* to *Chadha*, majorities of the justices used statutory construction to react to concerns about delegation in both protected freedoms cases and more routine cases. Never in this era did a majority vote to hold an ordinary regulatory statute unconstitutional, but a majority did strike down delegations under the rubrics void for vagueness and due process and as a response to the legislative veto. Yet the Court failed adequately to explain why it opposes delegation in some cases but not in others. More striking still, no majority since 1948 wrote at length in defense of the generally permissive approach to delegation in workaday cases, despite the forceful arguments presented in concurrences and dissents.[75]

Mistretta v. United States, decided in 1989, presented the Court with an opportunity to rethink or explain its approach to delegation. It did neither. In an eight-to-one decision, the Court rejected a delegation challenge to a statute that empowered a commission to make rules controlling criminal sentencing. The majority stated that "Congress generally cannot delegate its legislative power to another Branch," but then used *Hampton & Co.*'s intelligible principle test and its lesson that governmental convenience is the hallmark of the delegation doctrine to uphold the delegation. The majority found there was an intelligible principle in the statute's statement of the goals for sentencing guidelines—such as punishing criminals and deterring crime—and the procedures and format that the commission should use to issue its rules. Justice Scalia pointed out in dissent that the statute's recitation of these goals left the commission a long way from knowing whether the sentence for any given crime complied with the statute. The commission could, after all, choose from among a warning, a minor fine, a short jail sentence, a long jail sentence, and death. The Court did not respond. Moreover, the Court did not explain why *Mistretta* was not a protected freedoms or void for vagueness case, although the commission has the power to make rules that decide what conduct results in a prison term or execution. Instead of responding to the recent criticisms of its approach to delegation, the Court reasserted the propositions that the intelligible principle test vindicates the purposes of the delegation doctrine and that delegation is necessary. *Mistretta* essentially refused to reconsider delegation.[76]

This chapter began by promising that a look at history would support three conclusions. First, *Americans have generally sought a lawmaking process that is democratically accountable, that safeguards liberty, and that allows the government to protect the public effectively.* The Framers and the New Dealers sought to achieve precisely these goals, and the modern Supreme Court claims that its approach to delegation achieves them as well.

Second, *opposition to delegation is not peculiar to business, and authorities other than the Supreme Court that opposed the New Deal have believed that the Constitution bans delegation.* Some railroads supported the ICC as a means to forestall detailed statutory rules,[77] big business favored the NIRA,[78] and, as Chapter 4 will show, big business in modern times sometimes favors broad delegations to federal agencies to forestall more aggressive regulation by Congress or the states. Civil libertarians, advocates of more forceful regulation, and liberal scholars and judges have raised concerns about broad delegations. From the debates over the ratification of the Constitution to the late 1920s, the Framers and the Supreme Court said that Congress may not delegate its legislative power. Supporters of delegation sniff that this was nothing but talk, since only two Supreme Court cases, *Panama Refining* and *Schechter*, ever struck down delegation to public officials, and the Court previously had upheld many statutes that did delegate.[79] However, three cases did strike down statutes on delegation grounds before the New Deal, and the Court's not striking down more is explicable by the scarcity of opportunities and by their inflated concept of expertise, which blinded them to the existence of delegations.[80] Since the New Deal, the Court has responded to delegation concerns in *Kent v. Dulles* and its progeny, as well as in *Chadha* and some more routine cases.

Third, *Americans repeatedly have made the mistake of believing that they could prevent lawmakers from using public power for private purposes by creating a system that would put virtuous lawmakers in charge.* We have made this mistake in many forms. The American Revolutionaries thought that, although imperial officials made laws to benefit themselves and their friends, elected state legislatures would put the public first. The Framers thought, although concentrated interests could induce elected state legislators to ignore the broader and more diffuse interests of the general public, the national Constitution would produce lawmakers who would be "disinterested and dispassionate umpire[s]."[81] Advocates of delegation believed that big business used its power to keep Congress from responding to broad public needs, but that delegation would allow experts, insulated from politics, to use science to make decisions in the public interest. And critics of agencies argued that regulated industries had captured the regulators but "public interest groups"—nonprofit organizations that profess to be virtuous defenders of the public interest—would use the opportunities for judicial review that narrow delegation offers to reinstate the broad public interest.

The enduring hope for public virtue is understandable but childish. Most individuals have enough trouble truly loving those with whom they are intimate, so that truly loving the public seems unlikely.[82] We should choose our means of making law without listening to protestations of virtue.

Delegation in Practice

PART III

MODERN POLITICAL SCIENTISTS HAVE SYS-
tematically explained how "concentrated
interests" can entice and pressure lawmakers to enact statutes harmful to the
great majority of the electorate.[1] A concentrated interest is a group whose individual members have a far larger stake
in a policy issue than do members of the
general public. Because a concentrated
interest can organize itself more readily
than the general public, it can assemble
the experts and money needed to understand the real consequences of what lawmakers do with its issue and to reward
and punish them accordingly, through
contributions and other favors to them
or to their electoral opponents.

A manufacturer of a patented pesticide is a concentrated interest when the
government decides whether to license
the pesticide; the benefits of the license
fall heavily on the manufacturer, while
the potential costs, should the pesticide
be licensed although unsafe, fall diffusely
on the public. So the manufacturer, but
not an average citizen, will follow the
decision-making process closely and pressure officials to act favorably. That same
manufacturer will not have a sufficient
incentive to follow and intervene in governmental decisions that affect it diffusely, a decision, for example, to spend
public money on pork-barrel projects.
Many sorts of persons or groups—busi-

nesses, unions, or "public-interest" groups[2]—can be "concentrated interests" on issues of special concern to themselves.

In this part of the book I consider how delegation actually has affected the power of concentrated interests to influence lawmakers to disregard the public's interest. The navel orange marketing order discussed in Chapter 1 is used in Chapter 3 to illustrate that experience with broad delegation. Regulation of air pollution under the Clean Air Act is introduced in Chapter 4 to illustrate the experience with narrow delegation and with Congress making law itself. Generalizing from these experiences and others, in Chapter 5 I will describe how delegation changes the politics of lawmaking and why Congress delegates.

Broad Delegation: Regulating Navel Oranges

THE NAVEL ORANGE MARKETING ORDER IS A particularly apt illustration of broad delegation: the marketing order program was a centerpiece of the New Deal approach to lawmaking, and navel oranges have been regulated, with brief interruptions, from the program's inception.

Broad delegation aimed to overcome a perceived weakness in lawmaking in Congress—namely, that concentrated interests use their superior ability to pressure legislators to do their bidding. The lawmaking process would be changed in order to (1) insulate it from legislative politics, (2) base decisions on the advice of experts, and (3) keep the lawmakers' focus on a reasoned understanding of the broad public interest.[1] With the navel orange marketing order, however, delegation failed to work as promised. Legislators themselves helped concentrated interests to dominate the agency's lawmaking process, experts were subordinated to politicians, and short shrift was given to the broad public interest.

How the Statute Was Supposed to Work

The Agricultural Adjustment Act delegated to the secretary of agriculture broad discretion to make agricultural marketing "orderly." As Frank Easterbrook has observed, "'orderly' marketing is a wonderful euphemism" for price fixing, but the phrase provides little guidance on which crops should have marketing orders, how to apportion the market between growers, or how high to fix prices at the expense of consumers.[2] Thus the statute delegates broadly.

Under the statute the marketing orders need not themselves state the quotas and other rules; they may set up the procedures through which the secretary will promulgate and administer those rules. The marketing order may set up a committee of growers and others to recommend quotas to the secretary and to help to administer the order.[3] Neither the order nor amendments may go into effect unless the secretary determines through a referendum or other means that the affected growers support it. Nonetheless, the secretary, as the guardian of the broad public interest, has authority to impose a marketing order that growers oppose, to withhold or terminate a marketing order that growers support, or to refuse to turn into law the recommendations of the growers' committees on quotas. In such decisions, the secretary would rely on the advice of economists and other experts in the Agricultural Marketing Service of the department.[4]

How the Statute Actually Does Work

Sunkist dominates the growers' committee that advises the secretary of agriculture on the marketing order governing California and Arizona navel oranges, the Navel Orange Administrative Committee (NOAC). The order provides that the secretary appoints NOAC's members; in fact, the secretary routinely appoints the nominees of the orange industry. The order allows Sunkist to nominate five of the eleven NOAC members. Handlers and growers not affiliated with Sunkist nominate five other members, with the larger handlers and growers getting a relatively larger voice. These ten industry members then nominate an eleventh and final member who is supposed to represent the public. Sunkist is linked to NOAC by a direct telephone line and NOAC's staff is covered by Sunkist's pension plan.[5] The voice of consumers is effectively excluded from this structure. Sunkist is able to dictate NOAC policy, as long as it keeps a few large handlers happy.

While the statute provides that crop committees such as NOAC shall recommend policy to the secretary rather than decide it, Lawrence Shepard notes that NOAC and other crop committees "enjoy a high degree of autonomy."[6] The procedure of the agriculture department for deciding how many oranges can be sold to consumers exemplifies NOAC's power. The Administrative Procedure Act requires that before promulgating a rule, an agency must give the public notice of the proposed rule in the *Federal Register* and an opportunity to comment upon it in writing. An agency may dispense with such notice and opportunity for comment only to the extent justified by an emergency or other good cause. But the agriculture department promulgated weekly navel orange quotas for thirty-five years without giving advance notice in the *Federal Register* or allowing the opportunity to comment in writing to anyone but NOAC. After a recent court ruling that some aspects of these procedures were illegal, the department has improved them slightly.[7]

Sunkist has used its political power to defeat a variety of threats to its control of the navel orange business. In 1974 the Cost of Living Council, a cabinet-level committee seeking to reduce inflation, persuaded the department to raise quotas. The council had to abandon its recommendation after influential legislators and the White House sided with Sunkist, which urged retention of low quotas. In the mid-1970s the Federal Trade Commission brought antitrust charges against Sunkist, but Sunkist's lawyer, according to a former partner, "went up to the Hill and had a rider put in the FTC's appropriations bill that cut off the funds for the investigation."[8]

In the early 1980s the Office of Management and Budget (OMB) tried to eliminate the most anticompetitive aspects of marketing orders as part of its deregulation campaign. The secretary of agriculture was about to announce a decision in 1983 to end the marketing order for lemons, but he reversed this position a few days after a White House breakfast meeting attended by James Lake, Sunkist chairman John Newman, presidential adviser Edwin Meese (a longtime friend of Newman's), Secretary of Agriculture John Block, and others. The *New York Times* quoted one participant as saying that, although no political pressure or threats of withdrawing support were made at the meeting, "to be honest . . . it may have been said that it just doesn't seem right that after all of these years in which we've supported Reagan, when he was Governor and later when he ran for President, that he would want to do this to the majority of the growers who say the marketing order is good for their industry, and who have heard him say for years that he wants to get 'nameless, faceless government bureaucrats off the backs of the people.'"[9]

At the behest of Sunkist's friends in Congress, the House Appropriations Committee subsequently attached a rider to an appropriations bill that prevented OMB from using government funds to review marketing orders. This rider made marketing orders the only regulatory program exempt from such review. Representative Barney Frank led a floor fight to oppose the rider but lost in a 319 to 97 vote. Most of the legislators voting to shield marketing orders from scrutiny came from districts that do not grow crops covered by marketing orders, including such representatives from urban and suburban areas as Ron Dellums, John Dingell, Dan Rostenkowski, and Henry Waxman. (Yet some of these same legislators signed a letter to the secretary of agriculture in 1992 citing the need to feed hungry children as a reason to end all marketing orders.)[10]

In 1984, at the urging of the Consumers Union, Secretary Block sought to reduce the hold of Sunkist and other large handlers on NOAC by proposing several amendments to the order. One, for example, would have reduced Sunkist's seats on the committee from five to four. Sunkist had been able to veto proposed changes to the marketing order because, under the statute, coops such as Sunkist have the option to cast the votes of their members as a bloc in referenda on amendments to the order and referenda questions always were posed in the form of whether to amend the order or let it stand, rather than on whether to amend the order or terminate it. According to Deputy Assistant Secretary John Ford, who served under Block,

> any Secretary of Agriculture over the period of the last decade or two decades had lost all authority in its entirety to control any aspect of the fruit and vegetable marketing orders for the simple reason that by passively giving up the right to require amendments [to the marketing order], that the statute and the regulations gave him the authority to require, the control, authority, and obligation of the Secretary under the AMAA had been diminished to the point of zero.[11]

After giving notice and receiving comments, Block formally decided this time to mail ballots to growers giving them a choice between accepting his amendments, including those lessening Sunkist's power, or terminating the order. On the following day, July 25, 1984, Sunkist applied intense political pressure to Secretary Block through members of Congress and the White House. On July 26 Block told Ford that he would reverse himself, as Sunkist would get Congress to pass an appropriations rider that would limit his power to change marketing orders and would respond to the referendum with a kind of scorched-earth policy. According to Ford, the president of Sunkist, Russell Hanlin, told Secretary Block that "Sunkist would bloc vote out the order, would make the Secretary personally responsible for it, and that it would chill President Reagan's re-election chances in the State of California." So Sunkist kept its five seats on NOAC and its de facto line-item veto over amendments to the marketing order that the secretary had concluded were in the public interest. (In 1992, a federal appeals court ruled that the secretary acted illegally in changing the procedures for this referendum at Sunkist's behest because he acted without giving the public notice and an opportunity to comment on this change in referendum procedures.) Ford maintained, "Since the July 26th reversal, the Department reverted to its passive role of not interfering with whatever the industry committees want."[12]

In 1984 an organization of independent growers asked the Department of Agriculture for the list of orange growers it had prepared for a referendum in order to mail them literature critical of the marketing order. The department refused; although it offered to mail the literature from the organization of independent growers to growers before referenda, it reserved "the right to review any and all materials." Unwilling to submit to such censorship, the independents brought a Freedom of Information Act suit against the department seeking the growers' names and addresses. The Department of Justice refused to defend the Department of Agriculture's position, and the latter eventually promised to provide the list. Sunkist then sued to keep the list secret, allegedly to protect the growers' privacy. Since having one's name and address on a list of orange growers hardly seems like much of a secret, it would appear that Sunkist's interest really was in preserving its own power. The judge ruled against Sunkist.[13]

So the independent growers got the 1984 growers' list, but not until after the 1984 referendum. To prevent them from getting an up-to-date list for the next referendum, to be held in 1988, Sunkist got Congress to enact another appropriations rider that forbids the use of government funds to release information about growers.[14] The department interpreted the rider to mean that it is forbidden from providing names and addresses in response to a Freedom of Information Act claim, even if those wanting the list bring in their own paper, copying machine, and generator. A federal court ultimately ruled against this interpretation, but the growers opposing Sunkist did not get an updated growers list until after the 1988 and 1991 referenda.[15]

Nonetheless, Sunkist knew that it would have difficulty getting the support in the 1991 referendum needed to continue the marketing order. By its own terms, the order terminates if it fails to get the support of three-quarters of the growers who voted in a referendum upon it.[16] A longstanding provision of the statute, however, gives a cooperative such as Sunkist the option to cast the votes of its members as a bloc. Through a bloc vote, Sunkist could cast the votes of all its members to sustain the order. Sunkist would thereby disenfranchise members who would have voted to terminate the order and get the benefit of the votes of the substantial portion of its members who would not have voted at all. Yet, to exercise the bloc-vote option would conflict with the department's policy, announced in 1982, that cooperatives not exercise it and with a provision of Sunkist's bylaws that guarantees its members the right to vote in referenda.

Sunkist first sent a letter to its members to solicit their advice on whether and how to exercise its bloc-vote option.[17] In a straw poll of its members, most did not participate, but those who did split almost evenly. Ignoring its own by-laws and the opposition to the marketing order within its ranks, Sunkist then cast all of its members' votes for continuing the marketing order. Of the individual growers who did not belong to Sunkist, 42 percent voted for continuance and 58 percent voted against. As Sunkist acknowledged, without the bloc vote, the marketing order would have been defeated.[18]

What the Navel Orange Marketing Order Suggests about Broad Delegation

The navel orange marketing order illustrates the opportunity that broad delegation affords a concentrated interest to disproportionately influence the laws of critical importance to it.[19] Sunkist's disproportionate influence is not unusual. Indeed, Sunkist encounters more opposition than do many other concentrated interests. Various citizen groups, such as the Consumers Union, have opposed Sunkist, but the limited funding available to them generally makes their interventions episodic. In addition, some independent orange growers and handlers have battled Sunkist over the marketing order before the Department of Agriculture and in the courts for over a decade. Most concentrated interests do not encounter such fierce resistance because no individual opponent has a sufficient personal economic stake. Sunkist did meet persistent resistance from two talented individuals. One grower-handler, the late Carl Pescosolido, spent over half a million dollars on the fight.[20] His attorney, James Moody, has donated about a million dollars' worth of his time. Yet Pescosolido's and Moody's resources are tiny compared to Sunkist's.

The regulation of the navel orange market illustrates broad delegation's failure to deliver on its three promises—to insulate lawmaking from the tandem of Congress and concentrated interests, base law on expertise rather than political power, and focus lawmaking on the public interest.

Failure to Insulate Lawmaking from Politics

Delegation did not insulate lawmaking from Sunkist's influence; to the contrary, it let Sunkist's agents in NOAC draft the law. Members of Congress with close connections to Sunkist stifled interference from agency experts who thought the marketing order was contrary to the public interest. Said former deputy assistant secretary Ford, "We found [in the early 1980s] that over recent decades the Secretaries of Agriculture had lost all authority to have any oversight that the Congress clearly expected a Secretary to exercise . . . "[21]

Rather than insulating lawmaking from legislators and concentrated interests, broad delegation helps to insulate Congress and the White House from political accountability for supporting laws that are harmful to the broad public interest. In the orange situation, elected officials and their staffs support Sunkist by appealing to agency officials in private. The legislation they enacted left them immune from political harm. The delegation itself is framed in terms of attractive abstractions such as "orderly" markets. The appropriations riders used to shield marketing orders from the scrutiny of the FTC or the OMB were framed in terms of other attractive abstractions, such as privacy or leaving agricultural policy to the experts in the Department of Agriculture,[22] rather than in terms that might reveal legislative support of high prices to consumers. These appropriations riders do not attract the same level of public attention as legislation to raise the price or cut the supply of a widely used commodity. They rarely come up for discussion or vote on the floor. Only a specialist in agricultural marketing orders would even know that many riders concerning the orders appear in each year's appropriations bill. As an aide to a legislator who worked closely with Sunkist said with some glee, there is "nothing in the legislative history," and even finding the riders "drives an ordinary tracer crazy."[23]

Failure to Base Law on Expertise and Reason

Decisions about the regulation of the orange market are responsive to political power rather than expertise and reason. The Department of Agriculture explains its regulatory decisions as aimed at maintaining an orderly market. But the General Accounting Office (GAO) found in 1985, half a century after the program began, that the department had still not defined what it meant by an "orderly market" and so had no standard with which to judge proposed marketing orders. In adopting the marketing policy for the 1990–91 season, the department flatly refused to say what it meant by an orderly market.[24] When experts at the FTC, the OMB, and even the Department of Agriculture challenged the marketing order at various times, the accuracy of and reasoning behind their challenges were not put to the test in the administrative process. Rather the experts were stopped through the exercise of naked power.

Failure to Focus Lawmaking on the Public Interest

Delegation has produced a decision-making process that displays an evident lack of concern for the public. The Department of Agriculture sought to fine Carl Pescosolido thousands of dollars because, after selling his quota of oranges, he had donated 115 tons of the leftover oranges to charity. A department official, asked whether the oranges should not be used to feed the poor rather than be left to rot, replied, "Oranges are not an essential food. People don't need oranges. They can take vitamins."[25]

The department denied the public at large an opportunity to comment on its regulations for thirty-five growing seasons. Consumer interests are all but excluded from NOAC, the entity that effectively decides the price of navel oranges. Congress has tried to deny growers who believe that the marketing order hurts their interests the opportunity to contact other growers on the pretext of protecting privacy. As one scholar concluded, the regulation of navel oranges is "a textbook illustration of 'economic' or 'capture' theories of regulation," in which a concentrated interest is able to dictate the law for its private advantage.[26]

It is tempting to dismiss the navel orange marketing order because of its flawed objective—trying to make a competitive market "orderly" through regulation. But when a statute has a good objective, broad delegation can do even more harm by allowing concentrated interests to thwart that objective and also pervert regulation to its own ends through the same techniques used by Sunkist.

Narrow Delegation: Regulating Air Pollution

CHAPTER 4

THE CLEAN AIR ACT OF 1970 WAS THE FIRST instance of narrow delegation and became the template for many other statutes. Subsequent amendments to the Clean Air Act reflect the changing tactics used by Congress in trying to control agencies and provide a survey of the evolving state of the art in narrow delegation.

While critics of agricultural marketing orders never blamed broad delegation for the harm done to the consumers, critics of federal air pollution regulation did, in 1970, blame broad delegation for stymying efforts to clean up the air. They argued that the failure of Congress to make hard choices left the pollution control agency vulnerable to pressure from concentrated interests. Congress reacted to this criticism not by deciding to make the laws itself, but instead by delegating in a new way: in the Clean Air Act it gave the agency elaborate instructions about the goals that it should achieve and the procedures for promulgating them. Congress claimed to have made the hard choices and to have reduced the agency's job to using its expertise and resources to implement the policy that legislators had made.

But, in elaborating goals and procedures, Congress failed to reduce the agency's job to matters of expertise and detail.

Legislators hid their continuing failure to make the hard choices and pressured the agency to ignore the goals stated in the statute. Furthermore, as this example will reveal, narrow delegation had the perverse side-effect of delaying, complicating, and rigidifying the process of making environmental laws.

How the Statute Was Supposed To Work

The Problem for Congress in 1970

The early impetus for the federal government to take the lead in regulating air pollution came, surprisingly, from automobile manufacturers and electric utilities rather than from environmental interests. Until 1965 Congress had left the job of regulating air pollution mainly to the states.[1] When a few states began to regulate in earnest, the auto industry became concerned that many states would enact strict limits on emissions from new cars. The industry sought advice on how to minimize its regulatory burdens from Lloyd Cutler, a prominent Washington lawyer. He suggested that Congress should be persuaded to delegate broad authority to an agency that would have the exclusive right to set limits on emissions from new cars and trucks. The industry took his advice and persuaded Congress to enact a statute in 1965 that gave such authority to the secretary of the Department of Health, Education, and Welfare (HEW).[2] In 1967 electrical utilities persuaded Congress to pass a statute designed to minimize state regulation of their emissions.[3] That statute directed each state to adopt air quality goals consistent with federal assessments of the effects of various pollutants and then to adopt a plan to achieve the goals. Industry hoped that this process would slow down and temper the states' more aggressive strides towards strict controls on emissions. The statute also provided that if a state failed to follow the process specified, HEW was to act in its place.

The HEW responded to these statutes as industry had hoped. Its limits on auto emissions were sufficiently lax that manufacturers could comply by installing inexpensive off-the-shelf hardware. Similarly, its administration of the 1967 statute suggested that states need not hurry to adopt plans.[4]

The HEW *failed to act vigorously* against pollution for the same reason that the Department of Agriculture *had acted vigorously* to increase the price of oranges: the concentrated nature of the regulated industry.

In the late 1960s, the potential costs of strict auto emission standards fell in the first instance primarily on General Motors, Ford, and Chrysler, while the potential benefits accrued to everyone who breathed polluted air. Each of these manufacturers had far more interest than the average citizen in understanding the regulatory issues and in pressuring officials to decide them in its favor. Although there were more electrical utilities than auto manufacturers, utilities' interests still were far more concentrated than those of the average citizen and, in addition, utilities had effective trade associations. Thus they had information and organization that allowed them to participate more effectively than the average citizen in the administrative process. Regulation, consequently, failed to require polluters to take many steps in which benefit to the public would have outweighed costs.

The sudden emergence of the environmental movement at the end of the 1960s took away some of the industries' informational and organizational advantages. The upsurge in concern about the environment brought the public a crash course in air pollution. Lead stories in the daily press and network news of 1970, for instance, told of smog in Southern California that kept children home from school and of a summer-long air pollution alert throughout the Northeast corridor.[5] The public was told not only that weak regulation imposed costs upon it but also that Congress shared the blame. Ralph Nader blamed the "collapse" of air pollution control on Congress in general and on Senator Edmund Muskie, author of the 1967 act, in particular.[6] Environmental organizations targeted especially "dirty" legislators for opposition in forthcoming elections. Legislators sensed that it was at them that the public had begun to direct its anger about pollution.

Congress felt the need to respond. After Ralph Nader had criticized existing air pollution legislation for failing to make the hard choices—in other words, for delegating broadly—Senator Muskie, who wanted to ride to victory as the champion of ecology in the 1972 presidential election, and President Nixon, who would run again in 1972, competed to offer air pollution bills that seemed decisively to protect the environment.[7] The question was in what form to make those hard choices. Broad delegation was the problem and therefore not an option. Congress could instead enact law itself—that is, the rules of conduct limiting emissions. But legislators voting for any realistic set of rules would inevitably draw fire, both from environmentalists for regulating too weakly and from industry for regulating too harshly. So the 1970 Clean

Air Act delegated generally, but in a new way that appeared to make the hard choices.[8]

The Goals of the 1970 Clean Air Act

The 1970 Clean Air Act promised to protect the public's health by the end of the decade. Senator Muskie, the act's author, declared that his statute "intend[ed] that all Americans in all parts of the country shall have clean air to breathe within the 1970's." He claimed the act made a legal right by imposing on officials the duty to take specific actions by specific dates and by authorizing any citizen to sue officials or polluters who failed to perform their duties. The act assured "that Federal and State agencies [would] aggressively pursue their responsibilities." In Muskie's words, it would "face the air pollution crisis with urgency and in candor. It [makes] hard choices."[9]

The act's central mechanism for ensuring the protection of health within the decade began by identifying the most important pollutants —those that are harmful and come from many sources. The administrator of the Environmental Protection Agency (EPA), which was created in 1970, formally had identified five such pollutants before the statute's enactment. The act mandated that he publish a list of additional pollutants in this category within a month of its enactment —the Senate report on the bill identified five pollutants that it expected would be on the list—and added that he must list other pollutants revealed in the future to be similarly harmful.[10]

The listing of a pollutant as harmful and issuing from many sources triggered a series of mandatory duties leading, theoretically, to the elimination of that pollutant's threat to public health. Within fifteen months of listing a pollutant, the administrator was obligated to promulgate "national ambient air quality standards" sufficient to protect health from that pollutant.[11] An *ambient standard* was to govern the concentration of a pollutant in the air we breathe, while an *emission standard* was to govern the rate at which a pollutant could flow into the air from a smokestack or tailpipe. The act did not make national ambient air quality standards enforceable directly against polluters, but rather required each state to have a plan that limited emissions enough to achieve the ambient standards. Specifically, within nine months of the promulgation of a national ambient air quality standard for a pollutant, it read, "[e]ach State shall . . . adopt and submit to the Administrator" plans to implement, maintain, and enforce the ambient standard for that pollutant.[12] Within another four months, the administrator was obligated to approve or disapprove the state plan; he could approve a plan only if the rules limiting emissions ensured compliance with the ambient standards within five years of the plan's approval.[13]

Putting the act's deadlines end-to-end meant that the entire nation would attain the national ambient air quality standards for the first group of five pollutants by 1977 and the second group of five pollutants by 1978. The act also required the EPA administrator and the states to deal with harmful pollutants that did not come from many sources, through an analogous series of mandatory duties. Hence, the Senate report could claim that "there should be no gaps" in fulfilling the promise "to assure the protection of the health of every American."[14]

To help the states achieve the national ambient air quality standards, the act also provided for federal rules limiting emissions on *new* stationary sources (for example, factories) and *new* mobile sources (for example, cars and trucks). The administrator was to list each category of stationary source (such as power plants) that "may contribute significantly" to harmful air pollution and then promulgate "New Source Performance Standards" limiting emissions to the extent economically and technologically feasible—an elastic standard. The administrator also had to prescribe emissions standards for any harmful pollutant from any class of new motor vehicles, again taking account of feasibility. Congress itself, however, required the administrator to order a 90-percent reduction in emissions of three pollutants from new passenger cars by specific dates.[15]

The act seemed to take account of economic and technological feasibility without compromising its unconditional vow to protect public health. As already noted, Congress directed the administrator to consider feasibility in establishing standards for new stationary sources and new motor vehicles. Although Congress had flatly directed that emissions from new cars be reduced by 90 percent, it also directed the administrator to grant a one-year extension if the auto manufacturers had tried diligently and still had fallen short, and it invited them to seek a statutory amendment if still more time was needed. However, to ensure the protection of health, the act directed the administrator to ignore feasibility when he established the national ambient air quality standards as goals that must be met.[16]

The states were directed to adopt emission limits on existing sources or additional emission limits on new sources to make up any difference between what the federal emission rules achieved and what attainment of the national ambient air quality standards required. The act generally allowed a state to regulate any source it chose, to any extent it chose, or not at all, so long as the state's plan as a whole achieved the federally mandated result.[17] Senator Muskie had presented this feature of the act as an attraction for the states:

> State and local authorities would be able to pursue options among a broad array, seeking a possible way of controlling or preventing air pollution that is most responsive to the nature of their air pollution problem and most responsive to their needs. In my judgment, the bill would give the State and local authorities sufficient latitude in selecting ways to prevent and control air pollution.[18]

The act thus promised both to protect the public health from air pollution *and* to protect the economy from infeasible controls. It was no wonder that Congress passed the 1970 Clean Air Act all but unanimously and that President Nixon signed the bill with fanfare.[19]

The Hard Choices That Congress Failed to Make

The act avoided facing the conflict between its twin promises of protecting health and the economy. If feasible rules limiting emissions fell short of achieving the national ambient air quality standards, the act's sponsors recognized that "[s]ome facilities may be closed."[20] But they added that this unpleasant possibility would encourage industry to develop the technology needed to achieve presently infeasible emission limits. This theory has been called *technology-forcing*.[21]

Technology-forcing and, with it, the Clean Air Act's promise to protect health and the economy, depended on some governmental authority actually imposing rules on pollution sources sufficient to protect health, regardless of feasibility. Congress called upon the states to make up the difference between the consequences of the economically sensitive national pollution rules and fulfillment of the congressional promise of health. So the states were left regulating those sources whose control would spark the fiercest opposition—existing sources, such as factories that already were built and employing people and cars and trucks that already were sold and being driven by voters. Moreover, the states had to regulate these sources beyond the point of economic or even technological feasibility in order to honor the act's flat promise to protect health at any price.

The severity of the laws that the act required the states to place upon their citizens became manifest only after the EPA administrator issued the first national ambient air quality standards, which were no stricter than the act's sponsors had expected, and the states began to prepare their plans. Measures needed to achieve the ambient air standards within the statutory timetable included cutting gasoline use in the Los Angeles area by over 80 percent, eliminating 30 to 40 percent of the parking in the business areas of Manhattan, and requiring public utilities to burn more expensive fuel, which helped raise the cost of electricity.[22]

Voters who had embraced the act's goals in the abstract resisted when the abstractions turned into laws applicable to them. Drivers in Los Angeles reacted vehemently to proposed gas rationing. Drivers in New York, and later in Los Angeles, engaged in massive resistance against laws that set aside special traffic lanes for buses and car pools.[23]

The question then became how the act would overcome such obstacles to fulfilling Congress's promises of healthy air. Congress had claimed in 1970 that citizens could use the courts to force the issuance of laws needed to protect health. But it had fudged the issue of who must issue the laws and had failed to decide what laws the courts could insist upon.

Who has the duty to impose the infeasible rules that the act requires?

State officials could not be expected to cooperate for long in a scheme in which they would bear the blame for costly and unpopular laws while federal legislators and the president could take credit for having cleaned the air. By 1973 most states were simply failing to submit plans to deal with pollution from cars and other mobile sources.[24]

The authors of the act had made no realistic provision to cope with this predictable reaction of state and local officials. The act says that a state "shall . . . adopt and submit" a plan to EPA. This seemed to mean that, as the Supreme Court said, Congress was "taking a stick to the States." But since the statutory remedy for the failure of a state to adopt a plan was for the EPA administrator to promulgate a federal plan for that state, states had no real duty to comply, only an option to act first.[25]

The EPA lacked the capacity to adopt and implement federal clean air plans. For many cities, a statutorily sufficient plan would require controversial choices about the building of new plants, the operation of old plants, the construction of new highways, the location of new shopping centers, and more. The act gave EPA the duty to make such controversial decisions in many locales of many states at once. Members of Congress, in debating the act, had not spoken of national takeover of state and local land use and transportation policies and had not provided the administrator political support for such actions. An effective plan, moreover, must not only specify decisions, but provide the means to implement them. Was EPA to deploy field inspectors to check smokestacks and tailpipes? Could it take over local regulatory functions that significantly affected pollution levels, such as zoning and traffic management? Could EPA command the states to carry out such functions? The act, as generally interpreted, required EPA itself to implement the federally promulgated plans. However, EPA had neither the political mandate nor the resources to promulgate and enforce the unpopular rules that attaining the goals of the act required.[26]

How clean should the air be made?

Congress had not defined the clean air goals with sufficient clarity for the courts to enforce them in actions against the agency. The statute required that the national ambient air quality standards be set at a level that would "allowing an adequate margin of safety . . . protect the public health" but provided no guidance on the meaning of the word *adequate*. Toxicologists usually want chemicals in foods, such as preservatives, limited to concentrations lower than a hundredth or a thousandth of the amounts known to have produced an adverse effect in laboratory animals, or even less. Since reducing air pollution to such levels would require repeal of the Industrial Revolution, the administrator inevitably had to balance health risks and the costs of pollution control in deciding what margin of safety was "adequate."[27]

Even more fundamentally, EPA's duty to "protect the public health" presumed that the agency could demonstrate that there was some ambient concentration of a pollutant above which the air was risky and below which the air was healthy. Congress, however, knew there was no such threshold, so that one could speak only of degrees of risk. Reflecting on the 1970 act, Senator Muskie later stated: "Our public health scientists and doctors have told us that there is no threshold, that any air pollution is harmful. The Clean Air Act is based on the assumption, although we knew at the time it was inaccurate, that there is a threshold. When we set the standards, we understood that below the standard that we set there would still be health effects."[28]

Setting the health-related standards does compel a discretionary balancing of health and economic concerns, as opposed to the broad promise of Congress that the standards would protect health.

How should the burden of cleaning the air be allocated?

Congress also failed to decide how to allocate among pollution sources the burden of cleaning the air. This deficiency meant that EPA had no guidance and, more important, no political support in deciding who had to pay to meet the ambient air standards.

There was no right way to apportion this burden. The administrator might logically have decided to impose emission limits designed to achieve:

- equal-percentage reductions in emissions from all sources;
- reductions in emissions from each source proportionate to its contribution to the worst ambient concentrations;
- the same emissions from all sources of a particular type; or
- other goals, such as minimizing adverse effect on employment.

These different principles would lead to far different results. The administrator was also required to decide whether to allow new sources to be built because, if a plan only barely attained the clean air standard, no margin would be left for new sources. The scope left for new sources potentially affected both property values and the creation of new jobs.

Congress also had failed to provide guidance on allocating the cleanup burden between states. The act purported to deal with interstate air pollution by requiring a state plan to contain "measures necessary to insure" that pollution from that state "will not interfere" with achieving the ambient standards in any other state. This language said nothing about division of the cleanup burden between sources in two or more states that together contributed to a violation of a national ambient air quality standard.[29]

The act's failure to allocate the cleanup burden encouraged companies to avoid developing new pollution-control technology because the states or EPA would tend to place more of the burden of reducing pollution on those companies that could do so most economically. Congressional failure to make the hard choices on allocating the cleanup burden undercut technology-forcing, which was the way it had proposed to reconcile its conflicting promises to protect both health and the economy.[30]

How the Statute Actually Worked

Legislators and President Nixon, both of whom had played environmental hero for environmentalist constituents by enacting the Clean Air Act, proceeded to play economic hero for their business and labor constituents by opposing EPA's efforts to implement the act. The White House under President Nixon—and *all* of his successors—pressured EPA to go slow on a wide range of issues.[31] In one controversy in which I represented citizen environmental groups, Senator Thomas Eagleton of Missouri, who had worked closely with Senator Muskie during the 1970 enactment, pressed the EPA administrator to take the financial impact on Missouri's lead industry into account in setting the national ambient air quality standard for lead, although the act clearly prohibited taking costs into account.[32] In a second case in which I represented citizen environmental groups, almost the entire New York City congressional delegation (which had vigorously supported passage of the Clean Air Act) opposed with equal vigor the ruling of a federal judge that required New York State to implement a key strategy in its clean air plan—placing tolls on the bridges owned by New York City.[33] The state itself had chosen this strategy to raise funds to improve mass transit as a means to reduce automotive pollution, but it tried to avoid honoring its commitment when opposition arose, particularly from Brooklyn motorists. Representative Elizabeth Holtzman, who had attained national stature in the Nixon impeachment proceedings, led the Brooklyn congressional contingent in a march over Brooklyn Bridge to protest the tolls. She proclaimed her continued support for clean air but did not suggest what burdens she would agree to impose on her constituents to clean the air. In wondering at this time how members of Congress could get political credit both for advocating a goal and opposing the inevitable costs of its achievement, I first started to ask myself whether delegation is desirable.

The EPA could not ignore the protests from elected lawmakers on the basis that the act required it to take the protested steps. As the previous section showed, the act was none too clear on the key questions of how clean to make the air or how to allocate the burden of paying for the cleanup. The agency had to take its legislative critics seriously, because they could amend the act, cut the agency budget, object to agency appointments, or hold prolonged oversight hearings. The agency similarly had to take its White House critics seriously, because the president can fire the administrator or other agency appointees.[34]

Legislators, the president, and EPA wanted to trim the duties that the Clean Air Act imposed, yet avoid the embarrassment of taking back the promises that the elected lawmakers had made with so much self-congratulation in 1970. They did so by employing five techniques described below (see also table 1):

1. *Use prosecutorial discretion to allow firms to violate laws.* If a state or the EPA was unwilling to enforce a law in the state's plan, they could ignore violations or write compliance schedules that allowed sources to do less than the law required.[35] The EPA generally did not require states to compensate for lowered demands on some sources by imposing tougher emission reductions on other sources.[36] However, under-enforcement was far from an ideal solution, because the act gave citizens the power to bring their own enforcement actions.[37]

2. *Do not adopt unpalatable emission laws.* Officials tried to avoid incorporating unattractive laws in a plan. The EPA dropped a law requiring severe gas rationing, which it had earlier imposed as necessary to meet the ambient air standard in Los Angeles because the public had reacted to it with understandable anger. Although the 1970 act required states to take whatever action was necessary to meet the ambient air quality standards, EPA refused to prevent major new pollution sources from being built in areas that would not achieve the standards by the act's deadline. Congress itself forbade EPA from imposing a number of unpopular strategies. Including only palatable laws in state plans ignored the act's requirement that the plans be sufficiently stringent to attain the ambient air quality standards.[38]

3. *Approve plans inadequate to meet ambient standards.* The Environmental Protection Agency approved as sufficient to meet the ambient air standards plans that actually were inadequate. As a 1989 Senate report recognized, EPA used a number of strategies to justify its claims:[39]

Table 1   Promise and Practice under the Clean Air Act of 1970

Promise	Practice
The goal: health.	**The problem is resolved.**
↓	↑
Identify and list pollutants that are harmful and come from many sources.	Leave harmful pollutants off the list.
↓	↑
Set ambient standards to protect health, regardless of feasibility.	Set ambient standards with eye to feasibility.
↓	↑
Develop state plan to meet ambient standards by:	Approve plans inadequate to meet ambient standards by:
• monitoring air quality at worst locations,	• not monitoring air quality at worst locations,
• calculating emission reductions needed to meet ambient standards, and	• manipulating air-quality projections to predict compliance with ambient standards,
• identifying sources that can reduce emissions.	• taking credit for illusory emission reductions.
↓	↑
Adopt laws reducing emissions enough to meet ambient standards.	Do not adopt unpalatable emission laws.
↓	↑
Require firms to comply with laws or shut down.	Use prosecutorial discretion to allow firms to violate laws.
↓	↑
The goal is realized.	**The problem: a political commitment and legal duty to implement an impossible act.**

Note: The left column (read from top to bottom) presents the promise of the Clean Air Act, according to which a series of mandatory duties would translate the goal of health protection into reality. The right column (read from bottom to top) presents the techniques used to avoid establishment or enforcement of politically unpalatable laws by subverting the duties imposed by the act.

• *Neglecting to monitor the worst locations.* Achieving the ambient air standards everywhere, as the act dictated, required knowing where they were violated and by how much, because pollution levels vary greatly. Using few monitors and placing them away from big factories or busy streets makes pollution appear less severe than it is.[40]

• *Manipulating air quality projections.* Determining whether the laws in a state plan would achieve the ambient air quality standards required predicting their impact on future air ambient quality. The states and EPA manipulated such predictions to show that palatable controls would achieve the ambient air standards. An EPA deputy general counsel wrote, "When modelling results began to show that in many cases not only the suggested new pattern of emissions, but the existing one as well, violated air quality requirements—thereby suggesting a legal duty to impose more control—the EPA significantly revised its modeling requirements."[41]

• *Taking credit for illusory emission reductions.* States exaggerated, even doubled, the reductions in emissions that the laws in their plans would achieve.[42]

4. *Set the ambient air standards with an eye to feasibility.* Although the act promised to protect health without regard to cost and so required the administrator to ignore cost in setting the ambient air standards, the administrator did take the cost of attaining these standards into account. As Senator Muskie recognized in 1977, the ambient standards represented a "pragmatic judgment." In fact, President Carter and his successors required EPA to prepare a formal analysis of the cost of complying with the ambient standards, but the agency had to deny that it paid attention to the cost analysis in setting the standard to protect it from court challenge.[43]

5. *Leave harmful pollutants off the list.* Since listing harmful pollutants triggered duties under the act, EPA forestalled those duties by not listing additional pollutants. The 1970 act listed five initial pollutants but the sponsors of the act promised that the agency would include five additional ones, and later add any other harmful pollutant that came from many sources. The EPA listed only one of these five additional pollutants, nitrogen oxides, in 1971 and then stopped. The courts ordered it to list another, lead, in 1976 in response to a lawsuit that I brought for the Natural Resources Defense Council and other citizen groups. The agency has listed no pollutants since.

The 1970 act also required EPA to list any harmful pollutant that is not widespread but causes cancer or is otherwise particularly hazardous. However, EPA listed only eight such pollutants through 1990, although it knew of about two hundred that it had not listed. A 1990 EPA study of some plants emitting some of these pollutants found that fifty-two plants presented cancer risks to the most exposed individual of greater than 1 in 1000, seven plants presented risks of greater than 1 in 100, and one presented a risk of greater than 1 in 10.[44]

What Congress Did after Its Deadline for Protecting Health Had Run Out

Many states did not meet the supposedly inflexible deadline of achieving the original ambient air standards by 1977. In that year, Congress postponed the deadlines for meeting the ambient air standards to 1982 for some pollutants and to 1987 for others.[45] It used procrastination, as it had in 1970, to obscure the infeasibility of its absolute promises.

Legislators, of course, did not acknowledge that they were just buying time but claimed that they were serious about meeting the ambient standards. They included provisions in the 1977 Amendments that allowed EPA to sanction states it found lacked plans to meet the standards on schedule. The agency, however, strove to limit use of its sanction authority for fear that Congress would weaken its powers.[46] As they had under the 1970 Act, EPA, the states, and pollution sources twisted the facts in order to approve inadequate state plans and papered over violations of the ambient air standards. According to the National Commission on Air Quality, EPA "approved virtually all states' projections that they would meet the air quality standards even though federal, state, and local officials privately acknowledge that such projections often were based on imprecise emission inventories and inadequate projection techniques, and that they often were overly optimistic." When those tactics did not work, the commission noted, EPA still usually found ways to avoid sanctioning the states.[47]

The inadequacy of the plans adopted under the 1977 legislation became evident as 1982 approached. Congress tried in 1981 and again in 1982 to enact additional amendments, but without success. Ann Gorsuch, the EPA administrator, threatened to impose sanctions but relented when environmental groups criticized this initiative as an effort to disparage the Clean Air Act and prompt Congress to pass weakening amendments.[48] Congress spent considerable time in each year after 1982 trying to amend the act, all without success until 1990.

In 1990 the air most people breathed still violated one or more of the ambient standards. Congressional committee reports pointed a finger of blame with great specificity at everybody but Congress, which they faulted, if at all, only in the most general of terms. A Senate report maintained that "the responsibility for the widespread failure to meet the ambient standards rests with both States (and local governments) and EPA."[49] So, the amendments passed in 1990 built upon past legislative failures, rather than correcting them.

The 1990 amendments grant extensions to the deadlines for meeting the ambient air standards of a few years to twenty years, depending upon the pollutant and the severity of the problem in a particular air quality–control region.[50] Thus the complete health protection the 1970 act promised to deliver by 1977 was postponed by the 1977 amendments until 1987, and will now theoretically arrive in 2010—the year in which the sequel to the futuristic movie *2001* is set.

The 1990 amendments also provide that states which have not attained the ambient air standards must impose various kinds of pollution control strategies, with more severe strategies required in the most polluted areas.[51] The Act generally calls upon EPA to issue regulations fleshing out what the states must do to satisfy these requirements. The 1990 act thus removes much of the flexibility that the 1970 act supposedly gave the states.

Like the 1977 amendments, the 1990 amendments tighten the emission limits on new cars that Congress originally enacted in 1970.[52] The 1990 amendments also deal with acid rain largely without delegating. I will discuss those provisions in Chapter 9.

What the Clean Air Act Shows about Delegation

Congress promised that narrow delegation would make the hard choices by giving agencies specific instructions on what goals its laws must achieve and through which procedures they must be issued. But, as we have seen, the Clean Air Act did not make the hard choices, and the failure of narrow delegation was not caused by the particulars of that act. From the Clean Air Act experience we can draw the general conclusions that (1) delegation does not provide a way for legislators to make the hard choices, (2) narrow delegation, in particular, is not a sensible way to resolve public controversies, and (3) narrow delegation introduces a staggering degree of delay, complexity, and confusion into lawmaking.

1. *Delegation does not provide a way for legislators to make the hard choices.* Congress made only one law in the 1970 act—the one limiting emissions of three pollutants from new cars by 90 percent. Otherwise, it decided that EPA and the states should make the laws. In its lengthy instructions on how they should do so, Congress sidestepped the two hardest and most fundamental choices: how clean to make the air, and who should bear the cleanup burden. Moreover, legislators artfully exploited the ambiguity in the act to convey quite different impressions to different constituencies. While the general public believed that Congress had taken a strong stand in favor of health, industry believed that the process for dealing with ambient pollutants would be sensitive to economic constraints. Indeed, corporations did not even challenge the first set of national ambient air quality standards in court, although the statute theoretically required their attainment by 1977.[53] The deception deprived everyone of two key advantages provided by the statutory resolution of a major social conflict—knowing how one was represented in Congress, and an authoritative resolution of the dispute upon which to base expectations and plans. The Clean Air Act left the electorate unenlightened and future clean-air policy undetermined.[54]

The lengthy instructions included in the act fooled not only the public but legal experts as well into believing that Congress actually had made the hard choices. Louis Jaffe, in a well-known article written shortly after the passage of the act, argued that in such statutes Congress would make the hard choices, although it did not make the rules of conduct, so long as the "reformer"

> secures a specific and firm political judgment from Congress which will resolve, to the degree appropriate formulae permit, the sharp conflicts of interest which are likely to be incapable of resolution by an agency. . . . The statutory language may be more or less general in terms; what counts is the statutory history. The key to success is the strong and persistent public opinion which demands a response to a given problem, which is sufficiently organized to press for the detailed legislative solution required, and which will, ultimately, keep the administration on the job of implementing it.[55]

The 1970 act sought to do just this, as Jaffe acknowledged. Its legislative history stated, as precisely as possible, that health was to be protected at any price.[56] Furthermore, opinion polls and the activity of environmental groups show a high degree of continuing public support for that goal in the abstract. Nonetheless, EPA found it was one thing to have Congress stand behind the principle of clean air, and quite another to have Congress stand behind particular laws. Not having voted for any particular laws, legislators were free to oppose whatever agency-made laws their constituents disliked. They could always find a way of saying, in effect, "I'm for the environment, but EPA is going about protecting it the wrong way." The act's "legislative history" thus failed to protect EPA from the legislative present.

Congress could not have avoided the hard choices if it had made the laws itself nor could it have made the hard choices if it delegated in some other way. Stating the laws would have made manifest to the public and industry alike the conflict lurking below the surface of the act, by making clear who was to do what. Not surprisingly, the mandated 90-percent reduction in emissions from new cars—the only law specified in the act—sparked the hottest debate in Congress.[57] In contrast to a statute that makes law, a statute that delegates speaks to what the laws shall be in, at most, indirect and abstract terms, specifying only the goals that the agency's laws must achieve. The ambiguity inherent in such instructions ordinarily gives the agency broad discretion in shaping its laws and permits legislators to tell different constituencies widely differing accounts of what the statute will mean in practice. As William Rodgers has concluded, Congress typically uses complicated instructions to agencies in environmental statutes for the purpose of "dissembling and manipulation."[58]

Even if Congress did want to make the hard choices, it could not do so by instructing a delegate to achieve specified goals. Dictating an absolute goal usually makes no sense. Protecting health cannot be the absolute goal of pollution law because, as previously discussed, there is no clear dividing line between health and safety, and it is foolish to eliminate tiny risks at great cost. A candid Congress wishing to delegate would have to tell an agency to balance clashing goals, but then the agency, rather than Congress, would make the hard choices.

In 1980 Bruce Ackerman and William Hassler suggested a way for Congress to make the hard choice between health protection and the cost it entails, yet still delegate. Specifically, they argued that Congress should set a numerical target for EPA to pursue, for instance: "Achieve ambient air quality improvements that promise to add at least 25,000 years to the life expectancies of the American people by [a particular date]."[59] The agency could then decide what laws it would issue to achieve that goal. This would provide a way for Congress to decide how clean to make the air, but it would not address the question of how to allocate the cleanup burden. As long as Congress failed to make that hard choice, the EPA would still bear the political burden of imposing costs and would continue to encounter the fierce controversy that tends to paralyze decisionmaking. Congress could, in theory, go on to propose some other sort of numerical formula to govern how the agency should allocate the cleanup burden; however, if Congress really expressed in a verifiable way how clean the air must be made and how the burden of making it that clean should be allocated, Congress would itself have determined the rules of conduct. The only work left for the agency would be interpretation of the statutory instructions. In other words, Congress would have made the law, without delegation.

A second problem with Ackerman and Hassler's proposal is that numerical goals sound definitive, but often fail to make the hard choices in a meaningful way. In this instance, science lacks the capacity to produce hard specifications for the clean-air laws that the EPA is to issue because it is enormously difficult to assess the risk presented by chemicals. For example, a national study concluded that over seventy years, regular exposure of the population to certain doses of saccharin would cause somewhere between 0.22 and 1,144,000 cases of bladder cancer.[60] In areas of regulation other than environmental protection, agencies usually have still broader discretion because the connection between goals and laws in social and economic regulation rests upon the "soft" social sciences, which tend to have even greater levels of uncertainty than the "hard" natural sciences used in pollution control.

In sum, legislators cannot make the hard choices by delegation. Narrow delegation offers them a way to appear to make them without actually doing so.

2. *Narrow delegation is not a sensible way to make hard choices.* The effort of Congress to make hard choices by stating absolute goals got in the way of sensibly resolving the inevitable tension between minimizing the risk to health and minimizing the cost of pollution control. Under the act, the agency had to base its ambient standards on health concerns, to the exclusion of cost, but had to base its national emission

standards for new stationary and mobile sources on the economic feasibility of the reductions, to the exclusion of health considerations. Neither set of standards made sense. Whether a risk to health remaining in an ambient air standard is unreasonable depends in part upon the marginal cost of reducing the risk; similarly, what constitutes a reasonable cost for an emission control system depends upon the marginal benefit from a further reduction in emissions. So although trade-offs were inevitable, the decision to delegate in this way meant that the agency could not candidly discuss these trade-offs.

The legal obstacles preventing EPA from openly compromising the health-at-any-price goal have led to irrational results. The agency essentially stopped listing harmful pollutants to avoid the command that they regulate these pollutants without regard for the economic consequences.[61] While the sponsors of the Clean Air Act promised that official recognition of danger would prompt action, the act's absolute duties to respond to danger prompted officials not to recognize the dangers in the first place.

The unrealistic mandate for health at any cost responded to popular demand. But the statutory scheme perpetuated the lack of realism in public opinion. From 1970 down to the present, when pollsters ask whether health protection should be sacrificed to economic concerns, much of the public says no.[62] That is the question that the Clean Air Act pretends to answer, but it is the wrong question. People tend to think of *their* health being sacrificed to save *somebody else's* cost. The realistic question is, what costs would you bear to reduce risks to your own health. A statute that did not delegate would have posed that question. In contrast, delegation allowed the legislators who passed the Clean Air Act to avoid confronting the desires of their constituents to do the very things that make pollution. Congress spoke as if they represented *us*, forced to breathe pollution produced by *them*. In 1970 polls, few people labeled emissions from their own home furnaces, for instance, as pollution. In 1990, even after twenty years of experience with the 1970 act, the Senate majority leader, George Mitchell, could derive political advantage from arguing that health should not be balanced against the cost of pollution control.[63]

The public's unrealistic demand for health protection at any price also results in part from its appropriate distrust of public officials. When legislators first require their delegates to protect health at any cost, then work behind the scenes to prevent the delegates from carrying out those instructions, and later criticize those officials for violating the statute, citizens rightly doubt those officials' intentions and feel subject to risks beyond their control. From that perspective, commanding those in control to avoid the risk at any cost is understandable. In contrast, if legislators had to vote on the rules of conduct directly, constituents might feel more in control of their own destinies and take more realistic positions. Perhaps the relative control over their own destinies that California voters were allowed in deciding environmental rules in the 1990 "Big Green" referendum explains why this relatively pro-environment constituency rejected this measure at the same time that the United States Congress embraced the 1990 Clean Air Act with its health-at-any-price rhetoric at an estimated annual cost of from twenty billion to one hundred billion dollars.[64]

Supporters of the Clean Air Act claimed that its utopian goals produced the most important reductions in pollution,[65] but in fact the largest reductions came from the one legislated rule in the act, which limited new-car emissions. Regarding stationary sources, the states actually had adopted the most significant emissions rules *before* Congress enacted the federal mandate on national ambient air standards. So, while Congress acted as if it had to take a stick to the laggardly states, the states took the action and Congress took the credit.[66]

The air might well be cleaner today if Congress had enacted more laws that limited emissions instead of enacting aspirational goals. The prevalent idea that the statute we got was stronger because of delegation comes, I suppose, from the notion that delegation hides the cost from the public until it is too late to protest. This ploy proves more clever in theory than in practice, and, moreover, it patronizes the public. During the Clean Air Act hearings in early 1970 Senator Muskie said, "For the first time in seven or eight years there is a tremendous reservoir of public concern and support for effective action in this field. I think our primary challenge is to use that resource in developing the soundest and most effective legislation of which we are capable."[67] This potent public pressure might have provided sufficient support for the enactment of strong rules but instead was answered with complicated, prolonged administrative procedures. In those settings, public opinion is less powerful than in an open legislative battle, and industry's teams of lawyers and expert witnesses are more powerful. That is what deflated the promises of the 1970 act. That is why industry supported delegation in the air pollution area in the middle

1960s and why it has supported delegation in other environmental statutes since.[68]

The act's health-at-any-price stance led federal and state officials to conspire to violate the statute quite purposefully in order to reconcile it with economic and political reality. The National Commission on Air Quality, whose key members were legislators, documented such violations in copious detail. Yet the commission concluded that "the structure of the Clean Air Act is sound"[69] and hardly raised an eyebrow at the behavior of officials. When legislators enact statutes knowing that an agency will violate them, and indeed planning to abet the violations, they mislead the public and breed contempt for law.

3. *Narrow delegation introduces a staggering degree of delay, complexity, and confusion into lawmaking.* A statute that delegates neither protects those who face danger nor guides those who are to be regulated until an agency promulgates the requisite law. Even then, the courts may reverse agency-made law, Congress may change it, or the agency may bow to pressure and do so itself, especially with a change of presidents. Statutory laws also get overturned in court or changed, but with far less frequency.

One agency law on which I worked as an attorney representing the Natural Resources Defense Council limited the lead content of gasoline used by pre–1975 cars, which do not have to use lead-free gasoline to protect their catalytic converters. The EPA began the rulemaking process in 1971, promulgated the law in 1973 after I secured a court order to stop its delaying, and finally got it affirmed on appeal in 1976. The agency proposed amendments weakening or strengthening the law once in 1976, twice in 1979, once in 1980, four times in 1982, three times in 1983, once in 1984, four times in 1985, and once in 1986, most of which changes were promulgated.[70] The agency stopped proposing amendments once the market for leaded gasoline for pre–1975 cars lost economic importance and the industry stopped fighting the restrictions. In other words, the controversy became moot before EPA resolved it.

That episode of protracted rulemaking took place under a provision of the act which delegates in broad terms. The provisions that delegated narrowly were supposed to speed the achievement of regulatory goals, but the complexity of the narrow delegation consumed prodigious amounts of human resources and ultimately became a source of delay in its own right. Translating air quality goals into laws reducing pollution requires many steps, each of which is plagued with uncertainty and intricacy. Because the ambient standards must protect health with a margin of safety, which is a sensible goal, EPA is, in the words of one of its scientists, "always setting the standards at a level where the data is lousy."[71] The emissions reduction necessary to bring air pollution down to the ambient standard is also an uncertain quantity because, according to former EPA Administrator Douglas Costle, specifying that figure depends upon "a huge number of highly uncertain explorations into modelling, monitoring and meteorological impacts, emissions inventories and so on." For example, air quality monitoring is readily manipulated and so makes a "really silly" reference point for a control program, according to a leading air quality monitoring expert. Costle notes, "Modeling is becoming elevated to the same high art of gamesmanship as lawyering, and often a company finds it cheaper to hire modelers and lawyers than to put in pollution control equipment."[72]

The Clean Air Act, moreover, requires EPA to deal with each harmful pollutant by considering its impact at all places and from all sources through separate plans for each harmful widespread pollutant in each "air quality control region" in every state. Many states have multiple regions; Massachusetts was divided into 351 regions for some purposes.[73] The laws reducing emissions in each plan can themselves be quite complex. Plans typically vary emission limits from plant to plant within a region, and even from smokestack to smokestack within a single plant to avoid any emission reduction not strictly required by the act's ambient air goals.[74] Putting a state plan into effect or revising an old one requires two steps: adoption of a plan by the state and its approval by EPA.[75] Each is a separate rulemaking. During the period of federal rulemaking—which can last a year or two if there is any issue and more if it is controversial—the plan under state law will differ from that under federal law.

The impossibly complex job that the statute gave EPA and the states undercut the air pollution program in many ways. Two examples:

• The EPA may be years behind in approving or disapproving state-plan revisions. This delay affects industry's compliance with the plan and sows confusion about what version should be enforced. The agency can and does prosecute companies which are in compliance with the plan as revised by the state if they are in violation

of the unrevised plan. This is the case though EPA has delayed
unreasonably in ruling on the state revision.[76]
• The "plan" is not a single document but the various documents
issued by the state and EPA in adopting and revising the plan over
many years. Since the documents' relationship to one another is
not always clear and so many documents are involved—often filling
filing cabinets—sometimes neither the state nor EPA knows what
the plan in question requires of a pollution source. When the defendant in one enforcement suit demanded in discovery to see the
plan, EPA could not produce all the documents and had to dismiss
in a settlement that awarded attorney's fees to the defendant.[77]

It would be comforting, but wrong, to think that the delay, complexity, and confusion produced by the Clean Air Act is the result of
some unforeseen mistake in its design rather than the inevitable consequence of delegation. Delegation inevitably produces these results because an agency is left to make the law and rationalize it in detail, and
even then the law is not settled. Narrowing the delegation compounds
the problem by making the agency jump through additional hoops.
But the chief source of the difficulty is more insidious: legislators seem
to be unconcerned about imposing delay, complexity, and confusion
on their constituents when they delegate. Even in 1970 the Clean Air
Act's chief architects knew that it was unworkable.[78] Congress did not
change the basic structure of the act in 1977 but rather responded to
the problems by issuing additional instructions, thereby increasing
the excessive burden on the agency that had helped to cause the problems. For instance, the 1977 amendments dealt with uncertainty about
the contents of plans by requiring EPA to "publish" all plans at least
annually, even though a plan often is the contents of a filing cabinet.
The National Commission report, issued in 1981, acknowledged that
"it is seldom possible to obtain a copy of the current federally approved implementation plan for a given state."[79] Overall, EPA met fewer
than 15 percent of the rulemaking deadlines set under the 1970 and
1977 acts.[80]

In 1990 Congress again did not dismantle programs that had not
worked well before; it instead added still more instructions and created entirely new programs. One indicator of the extent to which Congress has multiplied instructions to the agency is the growth in the
length of the act: from approximately 8 double-spaced typed pages in

1965, to 76 pages in 1970, to 272 pages in 1977, and to 718 pages in 1990. The 1990 amendments require EPA to issue fifty major and thirty minor regulations within the next two years. The agency cannot possibly comply. Previous to 1990, it had managed to produce only seven or eight major regulations per year for air pollution, toxic-waste cleanup, and all of its other programs combined. In 1992 Representative Henry Waxman, one of the authors of the 1990 amendments, sued EPA for failing to meet thirty-one of its deadlines.[81]

Whether the Clean Air Act works somewhat better or somewhat worse than other narrow delegations, narrow delegation generally does evade hard choices, prolong public policy disputes, and sow delay, complexity, and confusion. As the political scientist Terry Moe concludes, "American public bureaucracy is not designed to be effective" but rather to advance the interests of "those who exercise political power."[82]

How Delegation Changes the Politics of Lawmaking

STATUTES THAT PURPORT TO GIVE LAWMAKING power to an agency actually entail a sharing of lawmaking power among several groups, including the agency, the most powerful members of the legislative committees with jurisdiction over the agency, their counterparts in the White House, and concentrated interests. Concurrently, political benefits accrue to legislators and the president. First, they can claim credit for the promised benefits of a regulatory program, yet shift blame for the disappointments and costs of the program to the agency. Second, with delegation they increase their opportunities to obtain campaign contributions and other favors from concentrated interests.

The Politics of Agency Lawmaking

Some observers of agencies argue that regulated industries and other concentrated interests often capture the agency and actually use it against the public. Other observers produce evidence that members of congressional subcommittees with jurisdiction over the agency use the agency to serve the interests with which they are aligned. Still others contend that agency personnel themselves are an interest group that strives at the expense of the public interest to increase their own pay, power, prestige, and access to lucrative private-sector jobs.[1]

Most political scientists see a role for all of the above—concentrated interests, congressional subcommittees, and agency personnel—in determining agency behavior.[2] Some use the term *subgovernment* to describe this constellation of interests that gathers around most agencies. Each part of a subgovernment stands to help and be helped by the others. In simplified terms, a concentrated interest, such as a regulated industry, can offer legislators money or campaign assistance in return for leniency by the agency toward the industry; legislators can offer the agency generous budgets in return for that leniency; and the agency can manifest leniency in return for the large budgets.[3]

Since each component of a subgovernment gains from agency laws that enrich these concentrated private interests, all of them have an incentive to work together to keep outsiders from disrupting their arrangement. Some political scientists call the triad of agency personnel, congressional subcommittees, and concentrated interests an "iron triangle" because it includes the most powerful forces at work in the broad delegations—those with unique access to information and the most direct control of the relevant agenda in the agency and in Congress.[4] One journalist noted that, although agricultural marketing orders hurt most of their constituents, legislators "who know about the orders are almost all protective."[5]

I prefer the term *subgovernment* because the *iron triangle* metaphor leaves out the president and his staff in the White House and the Office of Management and Budget. They have considerable power over lawmaking, given that the president appoints the top agency staff and can fire them as well, except in the case of so-called independent agencies. And even independent agencies need the cooperation of the president's staff, especially in the budget process. Those members of the president's staff with particular responsibility for the agency are part of the concept of the subgovernment.

A subgovernment does not have absolute power. Its members may have a falling out over the division of the spoils. Or, if the consequences on those outside its ranks are sufficiently severe, members of Congress or citizens' advocacy groups may try to intervene. In the agricultural marketing order program, however, a subgovernment repulsed such efforts to intervene for many years.

Narrow delegation in the Clean Air Act and in the statutes modeled after it changed the workings of subgovernment by giving private citizens the power to make agencies regulate industries in response to popular goals, rather than according to the industries' desires. Even though, as the Clean Air Act demonstrates, the members of a subgovernment can find ways of evading such instructions, private organizations have gained power by systematically taking advantage of the opportunities offered by narrow delegations. Although these organizations call themselves "public-interest" groups, they frequently represent only part of the spectrum of public opinion and have private interests of their own, such as obtaining money to fund their often substantial budgets and satisfying the ambitions of their staffs. Citizens' groups sometimes form alliances with legislators, agency personnel, or regulated industry. Because the affected subgovernment is no longer either "triangular" or "iron," political scientists search for new metaphors, such as *issue networks*, to describe these power relationships.[6]

What Legislators Get from Delegation

The Opportunity to Take Credit and Shift Blame

David Mayhew suggests that legislators delegate to facilitate taking attractive positions, because "in a large class of legislative undertakings the electoral payment is for positions rather than for effects." He continues:

> Regulatory statutes are the by-products of congressional position taking at times of public dissatisfaction. They tend to be vaguely drawn. What happens in enforcement is largely a result of congressional credit-claiming activities on behalf of the regulated; there is every reason to believe that the regulatory agencies do what Congress wants them to do. The ambitious "public interest" aims of the statutes are seldom accomplished.[7]

The agency then takes the blame for the failure to achieve the statute's popular goals and for the costs of any regulation actually imposed.

To explain why Congress delegates in some "legislative undertakings" and not in others requires a general sense of what motivates Congress when it legislates. The huge literature on that topic would take an entire book to analyze.[8] I will draw upon part of that extensive literature to explain briefly why Congress legislates and why, when it legislates, it sometimes delegates.

I start by assuming that legislators base their votes to a significant extent on looking good to the public rather than on doing good for the public. After establishing this assumption, I will use it to show why legislators sometimes enact laws that actually hurt the public. I will then discuss how delegation sometimes aids, but sometimes undermines, legislators' efforts to look good to their constituents.

Looking good to the public rather than doing good for the public.
Legislators traditionally claim to have dedicated themselves to "public service," which implies that they want to give the public the reality rather than the appearance of good government. As Chapter 2 suggested, we should greet such claims of public virtue with skepticism.[9]

Taking a fresh look at widely reported observations about modern legislators' behavior shows this skepticism to be well-founded. For instance, legislators use the public's money to give themselves huge advantages in reelection campaigns. Alan Ehrenhalt, the editor of a trade magazine for politicians and sympathetic to legislators, nonetheless writes:

> Through the 1980s, the U.S. House acquired and came to deserve a reputation as an "incumbent protection society" that organized itself in every possible way to guarantee the reelection of its members every two years. The devices used in this process are no secret: self-promotional newsletters, mailed regularly to thousands of households at taxpayer expense; weekend trips to the district virtually year-round, funded through regular staff allowances; constituent service offices, as many as three or four in some districts, organized to make friends with voters one at a time by tracing their lost social security checks, . . . and . . . countless other forms of vote-gaining kindness; committee hearings in the district, convened for the nominal purpose of investigating public policy but designed to provide favorable publicity for the member in whose constituency they are held.[10]

The public also paid for an advanced broadcasting complex that allows any legislator to produce sophisticated video clips and feed them by satellite to any local station in the country.

Legislators devote most of their own time, and that of their staff, to tasks of more benefit to themselves than the public: fund-raising, burnishing their images, pressing the flesh of their constituents, doing casework likely to lead to electoral support or cash contributions, "making floor speeches or inserting documents into the *Congressional Record* to impress the home audience rather than to persuade colleagues."[11] Of course casework helps the citizen on whose behalf it is done, but often at the expense of other citizens waiting to be served by the same agency.[12] As I will discuss in Chapter 9, legislators could provide such assistance to citizens without taking personal credit by setting up an ombudsman system not linked to any particular legislator, as is done in many other countries. Our legislators have no more right to attach their names to the help given to constituents through public funds than they have to sign personally the Social Security checks that go to their constituents.

A related example of legislators' preferring the appearance of good government to its reality concerns how they compensate themselves. For years, they sincerely believed they should get pay increases but refused to enact them to avoid looking bad to constituents. At the same time, they permitted themselves to accept money and other valuables from private sources. Such private compensation can cost the public far more than pay increases, because it is pregnant with the possibility of bribery. Only after long criticism did Congress stop members from pocketing leftover campaign funds and accepting "honoraria." Congress has still not clamped down on legislators' use of campaign funds for personal expenses.[13] The system of campaign contributions through political action committees suggests that donors believe they are getting something for their money. As former senator Alan Cranston acknowledged, "A person who makes a contribution has a better chance to get access than someone who does not." His chief fundraiser sought to deny that Cranston made any explicit bargain with a certain big contributor by arguing that "there are a lot of people who are not subtle about what it is they want, and there was no reason to have to deal with those people." In other words, a legislator *may* take money from a contributor who is subtle in asking for something in return. According to former senator William Proxmire, "contributions given to members of committees with jurisdiction over a contributor's industry are bribes, pure and simple."[14]

Some legislators probably are sincere in their protests that they put the public first, but their sincerity does not undercut my assumption. I have not assumed that looking good is the only motive in Congress, but that it is an important motive, and perhaps the major one.[15] Even a legislator who sincerely wants to put the public first must get reelected in order to continue to do good. Of course many legislators represent districts in which their reelection is almost assured, but such safe districts are often the result of assiduous, continuing efforts to build a good image.[16] Even legislators who win by large margins often act as if they fear that the next election will be close. As Ehrenhalt puts it, "The young congressman who finds his reelection margins climbing after a term or two toward 70 percent, who no longer attracts credible or decently financed opposition, is not noticeably less obsessed with reelection than his rare colleague who is genuinely vulnerable." Moreover, even a legislator representing a truly safe district may aspire to higher office or simply may crave popularity. In Elliot Richardson's words, Washington's leaders are "more interested in being petted and admired than in rendering the exercise of power."[17]

Craving electoral success or adulation, legislators can easily fool themselves into thinking that they put the public first. What one commentator wrote of clerics and psychotherapists also applies to many legislators:

Something is a bit odd about people who proclaim "I want to help other people". . . . Such people may be lured, knowingly or unknowingly, by the position of authority, by the dependence of others, by the image of benevolence, by the promise of adulation, or by a hope of vicariously helping themselves through helping others. Though some helping professionals have humbly and realistically perceived that they have something to offer and are willing to accept the responsibilities inherent in their calling, others use the role to manipulate their world in a convenient, simplistic manner, ultimately failing to take responsibility and using authority precisely to avoid it. For such people their job is not merely a way to earn a living: it is the essence of their lives.[18]

This description fits many legislators in general and their use of delegation in particular. Many members of Congress cling to their positions as to life itself, despite the relatively low official income, arduous hours, and frustration.[19] Their desperation is captured in the following excerpt from Veronica Geng's parody of a congressman's form letter:

Dear Constituent:
As the New Year is evidently under way, I am completing a nearly striving-packed decade as your full-time Representative in Wash-

ington, D.C. I want you to know how firmly I have urged you to support me, and how deeply I appreciate the authority you have vested in me to exceed my authority . . . [20]

A recent study of what legislators think of their jobs left the researchers unable to explain why people who dislike their jobs so much stay on so long.[21] Ward Just, "the Washington novelist's Washington novelist," suggests a plausible explanation. He has one of his heroes realize, in the course of unsuccessfully trying to get out of politics, that politicians chose "politics for the protection it afforded [from personal life]. . . . It was courage they wanted, though this was vulgar to admit. It was hard being your own man, because you did not know who that was, after so many years in the crowd."[22] Such an inability to face oneself might entail a fear of having to account to others as equals on a one-to-one basis, as a lawyer in private practice must with clients or partners. However, as long as legislators stay in politics, they have excellent odds of reelection and treat each other as independent potentates. Leaving office would require a descent from the pedestal.

Legislators need not find it hard to rationalize self-serving actions. Uncertainty about whether statutes can be enacted and what they will accomplish leads to blurring the distinction between the actions that will best serve the public and those that will look good to the public. Rationalizations for the politically convenient route are easy to contrive. For example, the idea of "orderly markets," the official reason for agricultural marketing orders, provides a handy pretext for a dreadful but politically advantageous program. Another formulation is this: A legislator may think, "I must vote as I do, because otherwise my opponent would win and that would be worse for the public."

How responsibility shifting affects legislation.
I offer a model of how legislators vote derived from the work of Morris Fiorina but relaxing some of his assumptions.[23] The model simplifies legislators' behavior, as its purpose is not to predict how any given legislator would react to any given bill, but to present systematically the kinds of factors that affect whether delegation shifts more or less blame than credit.

My model begins with the continued assumption that many legislators decide how to vote partly on the basis of how their vote will look to the public rather than whether it helps the public. In other words, they will tend to vote for a bill if they think that the public will perceive it as doing more good than harm, even though it might actually do more harm than good.

The public can misperceive the real effects of a bill that does not delegate if they fail to notice the ensuing harms and benefits, or to see their governmental origin. For example, most people do not understand that the government artificially inflates the cost of oranges; the average consumer's stake in the price of oranges is too small to make it worthwhile to investigate that question. Similarly, when officeholders build themselves a new office building, each individual voter bears little of the cost, which is spread broadly throughout the economy by taxation and government borrowing. In contrast to the diffusely spread costs imposed by the orange quotas or by a new government office building, their benefits are concentrated: on Sunkist, or on the contractors and workers who construct the building, as well as on the officials who use it. The relatively greater concentration of the benefits makes the beneficiaries more likely than the victims to recognize the source of the costs and benefits. The legislator will tend to vote for the action if the perceived benefit is greater than the perceived cost, even if the real benefit is less than the real cost.[24]

The disparity in the perception of benefits and harms arising from concentrated benefits and diffused harms is the traditional explanation of why legislators vote for pork-barrel projects and other actions whose real costs outweigh their benefits—that is, in Fiorina's terms, why they commit a "sin of commission." Conversely, diffuse benefits and concentrated harms may prompt legislators to vote against bills that would create more objective benefit than harm for constituents —that is, they commit a "sin of omission."[25]

The public also misperceives the effects of legislative behavior when delegation shifts some of the credit for benefit and blame for harm from the legislators to the agency. Fiorina assumes that some of the responsibility that belongs to Congress will fall on the involved agency even if Congress does not delegate, but that delegation will shift more of the responsibility.[26] As Douglas Arnold observes:

> Sometimes legislators know precisely what the executive will decide, but the process of delegation insulates them from political retribution. When Congress was unable to approve any of the standby gasoline rationing plans submitted by President Carter, presumably for fear [that voters would blame them for any resultant costs], the procedural solution was for Congress to delegate authority to

the president to draft and implement a plan *without* the need for specific congressional approval. Everyone knew the president would simply affirm one of the previously rejected plans; but by delegating authority, legislators insulated themselves from any political repercussions, should a plan ever be implemented and produce unpopular effects.[27]

Delegation often does not shift credit and blame equally. For example, a statute that delegates power to an agency to set prices to the advantage of an industry may succeed in shifting almost all the blame for the costs to the agency, because consumers do not understand the legislature's role in authorizing the price-fixing; yet a sophisticated industry will still credit legislators for a substantial share of its benefit.

Within this model, when will an individual legislator who wants to look good support a bill that delegates, when a bill that does not delegate, and when no bill? The legislator will prefer a bill that delegates to one that does not if the public would perceive the net benefits from the bill that delegates as greater than those from the bill that does not delegate.[28] The legislator will prefer no bill if neither bill produces perceived net benefits.

Several factors affect the perceived net benefits of the alternative bills and therefore how the legislator will vote. If a bill would in fact cause major harm or if the public would perceive readily the governmental origin of whatever harm it causes, the net benefits the public perceives will decrease and thus give the legislator an incentive to try to shift blame to the agency by delegating. Conversely, if a bill would confer a major benefit or if the public would perceive readily the governmental origin of whatever benefit it would achieve, its perceived net benefit will increase and so give the legislator more reason not to delegate.[29] So when all or most districts perceive a government action as beneficial, the statute is more likely to enact a law rather than delegate. This accords with Congress's decisions in 1970, 1977, and 1990 to set limits on auto emissions. Auto manufacturers are located in relatively few legislative districts; the constituents in most other districts perceived the costs of controlling emissions as falling on these firms.[30]

Legislators are also more likely to avoid delegation if doing so significantly would shift credit away from them or would fail to shift away much blame.[31] This may provide a further explanation of why Congress itself set auto emissions standards: delegation is unlikely to fool the auto industry, which is sophisticated in the ways of government and would recognize legislators' roles in imposing costs, but can undermine legislators' ability to claim credit for benefits with the public. Differences in the impact of delegation on perceptions of the legislators' role in creating benefits and imposing costs also helps to explain congressional willingness to make detailed decisions about pork-barrel spending and tax breaks. In these instances, legislators get little blame without delegation; those who lose (taxpayers in general) fail to perceive the cost to them of any particular pork-barrel project or tax break. Yet legislators have much to lose from delegation, which allows the executive branch to claim the credit from those who receive the benefits.[32]

Conversely, legislators are more likely to delegate if doing so would shift blame away from them significantly or would fail to shift away much credit. In contrast with delegating the power to control emissions from new cars, delegating the power to control emissions from such other sources as existing cars, factories, and apartment houses could shift blame away from legislators, because those connected with these other sources are generally less sophisticated than the auto industry. Moreover, companies could not have predicted what effects the early environmental statutes would have on them even if they had deciphered their terms.[33] Congress also has delegated decisions about closing military bases because, given a base's concentrated effect on a local economy, people whose incomes depend upon the base acutely perceive the harm of the closing and legislators' role in it, while the public in general underperceives the benefits of closing an unneeded base. Local businessmen and others adversely affected by the base closing are less likely to blame the local member of Congress if the decision comes from a national commission rather than in a military appropriations bill for which their representative voted. For similar reasons, Congress tried to use delegation to increase its salary.

The Clean Air Act example not only provides anecdotal support for Fiorina's model, but also suggests four additional ways, not mentioned by Fiorina, in which legislators can use delegation to manipulate how they appear to the public. First, Fiorina assumes, for the sake of simplicity, that delegation would change neither the benefits and harms done by a possible congressional action nor the degree to which the public would attribute these benefits and costs to the government.[34] In fact, the availability of delegation may prompt Congress to act differently than it would without that option, in order to change public perception of benefits and harms to its advantage. This complements the observations of political scientists that legislators tend to specify the benefits of legislation as clearly as possible but distance themselves from the costs by framing statutes "that are long on goals but short on means to achieve them."[35] The former representative (now governor) James Florio said of his time in Congress, "In order to come to agreement . . . one consciously strives for ambiguity in order to get people to sign on to things."[36] The Clean Air Act was designed to concretize the benefits—attainment of the national ambient air quality standards by a specific date—while obscuring the most politically problematic costs of achieving that benefit—the expense to industry of reducing emissions from existing stationary sources and the inconvenience to motorists of changing their behavior.

Second, in considering the probability that the public will identify benefit and harm with a legislator, Fiorina assumes this connection is beyond the legislator's control.[37] But delegation allows legislators to better pursue one of the goals assigned to them by Fiorina: either to identify with the government action or to distance themselves from it, depending upon how the action affects their district. A legislator whose district will benefit from an action will identify with what the agency does, thus increasing the public's sense that the legislator is responsible for the benefits (and also the losses) from the action. Another legislator, whose district will be hurt, will say that the agency has botched the job, thus diminishing the public's sense that the legislator is responsible for harms (and benefits).[38] If Congress could not delegate, legislators could not choose so readily whether to identify with or dissociate themselves from government action. The Clean Air Act illustrates this phenomenon; politicians variously distanced themselves from the legislation or identified with it, as political considerations made each course worthwhile.

Third, delegation enhances legislators' opportunities simultaneously to support the benefits of an action and oppose its costs, which is political heaven.[39] The 1970 Clean Air Act passed all but unanimously, but some legislators who had been its strongest advocates opposed EPA when it was compelled by the statute to impose costs on their constituents.

The fourth and final point is that delegation enables legislators to represent themselves to some constituents as supporting an action and to others as opposing it, which is also political heaven. Legislators, for example, can write different letters about the same issue to different groups of constituents, with each letter crafted to make the legislator appear to sympathize with that group's position. The legislator is helped in being all things to all people because letters to constituents about bureaucratic actions are more private than publicly recorded votes on statutory laws. Legislators can also intervene with agencies on behalf of particular constituents. Such casework allows a legislator to provide "the most intensely divisible of private political benefits."[40]

These four ways in which legislators can use delegation to maximize their credit and minimize their blame help to explain why delegation systematically produces the delay, complexity, and confusion that the Clean Air Act illustrates. As former EPA Administrator Lee Thomas put it, "Everybody is accountable and nobody is accountable under the way [Congress] is setting it up, but [the legislators] have got a designated whipping boy."[41]

While delegation helps legislators commit sins of both commission and omission by shifting blame for hurting the public, delegation can also—at least in theory—help legislators to avoid committing such sins by shifting blame for disappointing concentrated interests.[42] Using delegation to minimize the political fallout of closing military bases is a case in point. But when concentrated interests are large corporations, national unions, or other sophisticated players, delegation will not keep them from perceiving the legislators' role in their disappointment. These interests will strive to enlist legislators on their behalf, either by persuading them to intervene with the agency or by influencing their allies in Congress to demand a vote on their issue. In practice, delegation seems more likely to prompt legislative sins than to prevent them.

Nonetheless, legislators readily can think of delegation as good for the public. They are familiar with the several widely held theories that delegation is a necessity and a virtue.[43] Lawyers, trained as we are to think in terms of procedure more than substance, tend to believe that "officials will automatically translate good policy into law once somebody finds out what it [good policy] is."[44] Legislators, many of whom are lawyers, thus tend to think that statutes which delegate will actually achieve their fine-sounding goals, and to blame the agency for any shortfall.

I emphasize that my conclusion that delegation will prompt legislators to act in ways that harm the public depends critically upon the assumption that delegation helps legislators to shift blame to an agency. This assumption makes sense for American politics because legislators and the president are elected separately. Legislators do maneuver to shift blame to agencies. But this assumption would make much less sense for parliamentary democracies in which legislators choose the chief executive and voters cast their ballot for legislators primarily on the basis of the candidates' party affiliation.[45] A majority party in parliament that shifted blame to agencies would assign blame to its own party and therefore diminish its chances to stay in power. Because parliamentary systems thus tend to prevent legislators from using delegation to shift blame to agencies, reports that delegation works well in such systems should not reassure Americans that delegation is good policy under our Constitution. Similarly, Europeans may find it useful to consider the American experience with delegation in considering the political structure of the European Community (EC); much of the popular opposition to closer political union in the EC was prompted by fears that the union's structure gives too much power to unaccountable agencies.

Increasing Opportunities to Do Casework

Legislators want their constituents and potential contributors to request help in receiving favorable treatment from agencies. Doing such casework helps the legislator get votes, campaign funds, endorsements, and other favors. While agency enforcement of statutory laws creates opportunities for legislators to do casework, delegation often increases those opportunities by giving the agency the power to make the laws as well. Indeed, legislators' desire to do casework gives them a perverse reason to delegate in ways that create delay, complexity, and confusion. The late representative Ned Pattison acknowledged that "many members have an incentive not to reform bad laws since that would reduce their role as hero-ombudsman."[46]

Legislators have more chances to bestow favors on contributors when they delegate than when they enact a broadly applicable rule. If Congress proposes to enact a law instead of delegating, the interests potentially affected have a direct incentive to make contributions only to legislators whose votes are uncertain and only if the bill's outcome is uncertain.[47] Once the bill is enacted, this incentive to contribute ceases. If Congress proposes to delegate, the interests affected still have a direct incentive to make contributions to legislators whose votes are uncertain, if the bill's outcome is uncertain. But the interests also will have a direct incentive to make contributions to any legislator who does casework on resulting agency lawmaking, which can go on perpetually.[48]

In contrast, legislators might decrease the opportunity for payments by delegating instead of enacting a low-visibility rule applicable only to a few persons. The outcome of such legislation is usually highly uncertain and is resolved in committee. Affected persons have an incentive to cultivate the good graces of many committee members and of other legislators who can intervene with committee members. These incentives may help to explain why Congress legislates tax breaks and spending projects with such particularity.

What the President Gets from Delegation

The president, who of course influences the design of legislation through recommendations and vetoes, has different incentives from legislators. When legislators shift blame or credit to an agency, they shift it to presidential appointees. The incentives for legislators to delegate might appear to be disincentives for the president. However, three factors work to attract the president to delegation. First, statutes often are structured so that the disappointed expectations of would-be beneficiaries and the costs to others are perceived after the next presidential election. For instance, the 1970 Clean Air Act was structured so that the EPA administrator would deal with states' failures to adopt plans only after the 1972 election.

Second, presidents must take personal responsibility for laws embodied in statutes that they sign, but they can shift some of the blame for agency laws to the agency. Shifting blame is easy when an independent agency has made the law, because the leaders of such agencies do not serve at the president's pleasure. Presidents also often avoid substantial political losses they might sustain for the unpopular actions of appointees who do serve at the president's pleasure by taking no position on what the agency has done or even by expressing some disagreement. Indeed, even incumbent presidents try to "run against the government." President George Bush tried to distance himself from agency laws promulgated during his administration by declaring a ninety-day moratorium on new agency laws before the 1992 elections.[49]

Third, delegation enhances the president's ability to use his staff to do casework. It thereby allows the president as well as legislators to particularize constituents' perceptions of costs and benefits.

Presidents Reagan and Bush made much of separation of powers —but usually to defend executive powers from congressional encroachment and never to prevent Congress from delegating its legislative power to the executive branch.[50]

Delegation does not change the cast of officials who participate in lawmaking: legislators, agency heads, the president, and their staffs. But delegation does allow legislators and the president to shift to the agency blame for the costs of complying with the laws, blame for the failure to deliver promised regulatory benefits, and blame for the delay, complexity, and confusion that the process causes. Delegation also increases the opportunity for legislators and the president to do politically valuable casework.

Is Delegation Good Policy?

> Prudence, indeed, will dictate that Governments long established should not be changed for light and transient causes . . .
> —*Declaration of Independence*, 1776

PART IV

Delegation Weakens Democracy

THE CONSTITUTION GIVES THE PEOPLE CONTROL over the laws that govern them by requiring that statutes be affirmed personally by legislators and a president whom the people have elected.[1] Through delegation, these elected officials grant the power to make laws to unelected officials in the agencies. In theory, the elected lawmakers give the agency general instructions, oversee implementation of the directions, provide more specific instructions, and so on until the agency does what the elected officials want. In the words of Robert Dahl, proponents of such a government maintain that it grafts "the expertness of [Platonic] guardianship to the popular sovereignty of the demos," but he warns that it may instead graft "the symbols of democracy to the de facto guardianship of the policy elites."[2] When the elected lawmakers delegate, the people lose control over the laws that govern them.

Accountability through Congress

One way that the Constitution gives people control over the laws is to require majorities in the House and Senate to enact them. Constituents can refuse to reelect a legislator who has voted for a bad law.

The Supreme Court, in *Hampton & Co.*, tried to reconcile delegation with this classic notion of accountability by requiring that statutes state an "intelligible principle" to guide the agency.[3] This "transmission-belt" rationale for delegation fails because statutes can meet the Court's intelligible principle test and still not make the hard choices.[4] The intelligible principle test and related rubrics that require statutes to provide a "standard" or a "rule of conduct" might seem to be saying that the statute must state the law.[5] The holdings, however, give the rubrics a lesser meaning. Congress need not state the laws as long as it says something about the goals that should guide the agency when it promulgates the laws that actually will govern private conduct.

The something said about the goals is sometimes practically nothing at all, as in statutes, upheld by the courts, that tell agencies to act in the "public interest."[6] If Congress needs only to state its goals, it can avoid the hard choices. For example, *Mistretta* upheld a delegation to a commission of the power to make sentencing guidelines, because the statute stated the goals the guidelines should achieve and the format they should take, as well as the procedures for formulating them.[7] However, the statute gave the commission little guidance in deciding whether any given category of violator should serve time, pay a fine, or both, and in what amounts. Although one of the statute's goals is preventing violators from committing future crimes, it says nothing about how long to lock up a violator who poses a moderate but long-term threat, nor about how to balance that goal against the potentially conflicting goal of punishing offenders in proportion to their crimes. The statute is full of goals and empty of hard choices, as is the Clean Air Act. Indeed, as Chapter 4 showed, delegation would prevent Congress from making many of the hard choices, even if it wanted to.

Agency expertise cannot eliminate the uncertainty produced by a vague "intelligible principle." As Robert Reich—a defender of delegation—admits, agency politics "confounds the ideal of scientific policymaking on which the legitimacy of regulatory agencies is based."[8]

The Supreme Court also has argued that the people still control agency lawmaking because their elected representatives control the agencies.[9] Legislators can enact a statute that repeals an agency law and key members of the relevant subcommittees can pressure the agency to rescind or amend a law. This supposed accountability through congressional oversight depends upon a chain of command in which (1) the agency makes the law, (2) the legislators supervise the agency, and (3) the people supervise the legislators. But each of the links in the chain is weak.

The agency-law link.

When agencies are delegated issues too hot for Congress to handle, they often have even less political capacity to make the necessary choices.[10] So the agency may do nothing, take years to adopt a law, or make the choice case by case in low-visibility proceedings rather than by adopting a law. The upshot is that the agency avoids crystallizing the issue for congressional review.

The Congress-agency link.

Once an agency makes a law, Congress will probably not repeal it even if Congress would not have enacted it. Both the agency itself and the relevant subcommittees in Congress, as members of the subgovernment formed around the agency, maximize their power by minimizing scrutiny of the agency by Congress as a whole. They have a mutual interest in not informing other members of Congress of agency policy initiatives. Unless the agency's action causes a big stir, the subcommittees, which have the primary power to set the agenda in Congress, often can frustrate meaningful review of the agency.[11] For example, most members of Congress are ignorant of the agricultural marketing orders discussed in Chapter 3.[12] As a result, the agency is ordinarily unaccountable, except for egregious political sins, to most of Congress and therefore to most of the people.

Even if an agency promulgates a rule against the wishes of the relevant subcommittee and refuses to retract it, the subcommittee may well fail to secure a statute that formally nullifies the agency action. The president—whose support is needed unless the subcommittee has two-thirds' majorities in both houses—usually supports the agency. Moreover, the proponents of a statute must overcome the considerable obstacles to getting a bill to the floor in the House and the Senate and winning a majority in both. The bill could be blocked by one house. In essence, Article I's supermajoritarian requirement works to insulate agency action from oversight. As the Supreme Court noted in interpreting a statute, "[l]egislative silence is a poor beacon to follow in discerning the proper statutory route."[13] The Court contradicts itself when it argues that congressional oversight makes delegation democratic.

To ease the burden of blocking agency action—thereby giving the congressional side of the iron triangle more power within each subgovernment—Congress grafted legislative veto provisions onto hundreds of delegating statutes.[14] The Supreme Court declared the legislative veto unconstitutional in *Chadha*,[15] partly because the legislative veto was less democratic than the Article I legislative process. Yet delegation without the legislative veto is even more undemocratic than delegation with it.

The people-Congress link.

Even more important than the difficulties faced by Congress in holding agencies to account is the difficulty faced by the public in holding Congress to account for what the agencies do. As Justice Powell stated in a concurring opinion in *Chadha*, "Congress is most accountable politically when it prescribes rules of general applicability."[16] The classic notion of accountability required majorities in Congress to take personal, public responsibility for a law. To that end, Article I of the Constitution specifically requires that "the Yeas and Nays of the Members of either House on any question shall, at the Desire of one fifth of those Present, be entered on the Journal."[17] So a controversial law can take effect only if a sufficient number of legislators support it explicitly and on the record. In contrast, the oversight notion of accountability allows Congress to sustain an agency law through inaction or to change the agency law through the informal activity of a few influential members. This enables legislators to accede to a controversial law without having to assume any personal or public responsibility for it.

Without delegation, legislators undoubtedly would do all they could to obscure their responsibility for controversial rules. For example, they might ask agencies to recommend statutory laws or to frame statutory rules in terms difficult for the public to understand. But, in the end, legislators would still have to vote for the statutory laws. Rivals for reelection would be able to discover their responsibility for laws that harm the public and explain to constituents how their representatives had hurt them. With delegation, however, rival candidates search the congressional records in vain for any evidence of where the incumbent stood on the laws. The incumbent's ability to deny responsibility for most hard choices—with the exception of Supreme Court confirmations, tax increases, declarations of war, and a few other issues[18] —helps to make for political campaigns that have little to do with the merits of public policy and a lot to do with slogans and scandals.

Jerry Mashaw has tried in another way to reconcile delegation with democracy. He points out that since no one legislator is responsible for every provision in a bill, the way legislators vote provides only partial information on their individual views. A vote on a statute that delegates provides similarly partial information on each legislator's views. Mashaw asserts that "it is surely much more important that voters know the general ideological tendencies that inform those votes (prolabor, probusiness, prodisarmament, prodefense) than that [representative] X votes for or against [the] particular language of [a] particular bill." So he wonders "how exactly" an end to delegation would provide voters with better information?[19] My answer is that delegation allows legislators to convey information selectively, withholding opinions about the hard choices while providing opinions that embrace popular aspirations. The Clean Air Act and many other delegating statutes have passed by wide margins for this reason, not because Congress reached a consensus on difficult subjects.

Mashaw's argument, moreover, shifts the focus of accountability from the people's power over the laws that govern them to the people's influence on what representatives say. The ideological poses that legislators strike and the laws that emerge from agencies often bear little resemblance to each other, as the stories of the navel orange marketing order and the Clean Air Act illustrate. Indeed, delegation makes it possible for legislators to espouse internally inconsistent ideologies (for example, avoiding economic dislocation and protecting health). They need not join issue over inconsistencies because they are talking at the symbolic level of goals rather than at the concrete level of laws. Delegation changes the saw that politicians "campaign in poetry and govern in prose" to "they pontificate in person and govern through delegates."

The failure to join issue in the legislative arena not only makes the information conveyed to the public less useful but also makes what goes on in the legislative arena less interesting to the public. In the words of E. E. Schattschneider: "Nothing attracts a crowd so quickly as a fight. Nothing is so contagious. Parliamentary debates, jury trials, town meetings, political campaigns, strikes, hearings, all have about them some of the exciting qualities of a fight; all produce dramatic spectacles that are almost irresistibly fascinating to people. At the root of all politics is the universal language of conflict."[20] To illustrate this point, during the passage of the 1970 Clean Air Act the media focused far more on the proposed law to control emissions from new cars than

on the remainder of the bill, which, although more important to the
public, was less gripping because it did not rouse a fight. Taking the
law out of legislation removes the spectacle so vital to attracting the
interest of voters.

Delegation lets legislators change their roles from actors who make
hard choices on the record in dramatic confrontations to service pro-
viders who do favors for individual constituents in private, where they
can take whatever stance happens to please that constituent.[21] In a
book arguing that legislators have changed their roles since the 1940s
in ways that have increased their chances for reelection, Morris Fiorina
writes:

> So long as . . . congressmen . . . function principally as national
> policymakers . . . reasonably close congressional elections will nat-
> urally result. For every voter a congressman pleases by a policy
> stand he will displease someone else. The consequence is a mar-
> ginal district. But if we have incumbents who deemphasize contro-
> versial policy positions and instead place heavy emphasis on non-
> partisan, nonprogrammatic constituency service . . . , the resulting
> blurring of political friends and enemies is sufficient to shift the
> district out of the marginal camp.[22]

American legislators have had a security in office that politicians in
Eastern and Western Europe must envy. In the ten years spanning the
elections of 1984, 1986, 1988, 1990, and 1992, 97 percent of the House
incumbents who sought reelection won, with the great bulk of them
winning by margins of over 20 percent. Each of the seven members of
the House of Representatives who lost in 1988 "had some kind of
ethics taint."[23] Senators are defeated more frequently but still have
remarkable job security. In 1992, a year the public was said to be
angry at incumbents, 93 percent of the House members who ran for
reelection won. While fear of losing caused an unusually large number
of incumbents not to run at all, their fears typically arose from the
taint of scandal or redistricting. So delegation and the opportunities
for casework that it creates continue to shield lawmakers from responsibility for the laws that they make.[24]

Fiorina's explanation of increasingly secure congressional tenure
includes factors not directly traceable to delegation, such as the
growth of the federal pork barrel and the use of the congressional
franking privilege for electoral purposes. Although delegation is

only one reason why incumbents get more votes than they did in the 1940s, he shows that a small vote shift in favor of incumbents—from 3 to 5 percent—accounts for the increased security of congressional tenures.[25]

Accountability Through the President

The second way that the Constitution makes lawmaking accountable to the people is by requiring that statutes be presented to an elected president, who has the power to veto them. Delegation allows the president to avoid personal involvement in lawmaking; an appointee adopts the law, and, as discussed earlier, presidents frequently distance themselves from the controversial decisions of their appointees.

Nonetheless, in the 1984 case *Chevron U.S.A. Inc. v. Natural Resources Defense Council*, the Supreme Court implied that the accountability of legislators that is lost by delegation is somehow replaced by the accountability of the president:

> While agencies are not directly accountable to the people, the Chief Executive is, and it is entirely appropriate for this political branch of the Government to make such policy choices—resolving the competing interests which Congress itself either inadvertently did not resolve, or intentionally left to be resolved by the agency charged with the administration of the statute in light of everyday realities.[26]

The Court is trying to paint two losses as an overall gain. In truth, the public loses the right to have both its elected representatives *and* its elected president take personal responsibility for the law, and in exchange gets the right to have someone appointed by an elected president take responsibility for the law.

Even if, instead, the president had to sign off on every agency law, the resulting presidential accountability would be worth less than congressional accountability. The Framers included the requirement that bills be presented to the president not out of any sense that the president was more accountable than Congress, but rather because the president was less accountable to particular interest groups and so more inclined to protect liberty.[27] A president has less reason than a member of Congress to worry that a position taken on a particular law will affect reelection prospects. The president's responsibility for making law would, after all, be diluted by the electorate's concern about activities in other areas such as national defense, foreign affairs, law enforcement, and so on. In any event, voters who disagree with some controversial agency laws are likely to agree with others, and are likely to both agree and disagree with the laws that would be promulgated under the president's next electoral opponent. Since voters must endorse presidential positions wholesale, it is unlikely that the president will feel much political tension over any one agency law. Of course, voters must also choose positions wholesale when they elect members of Congress, but in any legislative district there are likely to be a limited number of issues of particular local interest. A position taken by an incumbent on any one such issue could cause 5 percent of the voters to choose the challenger, thereby producing a 10-percent swing. That possibility would force many incumbents to pay careful attention to constituents' concerns when voting for a law. Given the difficulty of holding the president accountable for the laws that bureaucrats adopt, it is no wonder that we tend to think of countries where only the chief of state is elected as undemocratic.

In sum, accountability through the president matters less than accountability through Congress and, whatever the potential worth of presidential accountability might be, delegation diminishes its value.

Delegation Endangers Liberty

BY *LIBERTY* I MEAN, AS DID THE FRAMERS, the people's right to be left alone by government except when some genuinely public purpose warrants intervention. When government is persuaded to regulate persons for a private purpose, it infringes upon their liberty. But the Framers chose not to include in the Constitution a provision directly prohibiting laws that serve only private purposes because, as noted in Chapter 2, they realized that people would inevitably disagree about whether particular laws served only private purposes. Instead, the Framers sought to protect liberty indirectly by adopting a lawmaking process in which enacting a bill tends to require broad public support *and* by adopting the Bill of Rights and other specific constitutional rights.

In this chapter I will show that these specific constitutional rights, as important as they are, fall short of fully protecting liberty. I will then argue that the Constitution's lawmaking process does provide some safeguards for liberty but that delegation undercuts those safeguards, and the alternative safeguards that delegation provides are less meaningful. Finally, I will point out some controversial value judgments implicit in the Article I process.

CHAPTER 7

Constitutional Rights Fall Short of Protecting Liberty

Some examples illustrate why the Bill of Rights has only a limited ability to protect liberty: Suppose a statute gives Peter's land to Paul for the sole reason that Paul had the power in Congress to secure the statute's passage. Of course, such a statute would recite some public purpose as a pretext. Nonetheless, a court would not have to say that Congress lied about its motive in order to strike down the statute because it violates Peter's Fifth Amendment right against having government take his property without just compensation.[1]

While constitutional rights suffice to protect liberty in this blatant case, consider in contrast a statute that functionally would give Sunkist the power to determine how many oranges each grower could sell for the sole reason that Sunkist had enough political power in Congress to secure its passage. Of course, that statute would recite as a pretext some public purpose, such as producing "orderly markets." A court could not strike down such a statute as a taking of private property because the government would not have invaded anybody's land or severely limited its use. Orange growers could, after all, still make a profit under this statute or could use their land for other purposes. The court would not hold that the public purpose asserted by Congress was only a pretext.[2] A judge could not directly ascertain what motivated the individual legislators who voted for the statute. Nor could a judge say that this scheme lacks a public purpose on the basis that many economists think that marketing orders do not produce orderly markets; such policy judgments are left to elected lawmakers.[3] The Sunkist example suggests that courts often cannot use the Bill of Rights to invalidate laws that infringe liberty through sophisticated regulation.

In enforcing the Bill of Rights and other constitutional rights, judges have adopted two strategies to minimize their interference with the policy judgments made by elected officials. First, the courts have found that some constitutional rights require that the government leave people alone, even if there is a genuine public purpose for intruding. Interpreting rights as absolute relieves judges from having to gauge the genuineness or importance of elected lawmakers' asserted public purpose. But judges can erect absolute bans on government intrusion only to protect certain aspects of life—such as what one says or how one worships—without rendering government unable to protect the public from important harms.[4] Second, although the courts construe some constitutional rights as invalidating a government intrusion if, in the judge's opinion, the governmental intrusion challenged in the case is more weighty than the public purpose that it serves, courts apply this balancing strategy only to relatively discrete aspects of life, because it substitutes the policy decisions of judges for the policy decisions of elected officials.[5]

So, in most instances, the only protection for liberty that the Constitution provides is in the lawmaking process set in Article I.

The Safeguards of Liberty in Article I

Article I obviously does not put an end to all selfish statutes. For example, tax and appropriations legislation often contain provisions for tax breaks and pork-barrel spending to benefit special interests. The failure of Article I to completely protect liberty raises the question of whether delegation really does any additional damage to liberty. I would answer that delegation disarms Article I's safeguards of liberty in four principal ways: (1) it balkanizes the lawmaking process by shifting power from one body, Congress, to many separate agencies, each attuned to only a small subset of all the interests; (2) it allows legislators and the president to shift some blame for the cost of government policies to the agencies; (3) it circumvents the supermajoritarian feature of Article I by allowing an individual or small group—an agency head or the majority on a commission—to make the law; and (4) it puts lawmaking and law enforcement in the same hands.

The balkanization of the legislative process.

As John Hart Ely has said, "one reason we have broadly based representative assemblies is to await something approaching a consensus before government intervenes."[6] Delegation shifts the power to make law from a congress of all interests (hence the name "Congress") to subgovernments typically representative of only a narrow range of interests. In many rulemakings, the regulated industry is the only private participant.[7] For example, in EPA proceedings to consider a state's proposed revision of its implementation plan under the Clean Air Act, the state agency and the regulated polluters are usually the only outside participants.

Shifting responsibility.

Delegation allows legislators and the president to escape some of the blame for selfish government policies while still claiming much of the credit, as discussed in Chapter 5. In one example, delegation distances legislators from the law increasing the price that voters pay for oranges. The Clean Air Act represents a more complex form of shifting blame to an agency. Congress ensured that EPA took responsibility both for the failure to meet the grand promises made by legislators and for the costs of achieving the emissions reductions that were enacted.

Allowing a bare majority to make law.

Shifting responsibility to an agency makes the passage of laws even easier than in a unicameral legislature. Article I, on the other hand, sought to do the opposite. Madison set out to curb the "facility and excess of law-making" by requiring that statutes go through a bicameral legislature and the president.[8]

Madison's conviction that interest groups that might prevail in a unicameral legislature would find it harder to prevail in the Article I process has been validated in recent political science literature.[9] This work suggests that the differences in the size and nature of the constituencies of representatives, senators, and the president—and the different lengths of their terms in office—increase the probability that the actions of each will reflect a different balance of interests. This diversity of viewpoint, plus the greater difficulty of prevailing in three forums rather than one, means that constituent support sufficient to produce a bare majority in a unicameral legislature will probably fail to get a statute through the Article I process.

The Constitution's method of protecting liberty is analogous to the supermajority requirements in the constitutions or charters of states, municipalities, and private corporations that are designed to prevent those in power from acting selfishly. Many state constitutions and municipal charters, for instance, require that states or cities may issue bonds or raise taxes above a set limit only if a supermajority of the voters approve. Corporate charters sometimes require that certain important actions must have the support of a supermajority of the stockholders.

Writers of law as enforcers of law.

Legislators cannot very well deflect criticism of a law contained in a bill on the basis that they want it enforced selectively.[10] A legislator who wants to please environmentalist constituents by voting for a bill to limit emissions from dry cleaners cannot assuage a contributor who runs a chain of dry cleaners by saying, "I will not enforce the rule against you." A law, accordingly, must have sufficient political support to overcome opposition from all those to whom its terms apply—in the example, all dry cleaners. Therefore each individual's liberty receives a measure of protection from those similarly situated.[11]

The legislator can, of course, try to narrow the terms of a statutory law to exclude its application to contributors, but the Bill of Attainder and Equal Protection Clauses provide some protection against drafting too narrowly.[12] The size of Congress also makes it more difficult, though far from impossible, to negotiate special exceptions to general rules. The Framers had good reason to say that the lack of separation of powers was "the very definition of tyranny."[13]

Delegation's Safeguards of Liberty

New Dealers believed that powerful industries used Article I to escape regulation needed to protect the public.[14] They thought that delegation would guard against selfish laws because (1) agencies act on the basis of reason rather than politics, (2) administrative procedures ensure that agencies focus on the public interest, and (3) the interests which the agencies regulate have the ability to protect themselves.[15] The New Dealers were unduly optimistic.

The agency as guardian of the public interest.

Agencies do not replace politics with reason; agencies pursue private interests, starting with their own. In Robert Dahl's words, "We should not overestimate the virtue of policy elites. Throughout the world policy elites are famous for the ease with which they advance their own narrow bureaucratic, institutional, organizational, or group interests in the name of the public good."[16] Administrative law practitioners in the United States know that the best argument to make to an agency is "This will benefit the agency."[17] Indeed some scholars suggest that the best way for Congress to direct agencies is to pay performance incentives to their officials.[18]

In thinking that agencies would protect the public against concentrated interests, proponents of delegation saw the agency staff as virtual representatives of the diffuse interests that cannot take part in agency lawmaking.[19] Such virtual representation has failed, just as it failed to protect colonial Americans in the British Parliament. As Richard Stewart, a prominent defender of delegation, admits, agencies "unduly favor organized interests, especially the interests of regulated or client business firms and other organized groups at the expense of diffuse, comparatively unorganized interests such as consumers, environmentalists, and the poor."[20] Worse still, diffuse interests typically find it even more difficult to press their case before an agency than before the legislature. They often have no direct representation in the administrative process. Effective representation typically requires specialized legal counsel, expert witnesses, and the capacity to reward or punish top officials through political organization, press coverage, and close working relationships with members of the appropriate congressional subcommittee. Usually only regulated corporations, their trade associations, unions, and other concentrated interests have the skill, organization, resources, and financial stake necessary to participate in this way. As a result, compared with the interests that lobby Congress, a much narrower spectrum of interests participates in the administrative process. So the Federal Trade Commission could decide in 1970 not to implement an American Bar Association recommendation to work more strenuously against consumer fraud in urban ghettoes, in part because "the poor and the weak could not offer political power and support" to the commission.[21]

The citizen action organizations that emerged in the 1970s changed this picture only in part. They gained some power because they used the same sophisticated methods as the regulated industries, but in the name of the public interest. However, such groups have the resources to participate in only a small portion of agency proceedings. For example, a survey of political action committees found that, of 3000 such groups considered, only 17 were concerned with environmental interests and only 1 with consumer interests.[22] Moreover, citizen action groups represent only a part of the spectrum of public interests that the iron triangle leaves out.

Administrative procedures as protection.

Defenders of delegation hope that even if agencies are not virtuous, they can at least be made more honorable through the Administrative Procedure Act's requirements for agency rulemaking.[23] The act requires that an agency must publish a notice of its proposed law in the *Federal*

Register (the daily issues of which contain several hundred pages of fine print), give the public an opportunity to participate in the rulemaking by commenting at a hearing or in writing, and accompany the final rule with an explanation of the reasoning behind it. The Act also provides affected persons with a right to seek judicial review of the agency's final decision.[24] Nonetheless, these requirements provide little reassurance that agencies are better than Congress at weeding out proposed laws that lack a public purpose.

When Congress makes law, it can and ordinarily does follow essentially the same procedures as agencies. After all, the rulemaking requirements in the Administrative Procedure Act mimic how the legislative process usually works. Proposals for legislation (bills) are printed and made publicly available, legislators and congressional committees announce that they are considering a bill, and the committees hold hearings and accept written comments. In addition, Congress typically explains its acts in committee reports and floor statements. But while Congress explains its acts voluntarily, an agency, like a court, must explain its reasoning.

By analogizing between agency decisions and judicial ones and pointing to the judicial review of agency decisions, New Deal supporters of delegation tried to drape agency lawmaking with the legitimacy of judge-made common law, which the Constitution accepts.[25] But agency lawmaking differs from judicial decisions in two critical ways. First, the requirement to explain restricts agencies' power much less than judges' power. A court must explain how its decision follows from precedent, while an agency need only explain that it stayed within its delegated authority, which usually affords it broad discretion. Agencies may depart from precedent as long as they offer a plausible reason.[26] Second, federal judges face less temptation than agency officials to shape their opinions for political ends. Unlike those officials, who are enmeshed in the politics of a subgovernment, judges have lifetime tenures, are largely immune to retribution from Congress, cannot accept favors from a party in a case, and are not supposed to speak in private about pending matters.[27]

Judicial review of agency laws does differ from review of statutory laws. While courts may overturn an unconstitutional law made either in an agency or Congress, they have the additional power under the Administrative Procedure Act to strike down an agency law that is "arbitrary, capricious, [or] an abuse of discretion" or "in excess of statutory . . . authority."[28] The requirement that agency laws not exceed legislatively granted authority provides only limited protection of liberty because, as noted before, statutes that delegate typically allow an agency broad discretion in deciding how to balance and achieve their conflicting goals. Even statutes that Congress claims will narrow sharply the agency's discretion, such as the Clean Air Act, generally still leave areas of broad discretion. The requirement that agency laws not be "arbitrary, capricious, [or] an abuse of discretion" also provides only limited protection to liberty because an agency can mask the real purpose of selfish or partisan laws by claiming that they protect the public. In the example discussed extensively earlier, when the Department of Agriculture buckled under to political pressure exerted by Sunkist, it justified its action in terms of "orderly markets" and other public-spirited rationales. The opponents of the navel orange quotas never succeeded in getting a court to find any aspect of the department's laws "arbitrary, capricious, [or] an abuse of discretion" on the merits. But, they persuaded courts to find that the department did not follow the statutorily required procedures. Such victories are, however, often pyrrhic because they require many years of expensive litigation by ill-financed opponents of concentrated interests. Meanwhile, the agency law remains in effect, and, should the agency lose, it often can repair the procedural defect in a few months.[29]

From the New Deal through the 1960s, courts remained reluctant to find that the agency acted arbitrarily because of respect for agency expertise and a desire to avoid trenching on policy decisions best left to the political branches of government. But, during the 1960s, when the arguments were raised that agencies were being captured by regulated industries and that expertise does not dictate agency decisions, judges began to grow uncomfortable with giving the agencies such latitude. In an effort to make judicial review more meaningful, without usurping the decision of Congress to delegate to the agency rather than to the courts, judges began to insist that agencies demonstrate that they had taken a hard look at all the public policy issues and that they justify their decisions in the deliberative, deductive style of courts rather than the political, predictive style of legislators.[30]

The agencies then learned to shield their laws from judicial reversal by presenting them as the product of reasoned analysis. A court that suspects that an agency has concealed the true basis of its decision still must take the agency at its word unless some evidence starkly shows its rationale to be a pretext.[31] Thus, in most cases, the court legitimately can overturn an agency decision only when some flaw in its reasoning is blatant. Courts sometimes find such errors in agency reasoning, but then the agency frequently announces much the same result as before, backed by a new explanation crafted to overcome the court's prior criticism.[32] Judicial opinions actually teach agencies how to avoid having their laws set aside. As scholars repeatedly point out, an agency usually can ensure that its actions will pass judicial muster by performing the "charade" of giving everyone a chance to object and then issuing a decision that dismisses each objection on a pretext geared to past judicial opinions.[33]

Nonetheless, cases trying to justify broad delegation suggest that judicial review provides a thoroughgoing check on agency lawmaking. For example, Judge Harold Leventhal has argued that

Congress has been willing to delegate its legislative powers broadly —and courts have upheld such delegation—because there is court review to assure that the agency exercises the delegated power within statutory limits, and that it fleshes out objectives within those limits by an administration that is not irrational or discriminatory. Nor is that envisioned judicial role ephemeral, as [*Citizens To Preserve Overton Park v. Volpe*] makes clear.[34]

Judge Leventhal overstates the extent to which judicial review controls administrative discretion in most cases. The case upon which he relies, *Overton Park*, helps to show why. The statute forbade the secretary of transportation to permit a federally funded highway to be built through any park if a "feasible and prudent alternative exists." The secretary approved a highway through Overton Park in Memphis, Tennessee, apparently on the basis that routing the road around the park would cost more and require the relocation of many people. The Court reversed the secretary by construing the statute to mean that a highway may go in a park only if no other site is possible; cost and disruption of the community are insufficient justifications. As the Court put it, "the very existence of the statutes indicates that protection of parkland was to be given paramount importance. . . . [i]f the statutes are to have any meaning . . ."[35] But the existence of the statute could and did mean that Congress wanted the secretary to make the hard choices between park preservation and holding down the cost of highway construction. According to one analysis, legislators saw the statute "as an ambiguous compromise between highway advocates and environmentalists."[36] The Court cannot count on the approach to judicial review used in *Overton Park* because, first, it misinterpreted the statute in that case, and, second, statutes in most policy areas must and do call for a balancing of goals rather than for making one of the goals paramount. Moreover, when judges bend the meaning of statutes to control agencies, the law becomes even less democratic. In any event, Supreme Court decisions since *Overton Park* have cut back on even the limited review that that case contemplated.[37]

Given the limited scope of judicial review, delegation protects liberty only in the superficial sense that a court will stop abuses that the agency has failed to cloak with skillful rationalizations. One option would be for Congress to put more "oomph" into judicial review by allowing judges to undo not only actions that are so wrongheaded or ineptly rationalized that they appear arbitrary or capricious, but also actions with which they simply disagree. However, judges lack the staffs and informational contacts needed to play such a policymaking role.[38] Changing the judicial office to provide the staffs and allow the contacts would, in essence, turn judges into agency heads. This would complicate the problem rather than solve it. And, more important, it would also be inconsistent with democratic accountability.

The power of the regulated.

In the New Deal vision in which the Brain Trust of government was to regulate the monied trusts of big business, the agencies would care for the little people while those regulated would have the power to take care of themselves. Sometimes, however, regulated concerns are small companies with little access to power—the small orange growers and handlers, for instance. As studies of the actual effects of consumer protection regulation sadly show, consumers are protected from producers less often than politically powerful producers are protected from their competitors, often small companies.[39]

Even big concerns can get pushed around in the regulatory process, especially during a political storm. For instance, during the scandals of the mid-1980s concerning the Environmental Protection Agency's handling of toxic dumpsites, regulated concerns found it difficult to persuade agency officials to approve innocuous actions.[40]

Which Safeguards Work Better?

The Supreme Court has expressed a clear opinion about whether Article I or delegation works better to protect liberty. In the *Kent v. Dulles* line of cases, the Court strained to interpret the statute as not delegating because, as it acknowledged, the Article I legislative process protects liberty better than agency lawmaking. Consistent with this belief, the Court's delegation cases do not argue that agency lawmaking does a better job of protecting liberty, but rather that delegation is a necessity of modern government.[41]

Even when the administrative process would avoid violations of liberty that the legislative process might commit, delegation does not necessarily prevent the legislative process from infringing liberty. After all, interests in Congress bent on infringing others' liberties can, if they have the votes, enact just the law they want even if Congress already has delegated lawmaking responsibility to an agency.

The Value Judgments Implicit in Article I

In crafting Article I to protect liberty, the Framers sought to make redistribution of wealth and regulation more difficult than in a unicameral legislative process. Since the appropriate extent of redistribution and regulation are questions that fill entire books, I will only suggest how they relate to delegation.

The Framers designed Article I partly to make redistribution of wealth more difficult than in a unicameral legislature. Nonetheless, the Article I process often redistributes from rich to poor, and delegation often does the opposite. For example, Congress has enacted rules that redistribute from the more to the less wealthy through social security and other entitlement programs. Indeed, Congress tends to legislate rather than delegate when it gives to the less wealthy because they are numerous, and some degree of redistribution appeals to a majority of voters. In contrast, some political scientists report that agencies are systematically biased in favor of the wealthy.[42] Ending delegation would not stand in the way of rules with redistributive effects that have broad popular support.

Because it protects liberty by placing obstacles in the way of enacting any statute, Article I tilts against regulation, unselfish as well as selfish. What comprises the right tilt—and there are many possibilities—is a debatable question. The Framers tilted against regulation because, in Charles Murray's words, they thought that "man acting in his private capacity—*if restrained from the use of force*—is resourceful and benign, fulfilling his proper destiny; while man acting as a public and political creature is resourceful and dangerous, inherently destructive of the rights and freedoms of his fellow-men." Murray adds, "It is really very difficult for people . . . to do anything very bad, for very long, when they are not buttressed by the threat of physical coercion."[43] So the Framers viewed "liberty" as freedom from the unjustified use of governmental power rather than the protection afforded by government regulation. In adopting the Constitution's process for making law, the Framers struck a balance between liberty, as they conceived it, and easing the protection of the public through regulation. By radically altering that lawmaking process, delegation violates the Constitution, as will I show in the next part of the book. The remaining chapters in this part show that although delegation makes it easier for government to infringe upon liberty, delegation is unlikely to result in more effective protection of the public.

Delegation Makes Law Less Reasonable

THERE ARE SEVERAL POPULAR GROUNDS for thinking that agencies can make more reasonable laws than elected lawmakers: the supposed expertise of agency officials; the supposed ability of agencies to cut through the gridlock that can result when Congress and the president disagree; and the supposed independence of agency officials. Each of these premises is flawed, however. In fact, the failed attempt to make law more reasonable through delegation has had the perverse effect of making law less reasonable.

The Theory of Agency Expertise

In the ideal picture of delegation, agency officials are experts who make technical decisions, and legislators are generalists who make broad policy decisions. The picture is incorrect, even in theory. Congress usually cannot delegate the technical issues in lawmaking without also delegating the broad issues of policy. Lawmaking after all is not just a matter of making expert judgments: laws inevitably reflect moral judgments about how to balance and attain competing goals.[1] According to Robert Dahl:

> No intellectually defensible claim can be made that policy elites . . . possess superior moral knowledge or

more specifically superior knowledge of what constitutes the public good. Indeed, we have some reason for thinking that specialization, which is the very ground for the influence of policy elites, may itself impair their capacity for moral judgment. Likewise, precisely because the knowledge of the policy elites is specialized, their expert knowledge ordinarily provides too narrow a base for the instrumental judgments that an intelligent policy would require.[2]

Perhaps for this reason as well as because of the politics of the appointment process, most agency heads are not scientists, engineers, economists, or other kinds of technical experts. From EPA's inception in 1970, seven of its eight administrators and six of its eight assistant administrators for air pollution were lawyers.[3] One observer has noted that "the New Deal concept of the 'expert agency' breaks down in the modern context of health and environmental regulation. An agency addressing complex scientific, economic, and technological issues must draw upon so many different kinds of expertise that no individual employee can know very much about all of the issues involved in a typical rulemaking."[4] Meanwhile, generalist legislators often vote on laws—such as those setting the emission limits for new cars—the merits of which depend upon the resolution of hotly contested technical disputes.

Although both agency heads and legislators often lack the expertise to evaluate technical arguments by themselves, they can get help from agency staff, government institutes (for example, the Center for Disease Control), and private sources (for example, medical associations, private think tanks, and university scientists). In addition, legislators request advice from committee staffs and the congressional Office of Technology Assessment.[5] By paying attention to the source, amount, and tenor of competing advice, agency heads and legislators can make judgments involving technical issues without fully understanding them.

In my experience, however, legislators choose politically convenient answers to technical questions. For example, in setting the emission limits on new cars in 1970, 1977, and 1990, Congress apparently was driven as much by politics as by technical information. Congress is free to decide in this way because the legitimacy and legality of its laws flows from political representation. In contrast, the legitimacy and legality of agency laws depends upon a reasoned explanation. Nonetheless, as the Clean Air Act experience illustrates, agencies also often find politically convenient answers to technical questions. The charade of rationalizing these answers makes agency lawmaking more complicated but not necessarily more reasonable.

The Theory of Quick Agency Decisions

Some political leaders fear that separation of powers, of which the Article I lawmaking process is a part, is unworkable, because it leads to gridlock when the president and majorities in the House and the Senate do not all come from the same party.[6] *Gridlock* is a value-laden word for a decision not to make a law; such a gridlock is no problem to those, such as the Framers, who believed that laws should not be made unless they have the broad support that usually is sufficient to get them through the Article I process. Solutions proposed by those who see gridlock as a problem vary from amending the Constitution to change the method of electing legislators to reduce the chance of divided government, to dispensing with separation of powers altogether by adopting a parliamentary form of government.[7]

Whether these proposals have any merit or not, delegation is no cure for divided government. Delegation might seem to be a cure because the statutes let an agency make law without the permission of the House, Senate, or president. But, as we know, the president, the legislators, and their staffs influence the agency. So, with delegation the stalemate often continues, but in a new context. Yet, because delegation has ostensibly given the agency the job of making the law, our elected lawmakers can shift to the agency much of the blame for failing to resolve the dispute. Delegation thus shortcircuits the nation's only authoritative method of resolving disputes about what the law should be and so puts protection of the public into an administrative limbo. The EPA's delays in producing the rules required by the Clean Air Act are typical of what happens under many other statutes.[8]

The supposed ability of agencies to protect the public quickly is more apparent than real for other reasons. The Administrative Procedure Act theoretically allows agencies to make law in two months, and even less in an emergency.[9] It is tempting to compare such potential speed with the years that can pass while bills languish in Congress. Yet, in fact, Congress can react quickly when it senses public support for quick action, while agencies ordinarily need years to make law.

Even if the agency process is faster than the Article I process, the protection that agency-made law offers may be illusory, because its lack of widespread support will make it less likely to be obeyed. For the law to be effective, according to Judge Learned Hand, "it must be content to lag behind the best inspiration of its time until it feels behind it the weight of such general acceptance as will sanction its pretension to unquestioned dictation."[10]

Even when agency laws do have widespread support, they are less likely to be obeyed than statutory laws and thus less likely to provide protection. Agency laws are more difficult to enforce partly because voluntary compliance is less likely. Someone wishing to avoid compliance can ask the agency to reconsider, petition a court for review, or enlist members of Congress to pressure the agency to change the law; someone wishing to avoid compliance with a statutory law faces the far more difficult task of persuading Congress to amend it or the courts to strike it down. Companies who might comply voluntarily with statutory laws do not do so with agency law, lest competitors get easier treatment through continued resistance.[11]

Delegation also increases the difficulty of enforcement because statutory laws are more likely to be taken as community standards of right and wrong than are agency laws. Agency laws lack moral suasion due both to their mutability[12] and their lack of generality as compared with statutory laws. Legislation that is not general often confers benefits—such as tax breaks, grants, or exemptions from regulation —rather than imposing regulatory requirements. Agency laws tend to be particularized because Congress, first, tells agencies to make laws that maximize the attainment of conflicting goals and, second, establishes regulatory procedures that allow its members to intervene in agency lawmaking on an ad hoc basis. As a result, officials make laws with case-by-case variations to accommodate a host of policy and political considerations, as with the air pollution limits that vary from factory to factory, even from smokestack to smokestack within a factory. The greater generality of statutory laws creates moral suasion: people tend to accept that what is fair for one is fair for all. Moral suasion in turn encourages voluntary compliance and leads to tougher sanctions against violators.[14]

The Relative Independence of Agency Officials

Agency officials, particularly those protected by civil service laws, are in many ways less beholden to concentrated interests than are legislators. From this premise, it is tempting to reason, as Bruce Ackerman and William Hassler implicitly do, that agencies are more prone than Congress to carefully aim their laws at serving the broad public interest.[15] Theirs is the most widely cited modern argument that broad delegation yields the best law, but their reasoning is flawed; as I argued in Chapter 7, for many reasons agency laws actually are more likely to serve private purposes than are statutory laws. However, the real force of Ackerman and Hassler's argument comes from their evocative telling of a story from which they draw the moral that delegation makes law more reasonable. As I will show, a close reading of the story suggests that delegation makes law less reasonable.

Their story is about the participation of Congress in the regulation of new power plants using fossil fuels. The 1970 Clean Air Act instructed EPA to set an emission limit for each category of new sources representing the greatest reduction achievable by reasonably affordable pollution control technology.[16] A key feature of this delegation was that EPA had to set an emission limit rather than require the use of any particular pollution-control device, so that firms were free to develop and use less expensive ways to meet the emission limit.

This feature threatened eastern coal mine owners and unions. The EPA had concluded that using a device called a scrubber was the best way to control sulfur emissions from power plants. The agency planned to set power plant emission limits on the basis of the emissions predicted to result if a scrubber were used in a plant burning eastern coal, which has a higher sulfur content than western coal. Eastern power plants could meet that limit more cheaply by switching from eastern to western coal than by controlling the emissions from eastern coal with a scrubber; installing and using a scrubber would cost more than transporting coal from the West. Since eastern power plants were the biggest customers of eastern coal mines, the coming emission limit on new power plants threatened the profits of mine owners and the jobs of miners. At the same time, environmentalists disliked the emission limit for their own reasons: they wanted scrubbers installed in all new plants so that these plants could be required someday to use low sulfur fuel *and* scrub their emissions in a hoped-for program to reduce acid rain.[17]

The eastern coal interests and the environmental groups joined forces to persuade Congress to make new power plants install scrubbers. In response, Congress included an ambiguous and arcane provision in the 1977 amendments.[18] It seemed to order EPA to regulate new power plants not by limiting how much sulfur they could emit but rather by requiring them to use a pollution-control device sufficient to achieve the largest-percentage reduction that EPA found was reasonably affordable. So instead of instructing power plants to restrict emissions to x pounds of sulfur per kilowatt of electricity generated, EPA would tell them to reduce emissions by y percent from the amount they would have emitted without a pollution-control device. Since a plant would have to install equipment sufficient to reduce emissions by that percentage whether it burned clean western coal or dirty eastern coal, the amendment seemed to mean that utilities would have to install scrubbers. The amendment thus seemed to eliminate the incentive to switch to western coal. The EPA ultimately issued a law along these lines.[19]

Ackerman and Hassler criticize the statutory amendment and the agency's law, because switching to western coal would have reduced emissions at a far lower expense to power plant operators and the ultimate consumers of electricity. They point to this waste and the disregard many legislators had for electricity consumers as evidence of legislators' willingness to enact special interest legislation. The remedy they prescribe is for Congress to delegate broadly.[20]

Ackerman and Hassler prescribe precisely the wrong remedy, because they implicitly assume that the legislative process is more vulnerable to concentrated interests than the administrative process. However, experience repeatedly has shown that the administrative process is not insulated either from legislative politics or from the influence of concentrated interests. Ackerman and Hassler inadvertently drive the point home themselves by pointing out that EPA could have used the ambiguity in the 1977 statutory provision to reach a much more efficient result but failed to do so partly because of strong pressure from legislators.[21]

The story told by Ackerman and Hassler suggests that, contrary to their assumption, delegation can increase the influence of concentrated interests on lawmaking. The statutory provision that required EPA to mandate emission reductions by a percentage rather than to an absolute level did not enact a law but rather narrowed the terms of the 1970 act's delegation. This delegation allowed legislators not only to take credit for helping eastern coal interests and environmental groups, but also to shift the blame for the resulting costs to EPA. At the time of the 1977 amendments, no one could estimate the cost to electricity consumers, because no one knew what law EPA would promulgate. Indeed, other provisions of the delegation called upon the agency to promulgate regulations that they were cost-sensitive, so that legislators could claim that they were concerned about pocketbook issues.[22] Moreover, the ambiguity in the 1977 amendment further diffused Congress's responsibility.

In contrast, without delegation, legislators could not have taken the credit for requiring scrubbers unless they had voted for a law that required their use. Such a law would have had a predictable impact on our electricity bills and so made its costs manifest. Congress nonetheless might have enacted such a bill if, for instance, the public believed protecting eastern coal was worthwhile, or if eastern coal interests were better at exerting political pressure in the Article I lawmaking process than public utility interests. Even in that case, legislators would have had to feel the costs of what they did more fully.

In a sequel to Ackerman and Hassler's story, Congress did, in fact, resolve the issue of sulfur emissions from power plants largely without delegating when it enacted the provisions of the 1990 amendments dealing with acid rain. Congress showed great concern for the impact of pollution control costs on electricity consumers at that time, and deleted the 1977 provision that required EPA to regulate new power plants in terms of percentage reductions.[23]

In sum, legislators' disregard for the broader public interests in the 1977 act was made easier by their delegating in the first place, not from their delegating too narrowly. Ackerman and Hassler's story suggests that delegation can exacerbate the disproportionate influence of concentrated interests. Although the insulation of lawmaking from concentrated interests is attractive as an abstraction, what delegation produces in practice is the insulation of lawmakers from blame for the costs that they impose upon the public.

Trying to Make Law More Reasonable through Delegation Is Likely to Have the Opposite Effect

So far, I have examined three factors that are supposed to make agency law more reasonable than statutory law—reliance on expertise, avoidance of the "gridlock" of separation of powers, and independence from concentrated interests—and have shown why they fail to produce the promised results and how the failed effort to rationalize lawmaking renders it more complicated and less responsive to the public. Now, I want to show that the ultimate goal of the enterprise—to substitute rationality for politics in lawmaking—is irrational.

A statute that delegates tries to make lawmaking comport with reason by ordering agencies to make rules reasonably calculated to achieve the beneficial public purposes of the statute. Compared to the political tugging and hauling upon which Article I ultimately relies to produce results sensitive to the clashing interests of voters, the calculated reason of the administrative process seems like a kinder and gentler way to make law. After all, voters and their representatives can fall prey to greed, hatred, or manipulation.

Yet the rationality supposedly inherent in delegation does not really protect the public from itself. Alan Watts argued that reason provides individuals with no protection against the parts of their own natures that they distrust:

> There is really no alternative to trusting man's nature. This is not wishful thinking or sentimentality; it is the most practical of practical politics. For every system of mistrust and authoritarian control is *also* human. The will of the would-be saint can be as corrupt as his passions, and the intellect can be as misguided as the instincts. . . . The alternative [to faith in our own nature], as Freud saw, is the swelling of guilt "to a magnitude that individuals can hardly support."[24]

Just as individuals have no alternative to trusting their natures, the body politic has no alternative to trusting the political process because delegation does not insulate agencies from politics. Trying to rise above politics through delegation makes the body politic suffer in ways analogous to the guilt suffered by individuals who try to rise above their human nature.

Delegation Shifts the Focus of Lawmakers from Protecting People to Casting Blame

By making impossible demands upon agency officials, statutes that delegate heap on them legal and political as well as psychological guilt. The Clean Air Act, for example, says that the law of air pollution should protect health and yet be sensitive to the economy. Similarly, statutes that delegate lawmaking authority over energy "institutionaliz[e] . . . inconsistent demands upon administrative agencies—for example, for both higher and lower gas prices and electric rates and more vigorous or more flexible regulation of coal and nuclear power."[25] When statutes say what laws should achieve rather than what they are, agencies often cannot make law that achieves everything Congress says it should. Moreover, agencies cannot make all the laws and complete all the lawmaking procedures in the time and with the resources that Congress allows.

Given Congress's unrealistic goals and deadlines for issuing laws, it is easy for a citizens group to charge, and to have a court declare, that agency officials have violated a statute. But the courts often can do little without forcing the agency to reduce resources devoted to some other statutory duty. As a judge frustrated by such a case put it:

> Well-meaning statutes are not self-implementing. . . . There is need of a massive commitment of funds, talent and purpose to these objectives.
>
> If the Court could do anything about it, the Court would. . . .
>
> These are matters of national policy, political priorities; and I would urge upon the parties with everything at my command that they consider the appropriateness of continuing to rely on courts to accomplish objectives which can only be effectively accomplished in a democracy by resort to the polls, resort to the political processes which the Constitution preserves.[26]

While the judge was correct in thinking that the policy conflict before him should be resolved by Congress rather than a court, it was Congress which had subjected the agency to suit for failing to fulfill impossible statutory duties.

Judges add to the unrealistic burdens upon agencies by insisting that they justify their decisions in the closely reasoned style of courts rather than the more frankly subjective style of legislators. According to Martin Shapiro,

> The result is a monstrous catch-22 for the agencies. They could tell the truth. That is, they could openly say in the rulemaking record . . . that the uncertainties they faced can at best be reduced to highly subjective probabilities. They could admit that their choices among the range of plausible probabilities has been prudential and has been heavily influenced by the political persuasions of those who won the last election. . . . If an agency tells the truth in this way, it subjects itself to almost certain judicial reversal on the grounds that it has acted arbitrarily and capriciously. . . .

> So instead of telling the truth, agencies can lie; this is mostly what they do these days. They can dress up each of their guesstimates . . . in enormous, multilayered costumes of technocratic rationality.[27]

For Shapiro, the way out of this catch-22 is for courts to stop minimizing the extent to which agency lawmaking is delegated legislative power.[28] But courts cannot fully acknowledge the political, discretionary nature of agency lawmaking without undercutting the argument that delegation is constitutional because judicial review confines agency lawmaking to rational deductions from legislated first principles.

Meanwhile, legislators, who escape the vulnerability that comes from making hard choices, feel free to perpetually scold agency officials for failing to achieve statutory goals, meet statutory deadlines, and make the correct decisions. Delegation thus contributes to our government's tendency to engage in "revelation, investigation, and prosecution" as a substitute for resolving issues directly.[29] The emphasis on casting blame and avoiding responsibility shortchanges the public.

Delegation Creates Wasteful Fantasies of Cheap, Effective Regulatory Protection

When legislators place impossible demands on agencies, they give their constituents false hopes of cheap, effective regulatory protection. Legislators talk as if authorizing an agency to make laws to achieve popular goals is tantamount to Congress's guaranteeing the achievement of those goals. With such talk, legislators may be fooling their constituents or, still worse, fooling themselves. Regardless, the superficially rational processes that delegation launches take on a reality of their own. Lawmakers and EPA personnel speak of the planning concepts in the Clean Air Act, for example, as if they are natural objects and behave as if showing achievement of the act's goals on paper is the same as achieving them.

Wed to the official fantasy, lawmakers take actions that harm the public. As one example, the public would not have suffered the huge costs of bailing out the savings and loan associations but for the fantasy created by delegation that regulation would keep the savings and loans solvent. James Tobin, a Nobel laureate and member of President Kennedy's Council of Economic Advisors, argued that the "'savings and loan crisis' is in a deeper sense a crisis of federal deposit insurance," which he favored abolishing except for accounts whose funds would be invested in treasury bills and the like.[30] He noted that under such a system depositors would have to accept low returns on the insured accounts or deposit funds in uninsured accounts. Depositors' interest in finding safe uninsured accounts would be likely to police financial institutions far more effectively than regulation did. Legislators could not have continued, and increased, deposit insurance if they had been politically accountable for the real cost of the insurance. Because they believed that regulation would prevent losses greater than the small premiums paid by savings and loan associations, legislators thought insurance came without cost. But Congress delegated the job of regulation, under pressure from legislators to be nice to their friends in the industry, and the agency failed to regulate effectively. Delegation allowed legislators simultaneously to do favors for savings and loan associations and to provide politically popular insured deposits without seeming to be imposing any liability on the government. Delegation thus turned the agency into a *deus ex machina* through which legislators appeared able to make all wishes come true. The illusion that was so beneficial to legislators cost the public a fortune.

The savings and loan debacle is only one instance of legislators' using delegation to create illusions for which the public may well have to pay dearly. Congress guaranteed private pension plans in the expectation that such plans are generally made financially secure through agency law. Some analysts fear that the guarantees will cost the taxpayers billions of dollars.[31] Congress will likely establish a national health plan whose financial integrity is based upon the assumption that an agency will use delegated power to reduce health care costs to an unrealistic extent.

Delegation Reduces the Public's Sense That Government Is Responsive

Law cannot protect the public from all harms, since some are trivial and others too expensive to abate; but it should, according to Charles Murray, give people the sense that government responds to harms "in a reasonably *predictable and understandable way* that corresponds with commonly shared principles of right and wrong within the community."[32] Lawmaking through the Article I legislative process is responsive, in the sense that legislators usually take into account the concerns that voters express about the benefits and costs of outlawing various harms. The disproportionate influence of concentrated interests undermines public confidence, but voters at least understand how that influence works.

Delegation further erodes public confidence in the responsiveness of government. Legislators make exaggerated claims for the outcome of delegations to agencies; years later their constituents find that the agencies have achieved little of what was promised. The public generally does not understand complicated delegations such as the Clean Air Act and, by and large, cannot tell what went wrong. Charles Murray describes how such an unpredictable, incomprehensible governance erodes public faith in government:

> If I live in a state where I cannot get a building permit for X except by paying a bribe, and my friend lives in a state where he cannot get a building permit for exactly the same X except by paying the same amount of money to a lawyer to represent him before the dispenser of building permits, what is the nature of the difference? The detached observer may know that in the corrupt state, I am dependent on the whim of the bureaucrat, who will probably sanction all sorts of bad building permits in return for a bribe. My friend lives in a state where it takes just as much money to use the law, yes, but the law is there, in black and white, and we may be confident that the law is sound and wise, else it would not have been written that way, and the dispenser of building permits is bound by that law, and will only say yes to a legally suitable building. We may hope all that.[33]

But those of us who do not understand the law—which includes most lawyers, most of the time—cannot distinguish the honest regime from the dishonest one. No wonder the public increasingly sees legislators as tricky and agencies as unreliable guardians.

Delegation Makes Citizens Less Reasonable and More Alienated

The fear of the citizenry that government is unconcerned about threats to their safety prompts hysterical demands, such as that government must eliminate all risk from air pollution, regardless of the cost. The irrational political climate makes lawmaking less reasonable.

There is another reason why delegation results in a political climate that is less rational. The Framers had hoped that Article I would, by pitting parochial interests against each other, force legislators to explain to constituents why the national government could not meet their every demand, which would in turn lead to more mature public opinion. But delegation prevents the lawmaking process from educating voters about the need to compromise on regulation by allowing Congress to promise everything to everyone.

Lawmaking should serve not only to provide rules to protect us, but also to construct a sense of community by explaining to us why we have the rules that we do.[34] Such explanations once were provided by elders talking about customs around a tribal campfire or leaders debating in an agora. The large size of our national community may have rendered in-person exposure to such discussions impossible, but it has not decreased our hunger to understand the origins of the rules by which we live. We pay great attention when we can see Congress directly joining issue on important matters, as in Supreme Court confirmation battles. If legislators had to make the difficult laws, they would have to vote yea or nay on questions about which they felt intense, conflicting political pressure. Such drama frequently would grab the public's attention. In contrast, delegation takes the drama out of lawmaking by letting legislators disappear and by removing fights from center stage—the House and Senate floors. Witnessing what happens in Congress no longer bonds citizens to the community. Rather they are alienated by exposure to the misleading self-congratulation that accompanies delegation.

Social Choice Theory Does Not Show That Delegation Is a More Reasonable Way to Make Law

Some supporters of delegation argue that social choice theory shows that legislatures can make stable decisions only if the legislative process uses irrational procedures.[35] My short answer to this is that such a conclusion depends upon an unreasonable definition of rationality. (Those readers uninterested in social choice theory should skip to the last paragraph of this chapter.)

Social choice theory aims to explain the logic through which groups form collective choices from individual preferences. The best-known tenet of this theory is Arrow's Theorem, which concludes that, under certain conditions, democratic choices cannot be stable. A particularly neat explanation of the theorem goes as follows:

Assume that three children—Alice, Bobby, and Cindy—have been pestering their parents for a pet. The parents agree that the children may vote to have a dog, a parrot, or a cat. Suppose each child's order of preference is as follows: Alice—dog, parrot, cat; Bobby

—parrot, cat, dog; Cindy—cat, dog, parrot. In this situation, if pairwise voting is required, then majority voting cannot pick a pet. . . . A majority (Alice and Cindy) will vote for a dog rather than a parrot; a majority (Alice and Bobby) will vote for a parrot rather than a cat; and a majority (Bobby and Cindy) will vote for a cat rather than a dog.[36]

Arrow's Theorem concludes that groups acting by a majority vote may fail to select one alternative among an array of choices because, however any one vote between a pair of choices comes out, the next vote between a different pair of choices may well result in an altogether different outcome.

Jerry Mashaw uses Arrow's Theorem to justify the loss of accountability inherent in delegation. As he puts it, "delegating choice to administrators is but another way of avoiding voting cycles through the establishment of dictators."[37] But while Arrow's Theorem may give Alice, Bobby, and Cindy a reason to delegate to their parents the task of picking their pet, it does not give Congress a plausible excuse to delegate to agencies the task of making law. Empirical research has shown that Congress is not prey to the kind of voting cycles that plague our imaginary children, while experience shows that administrative agencies do change their policies with some regularity. Moreover, the assumptions upon which Arrow premised his proof do not hold true in the United States Congress. For example, Arrow's Theorem assumes that voters' preferences are not arrayed along some continuum, but rather are topsy-turvy, like those of Alice, Bobby, and Cindy; but studies show that preferences within Congress tend to be arrayed along a liberal-conservative continuum.[38]

In addition, Article I was designed to enhance the stability of the legislative process. Even if the House or Senate were stuck in a voting cycle over dogs, cats, and parrots, an individual president would not be, and the president may veto any legislation. Of course, the House and the Senate can override a presidential veto if a two-thirds majority of both bodies so vote. But overrides of vetoes are unlikely to lead to voting cycles; theorists have recently shown, based upon some plausible assumptions about voting preferences, that a requirement that a body muster at least a 64-percent majority will ordinarily prevent voting cycles.[39]

Some social choice theorists argue that the properties of the Article I process that help enforce stability make it an undesirable decisionmaking vehicle. Mashaw suggests, for example, that the presidential veto adds a dictatorial element to the legislative process.[40] But Mashaw's "dictator" is an elected official; concern for democratic decisionmaking is hardly a reason to transfer lawmaking power from elected officials in the legislative process to unelected officials in the administrative process.

Mashaw and other theorists also criticize the legislative process because its outcome is determined in part by the elite that sets the legislative agenda. Who sets the agenda makes all the difference in the legislature of the three children picking a pet: a parrot will be selected should the agenda be an initial vote between *dog* and *cat* and a final vote between the initial winner and *parrot*, but with different agendas a dog or a cat would win. Still, the presence of an agenda-setting elite in the legislative process does not make it illegitimate. Any system of collective choice requires a mechanism to set the agenda.[41] For example, agendas are set when agencies are given their mandates and when agency leaders decide what issues to take up and in what order. The issue is not whether the legislative or administrative process have agenda-setting elites, but whether there is any reason to suppose that the system for setting the agenda in the legislative process is less fair or less accountable than the system in the administrative process. Many of the same people, leaders of the legislative and executive branches, set the agenda in both the legislative and administrative processes.[42] I prefer the legislative process because the agenda setting is done more openly than in the administrative process and accountability for the results is more direct.[43]

Some social choice theorists go even further; they charge that democracy is "meaningless because it is impossible to be certain that [decisions] are not simply an artifact of the decision process that has been used."[44] The structure of the decisionmaking process certainly does affect outcomes. For example, a unicameral legislative process would not make the same decisions as the bicameral (with presidential veto power) legislative process of Article I. Nonetheless, the effect that the structure of the decisionmaking process has on outcomes does not render democracy meaningless. Any decisionmaking system must be structured—whether it relies upon elected legislators or unelected administrators—and there is no reason to suppose that it must have any particular structure to be rational or meaningful. Many countries have decisionmaking processes that, like Article I, require concurrent majorities in bicameral legislatures, supermajorities, or other devices to ensure that decisions have broad support. Although any particular decision might come out differently with a different structure, the overall pattern of decisions will tend to reflect public opinion.

Delegation, however, makes decisions depend more on the structure of the decisionmaking process and less on public opinion. While Article I provides one structure for all legislative decisions, delegation allows different structures to be used for different decisions. Legislators can vary the terms of the delegation to enhance their influence or to give an edge to a concentrated interest. The consistent use of the Article I structure would leave less room for legislators to manipulate the structure of the lawmaking process.

The traditional reasons for supposing that we are protected better by agencies than by elected lawmakers over whom we have more direct control sound like the various reasons that parents give for telling their children, "We know what is best for you": expertise ("you won't understand until you grow up"), avoiding stalemate ("you can't make up your mind"), insulation from concentrated interests ("you hang out with bad kids"), and superior rationality ("you're not thinking straight"). Sometimes, the parents are right, but sometimes they are protecting themselves rather than the children. In delegating, lawmakers usually do not deliver the paternalistic protection that they promise, but they do treat us like children.

Congress Has Enough Time to Make the Laws

THE SUPREME COURT HAS SAID THAT TIME limitations require Congress to delegate but supports this conclusion only with the observation that the federal government does delegate.[1] Modern scholars who agree with the Court wrongly assume that the only alternative to delegation is for Congress to take over the entire workload of agencies and that the federal government must enact laws as complex as those the agencies now promulgate.[2] Most agency work, however, does not involve the exercise of legislative power. I will discuss this point in detail in Chapter 12. And, while Congress and the president do have to undertake one big portion of the agencies' current workload—making laws—Congress need not enact laws as complex and intrusive as those that it now requires the agencies to promulgate. Despite their busy schedules, legislators could find the time necessary. If circumstances do not permit a total abolition of delegation, there is a way to allow some delegation yet still largely achieve the goals of the delegation doctrine.

Congress Can Protect the Public with Fewer and Less Complex Laws Than Agencies Now Issue

Most people reflexively think of detailed, national laws as *the* way to deal

135

with substantial threats to the public. The modern Congress responds to such threats by enacting laws or by instructing an agency to issue them. But alternatives to detailed, national laws exist, including: (1) state or local laws, (2) private arrangements, and (3) relatively simple national laws that harness private arrangements to take account of varying circumstances. These alternatives currently are underused because of the self-interest of federal legislators.

State and Local Rules

Only in recent decades has the federal government supplanted states as the primary source of new law. One rationale for the national government to make law is that, when the citizens of one state harm those of another, neither state can regulate fairly. A classic example is interstate pollution. The polluting state would tend to underregulate because the cost of reducing pollution would fall on its citizens, while the benefits would accrue to citizens of other states. The recipient state would tend to overregulate for the opposite reasons. But the political incentives in interstate pollution are not nearly as skewed as the hypothetical suggests, because the emissions that cause interstate pollution often cause even more harmful intrastate pollution.

The Clean Air Act has since 1963 stated as the first finding justifying its existence that air pollution crosses state and local boundaries.[3] Yet, perversely, federal regulation under the act focuses more on intrastate than interstate pollution. A recent environmental law textbook concludes, "The control of interstate pollution provides an easy rationale for federal regulation of air pollution. . . . Despite this, . . . the control of interstate pollution would still have to be considered an unfulfilled promise."[4]

Another justification for national air pollution laws is that states may hesitate to regulate vigorously enough lest their industries move to states willing to trade environmental protection for economic development.[5] When it passed the 1970 Clean Air Act, Congress acted as if it had to take "a stick to the states."[6] Congress was both self-serving and wrong. Industry urged Congress to pass the 1965 and 1967 acts to inhibit strong state regulation of in-state polluters. Nonetheless, the biggest reductions in sulfur emissions were enacted by the states before, rather than after, the 1970 act. Even in the 1980s the states led the national government in implementing new methods of pollution control. According to Robert Crandall, "assertions about the tremendous strides the EPA has made are mostly religious sentiment."[7]

In any event, each state should be able to strike its own balance between environmental quality and economic development or between other threats to the public and the costs of reducing those threats. In one interesting example, William Ruckelshaus, as EPA administrator, faced a tough decision about how to regulate arsenic emissions. The agency was under a court order to set arsenic standards, and the regulations it proposed would have impact exclusively on a Tacoma copper smelter. Its emissions of 310 tons of arsenic per year posed a serious health risk. Even if the smelter installed fairly good pollution controls, experts argued, it would still create a significant risk of lung cancer; cutting emissions further might drive the smelter out of business and deprive up to 800 people of their jobs.[8] Ruckelshaus undertook to educate local citizens about the choice before him and asked for their advice.[9] National environmental groups criticized him for suggesting that health concerns could be balanced against employment concerns.[10] The people from Tacoma, however, generally appreciated his gesture.

The Tacoma case poses the question of whether national policy should trump the preferences of those whose health and jobs are at stake. The local government in Tacoma imposed tough sulfur dioxide regulations that resulted in the company shutting the smelter down.[11] Should states opt for high environmental quality, they also may attract employers for whom environmental quality is important, as has been the case in Vermont and some other states. Other states or cities will opt for lower environmental quality in favor of retaining jobs. Allowing different locales to pursue different preferences is supposedly a strength of federalism.

States should have the power to make these and similar choices in the various fields of regulation, unless we have a good reason to distrust state government more than we distrust national government. Two hundred years ago James Madison argued that interests were less likely to capture the national government than state governments because the nation is larger and more diverse than the states, but most modern states surpass the entire original thirteen in population and diversity.

State governments may appear more susceptible to concentrated interests when the federal government requires them to achieve popular objectives. The state legislators then must impose the regulations or levy the taxes needed to deliver upon the federal legislators' promises. Former New York City mayor Ed Koch said of a mandate to provide transportation for the handicapped passed while he was a Congressman, "I voted for that. You'd be crazy to be against that. When you are a member of Congress and you are voting a mandate and not providing the funds for it, the sky's the limit."[12]

The federal government looks less "progressive" when it has to pay the cost. In the cleanup of toxic waste dump sites under the Superfund program, Congress must take the blame for levying most of the taxes to pay for the program, while state politicians reap benefits for demanding that the national government do more to protect the public.[13] A truer test of the comparative abilities of federal and state governments to deal with problems arises when each acts on its own initiative without involving the other. From 1970 to 1990, as an example, while the federal government listed only 8 air toxics, various states regulated over 700.[14]

The federal requirement that state and local governments remove much of the asbestos in public schools nicely illustrates how blame-shifting and credit-claiming drive the decision to adopt federal rules. Some of that asbestos presents an acute threat to health, some a small threat, and some a threat so minuscule that removing it actually increases the risk. Regardless of the threat, removal is expensive. A wise decision requires weighing the costs and benefits of asbestos removal in each individual school. Instead of leaving the decision to individual school boards or the states, Congress enacted a statute delegating to EPA power to mandate asbestos removal.[15]

Why did Congress take the decision away from local school boards? Surely not because asbestos in schools threatens people in other states, nor because varying decisions about its cleanup would be a substantial factor in the siting of factories. Nor does it make any sense to believe that members of Congress care more about schoolchildren than do their own parents and local officials. The answer cannot be that the federal government knows more about the problem, because then the appropriate solution would be federal advice rather than a federal requirement. When EPA defended the low level of federal grants available to help states remove asbestos by saying that the federal government's proper role was to offer technical advice to school districts, Senator Barbara Mikulski responded, "If it's a local problem you shouldn't have passed a federal law" to solve it.[16] Senator Mikulski should have said, "If it's a local problem *we* shouldn't have passed a federal law." The reason for a federal law on asbestos in the schools is to enable our elected lawmakers to strike a pose in favor of children's health without having to take the blame for the great bulk of the cleanup cost.

Far from being immune to the concentrated interests that are active at the state level, the federal government is often a tool of such interests, permitting them to win battles that they would lose at the state level. Large construction contractors and labor unions, working with state highway officials, for instance, often persuade the federal government to issue requirements that result in a larger share of the state budget going to these interests. Interests centered on state highway departments or other state or local departments can win these fights at the federal level because they are more knowledgeable about the legislation and regulations directly affecting them than are state or local officials with general responsibility—such as the governor, mayor, or legislators—and have a more focused reason to make a concerted lobbying effort. Political scientists call the close working relationships between state and local departments, their counterparts in coordinate federal agencies and congressional committees, and allied private interests *vertical autocracies*.[17] These vertical autocracies are one kind of subgovernment.

Private Arrangements

Another reason that Congress would not have to produce as many laws as agencies now write is that current federal codes regulate matters that often are better left to private arrangements, such as ordinary private contracts and marketplace bargaining. Government-imposed laws are, after all, not the only way to deal with problems. In many subdivisions residents are protected from harmful land uses springing up next to their homes by private covenants with their neighbors as well as by government-enacted zoning rules.[18] Consumers more often avoid being overcharged by buying from a store that offers a good price than by relying on government laws on prices. Federal regulation does sometimes produce better results than private arrangements, but not always.

The Great Depression shook faith in the competitive market because, even after prices fell sharply, the demand for goods was still insufficient to avoid massive unemployment and bankruptcy. Businesses wanted the government to intervene to prop up prices, hold back supply, and thereby, it was thought, prime the pump of commerce. Distinguished economists published works in 1933 that supported these claims by arguing that competition could be fundamentally destructive. Their theories gained "sudden prominence." James Landis premised his case for delegation on the assumption that government needs to manage industries the ways that executives manage firms.[19] In this climate regulation supplanted marketplace competition to too great an extent.

Government cannot manage industries without delegation. For example, in the 1930s Congress by itself had no hope of enacting and updating agricultural marketing orders and industrial codes, given the great number of laws needed to set outputs for the many suppliers of the many agricultural and industrial goods sold in the market and the changes in those laws required by fluctuations in the conditions affecting supply and demand. However, the regulation of markets ultimately did little, if anything, to help end the Depression. Many industrial codes were not effectively enforced and, in any event, *Schechter* struck them down long before the Depression ended. Also, by 1935, support for the codes had waned so much that the Senate seemed likely to block Roosevelt's proposal to extend the NIRA. Soon after *Schechter*, the administration decided that the problem was not too much competition but too little, and so embarked on quite the opposite tack, an aggressive campaign of antitrust enforcement.[20] Modern economists tend to see the Great Depression as having arisen not from malfunction of the markets for particular goods—the problem that the industrial codes sought to address—but rather from insufficient demand brought about by bad fiscal or monetary policy. The managing of markets through regulation holds even less appeal after the breakdown of the centralized economies of Eastern Europe and the Soviet Union.

Nonetheless, as a *New York Times* editorial suggested in 1990, we continue to regulate many markets in which competition would work better.[21] The proponents of agricultural marketing orders claim they are necessary to achieve "orderly markets," although markets for most goods and services, including crops, work well without regulation of supply. The chief rationale for regulating the supply of navel oranges and a few other crops is that agricultural markets are relatively unstable: large supplies of a crop will drive prices down, which causes farmers to plant less of that crop, which results in a shortage, which drives prices up, which causes farmers to plant more of that crop, which results in a glut, and so on. The potential for a recurring cycle of feast and famine is created by the farmers' need to invest in growing a crop while having only imperfect information about the price it is likely to fetch.[22] But suppliers in many unregulated markets face precisely the same problem. A new bakery must invest in equipment long before the first loaves are baked or sold.

Yet most markets do not suffer cycles of feast or famine, because successful suppliers learn to avoid them. They anticipate the possibility of cycles and base future investments not on last year's prices, but on predictions about next year's. The average farmer of the 1930s may have lacked sophistication in such matters, but many farmers today understand agricultural economics and have access to projections of plantings and prices. They can also shift the risk of falling prices by entering into long-term supply contracts, or hedging their positions through the options or futures markets. Most of our fruit, vegetable, and specialty crops get marketed without quotas or other quantity restrictions. So, even if agricultural marketing orders made sense in the 1930s, today, according to one economist, "the government has about as much business controlling the sale of fresh oranges as it does controlling the sale of toothbrushes."[23]

Proponents of the marketing orders also argue that the perishability of agricultural goods requires regulation of supply in order to match it with demand. But such highly perishable goods as raspberries and oysters get marketed without marketing orders or other such regulation. The markets for unregulated crops are, if anything, more stable.[24] In any event, the Department of Agriculture's rationale for regulating navel oranges was that they are *not* perishable, as they can be stored for months on the tree. Without a marketing order, the department claims that growers would pick and market the entire crop at the beginning of the picking season, causing a glut in the fall and a shortage in the spring. That argument assumes that growers would sell when the market is low. In contrast, both the department's economists and consumer groups conclude that orange growers, when given a chance, make the sensible decision to take the probable price into account in deciding when to sell.[25] In this way the market would, on its own, iron out fluctuations of supply and price. As one grower put it, "I am continuously amazed and insulted by the [Department of Agriculture] and the NOAC that they still believe in this day and age of efficient educated farmers that the orange farmer is still too stupid to make decisions during the navel season as to the proper time economically to harvest or not harvest his crop."[26]

Private arrangements, whether through contracts or marketplace competition, cannot solve all problems, but they can solve some problems traditionally handled by governmental rules. For example, a Brookings Institution study concludes that the deregulation of truck and rail freight rates has helped shippers, who have saved an estimated twenty billion dollars annually largely by avoiding inefficiencies caused by regulation.[27] The interesting questions are why, since the public was being overcharged for many decades, Congress did not deregulate far sooner, and why it has not more recently built upon these successes through additional deregulation. By this point in my discussion, the answers should be obvious. The trucking industry is a powerful concentrated interest willing to support members of Congress who block deregulation and who intervene on their behalf before the agencies. The public, on the other hand, is unlikely to know that government regulation has increased the cost of transportation and still less likely to blame this harm on their representatives in Congress rather than administrative agencies.

A Congress not skewed toward regulation by delegation would, I think, decide to deregulate or decrease regulation in many industries where habit makes regulation seem a given. For example, some economists recommend ending price regulation of natural gas pipelines and electricity generation (but not distribution) because they believe that competition could adequately control prices and that regulation leads to waste. According to one policy analyst, "the major problem [with such proposals] is political. The new delegation came into being and remains in place because it, better than any of the technically superior alternatives, works politically."[28]

Simple National Laws That Harness Private Arrangements

Some problems require federal attention because both private arrangements and state law lack the capacity to work a satisfactory solution. The federal government usually responds with laws that tell people what to do in precise terms. Such complicated laws often backfire because lawmakers (whether elected or appointed) have trouble envisioning how such laws will work in every context, the various ways of circumventing them, and their many indirect consequences.[29] Scholars have suggested that, instead of complicated laws, the federal government should enact simple laws that would help private arrangements work better. One example is the proposal, discussed in Chapter 1, to promote energy efficiency by providing information and taxing energy rather than by directly regulating new vehicles and appliances. Another example, discussed in Chapter 8, would be to curtail deposit insurance, which, when supplemented by financial disclosure laws, would help market forces do much of the work now done so badly by the direct regulation of savings and loans and banks.

Government often could achieve its legitimate purposes with far simpler laws. Cass Sunstein suggests that the Occupational Safety and Health Administration's 3,617 pages of safety regulations—which prescribe workplace design and practices down to such details as the dimensions of ladders—might be replaced by taxes or penalties geared to employers' actual performance in reducing deaths and injury performance and by disclosure to employees of risks, "at least where the risk is one that reasonable, informed people might run"; this would facilitate bargaining about workplace safety.[30]

Broadcast regulation provides another area for a possible simplification of federal rules. The Federal Communications Act now directs the Federal Communications Commission (FCC) to award television and radio licenses to the applicant who would best serve the public interest. The act provides that the airwaves remain public property and that licensees must compete with other applicants to get their licenses renewed. However, in practice, licensees almost always get their licenses renewed and the FCC's regulation does not markedly change the content of a licensee's programming. The government lets private persons use extremely valuable public property—the airways —and gets in return neither "better" programming nor rent. Some scholars and policy analysts suggest that Congress should instead instruct the FCC to license the highest bidder after setting basic requirements for participation in the auction, including solvency and proficiency in operating the broadcasting equipment.[31] In this scheme, the federal government would give up its right to pick the "best" among qualified applicants—which has proved of little meaning—in return for capturing the economic value of a publicly owned resource. Even if it is too late to reform broadcast regulation in this way because the government has, in effect, made the airwaves the property of broad-casters, the example suggests that new problems need not be solved by complex national rules.

Congress has a vested interest in not giving this alternative fair consideration. The federal government's gift of something extremely valuable becomes an occasion for legislators to do casework. The FCC actually proposed the auction approach for the distribution of licenses for cellular telephones, after Congress had abandoned the notion that the Commission could hold hearings for each market area to determine which applicant could best serve the public interest. Congress responded by forbidding such auctions. The FCC's only recourse was to hold lotteries for these licenses, estimated to be worth thirty to forty billion dollars in total. Many citizens, some with help from their legislator's office, have entered the sweepstakes, and some have come away as millionaires.[32]

Congress Has Sufficient Time to Protect the Public Without Delegation

The chief executive officer of a large private organization usually delegates details to leave enough time to decide the broad issues of policy. New Dealers argued for delegation on the grounds that "time spent on details [by Congress] must be at the sacrifice of time spent on matters of broad public policy."[33] Yet Congress does not act like an institution too short of time to get involved in details, especially as it has turned from broad to narrow delegation. For example, the Clean Air Act and many other statutes give agencies copious instructions on the handling of many complex questions. The 2,823–page-long Internal Revenue Code legislates in great detail, often creating rules so specialized that they apply to only one taxpayer. Congress legislates about details on an even more massive scale in the annual federal budget, which in 1991 ran to 1,527 printed pages on five and a half pounds of paper. That budget, like others, not only decides broad policy —such as the allocation of funds among major program categories —but also dictates tiny particulars of program administration. For example, Congress decided that $2.5 million of the $55.3 billion gross Department of Agriculture budget should go for the planning, design, and construction of a Poultry Disease Laboratory and that it should be located in Athens, Georgia.[34] But, in delegating to agencies, Congress often leaves open broad policy issues.

I cannot prove that Congress would have sufficient time to make the laws necessary to protect the public by toting up the time that each of a legislator's essential tasks would take; calculating the time required involves too many variables. Instead, I will argue that Congress would have adequate time because (1) making the laws would often take less time than delegating and, in any event, (2) legislators could make much more time available for lawmaking.

The Scope of the Job for Congress Without Delegation

Congress already makes much law itself. It enacts relatively succinct though important laws, such as that forbidding discrimination in employment, and also mammoth codes dealing with personal and other income taxes. Congress also tends to enact laws when providing benefits, as in major parts of the vast entitlements programs and the annual budget.[35]

Congress could achieve the public purposes that it now pursues through delegation in far less time than agencies take to make laws and in less time than delegation takes Congress in the long run. Acting by itself, Congress would not have to go through the same laborious processes that it requires of agencies. Congress currently accompanies delegation with detailed instructions on substance and procedure that constrain agency discretion. Writing such instructions would be unnecessary if Congress made the rules. Congress could, however, ask for an agency's help in drafting law. For instance, it could require the agency to propose statutory language, prepare supporting analyses, and hold hearings on proposals. The agency's analysis undoubtedly would make use of the kind of information that now is considered in administrative rulemaking. Congress could, if needed, amend its procedures to expedite consideration of such agency reports because the agency would have already laid much of the groundwork. Even if Congress enacted an agency's draft with hardly a change, the process would differ from delegation in an essential way: members of Congress and the president would have to take responsibility for the law. The votes on most such laws might never become issues in future reelection campaigns, but the most controversial ones would. And since the incumbents could never anticipate with full confidence which of their votes would become a campaign issue, they would have to take their constituents' interests into account in most of their votes. Forcing elected officials to make explicit decisions is essential for democratic accountability and the protection of liberty.

James Landis, the New Deal's chief architect of the administrative process, advocated that agencies propose important laws but that Congress be required to vote on them before they could go into effect. He thought that this approach would forestall concerns about the constitutionality of delegation and would protect the public better than delegation. As he recognized, since controversy often paralyses the administrative process, "it is an act of political wisdom to put back upon the shoulders of the Congress" responsibility for controversial choices.[36]

Legislators spend more time delegating than they might spend in making the laws themselves. Delegation is time-consuming because instructing agencies on how to make the law is a complex task, as the length of the various Clean Air Acts suggests. Moreover, the issues that one Congress ducks by delegating often reemerge to consume the time of succeeding Congresses. Delegation also requires legislators to oversee agency rulemaking and provides the opportunity to spend time on casework.

To illustrate my conclusion that Congress could make the laws necessary to protect the public in less time than it now spends delegating I would like to examine how Congress could tackle the regulation of agricultural markets and air pollution without delegation. These illustrations will suggest that my various proposals for simplifying federal lawmaking, taken together, would reduce the scope of Congress's job to a surprising extent.

Regulating agricultural markets without delegation.
An end to delegation would force Congress to consider other ways of achieving the official purposes of agricultural marketing orders, namely, to make an orderly market and to increase growers' incomes. The first purpose would be served by letting the market decide supply, and the second purpose through an approach far simpler than agricultural marketing orders—making cash payments to growers. Paul Samuelson, a member of President Kennedy's Council of Economic Advisors and a Nobel laureate, argues that subsidizing growers through cash gifts is superior to schemes to raise the market price of crops (of which the agricultural marketing order program is one) for two reasons. First, raising the price encourages additional production of an already overabundant crop and therefore is a wasteful way to increase farmers' incomes. Second, a direct cash payment makes clear that the purpose

of the program is to subsidize income and therefore clarifies the policy choice for the public.[37] Such clarity might well mean that Congress would decide not to subsidize the beneficiaries of agricultural marketing orders.

If, however, Congress did decide to award these subsidies, its job would be easy compared to the secretary's present one. Congress would only have to state a subsidy formula for the secretary to use in making out the checks. The statute could be far simpler than the one that delegates the authority to issue agricultural marketing orders. And the legislators would not get involved in the numerous squabbles that rulemaking under that program has occasioned over the years. Furthermore, the statute could include an adjustment for inflation, so Congress could leave it unchanged for decades. The secretary currently must decide how to allocate the market among growers annually, how much of the crop to sell weekly, and how to treat exports, organic oranges, and myriad other issues that sporadically arise.

Regulating air pollution without delegation.
Congress could also deal with air pollution in less time-consuming ways than under delegation. It would have to make laws for only a small proportion of the hundreds of pollutants that EPA was supposed to regulate under the 1970 act and now has to regulate under the 1990 act. States themselves would, in most instances, adequately regulate highly toxic pollutants because, as previously explained, most pollutants that could cause significant interstate harm also could cause intrastate disaster. (If unacceptable interstate effects remained, Congress could still intervene.) Moreover, Congress could leave to the states decisions about whether and how to regulate traffic to reduce carbon monoxide. Twenty years of federal efforts to get states to achieve the national ambient air quality standard for carbon monoxide by regulating traffic has achieved little. I played a part in this effort when, as an attorney at the Natural Resources Defence Council, I helped secure a court order against the governor of New York State and the mayor of New York City to force them to implement various traffic reducing strategies. The court order did little good. Ross Sandler, the New York City Transportation Commissioner (previously my partner at the Natural Resources Defense Council) testified to Congress in 1989, "No matter where you look, and no matter how many times [traffic restrictions] are restated in transportation control plans, they have

simply not been done."[38] The federal government will not get cities and states to do much more about traffic than their own citizens want done; nor should it, since those citizens suffer most from the fumes and inconveniences of traffic jams.

Without delegating, Congress could help the states deal with pollution. It could instruct EPA to provide them with information on all harmful pollutants and propose emission limits for the states' consideration. Congress could also require sources of toxic chemicals to report to the states the nature and amount of their emissions, as indeed it already has.[39] The release of such information has prompted increased regulation, for example, in Louisiana, which is hardly an environmentalist stronghold.

Congress could deal with the pollutants that do have substantial interstate effects in much simpler ways than present law provides. Such pollutants are emitted by many different categories of sources —from automobiles, steel mills, and oil refineries to drycleaners, gasoline stations, and backyard barbecues. Congress never could craft laws to deal with every category of source from the most important to the least important. Nor would that be desirable, because the great bulk of the emissions come from a small number of source categories. Before extensive national controls were in place—that is, in 1970—more than half of the sulfur oxides came from a single category: large fossil-fuel industrial boilers, such as power plants. A few other categories accounted for most of the rest. Power plants, other large fuel burners, and motor vehicles accounted for over four-fifths of the nitrogen oxides, sulfur oxides and lead emissions, and almost half of the emissions of hydrocarbons and particulate matter.[40] If Congress had enacted laws for just these categories of sources in 1970, instead of giving a comprehensive but time-consuming mandate to EPA to regulate every harmful pollutant in a way that takes account of every source, the air pollution control program would have gotten off to a far faster start. Congress could then have asked EPA to suggest other pollutants or categories of sources that should be regulated because of their interstate effects.

When enacting laws for even a single category of source, Congress would want to take account of differences (1) from place to place in the harm that emissions cause, and (2) from source to source in the cost of controlling emissions. The Clean Air Act takes account of regional differences in the amount of harm emissions cause in various ways.

The ambient air standards implicitly require a lower emission limit on plants located close together than on an isolated plant of the same size.[41] Congress could take account of significant geographical variations in harm by setting different emission limits for different regions. The statute might enact a basic national emission limit, but then apply a tighter one in, for instance, the rustbelt, to account for the concentration of emission sources, and, as another example, the area upwind of the Grand Canyon and the other great national parks to protect scenic values. Although regional variations in the emission law would not take account of more localized circumstances, Congress could allow the states to deal with these variations by not preventing them from imposing emission limits more stringent than the federal ones.

The current Clean Air Act takes account of differences between sources in the cost of controlling emissions in a variety of ways. For example, a state plan may impose different emission limits on different sources. A statute that did not delegate could do the same. First, it might vary the emission limits to take account of the greater ease of controlling emissions in a new plant. Second, it could use economic incentives, such as pollution taxes. A tax on each unit of a given pollutant emitted would make it profitable for firms to reduce emissions until further emission reductions would cost more than the tax. Such an approach would reduce pollution most at plants that could do so most efficiently.

Emissions limits and economic incentives could be combined. The statute could allow the set limit for emissions to be exceeded on the payment of a tax. Or, as I prefer, the statute could allow a firm that emitted less than the emission limit to sell the quantity of emission rights that it does not use to another firm, which could then exceed the limit by that quantity. As the Environmental Defense Fund argues, such emission trading and other economic approaches would take account of differences between plants in the cost of pollution control and also give industry a profit motive to invent better pollution control techniques and use them.[42]

There is a large literature on such market-oriented approaches to pollution, most of it favorable. They have several advantages. Firms know better than government who can reduce pollution cheaply and are given economic incentives to act on that information. Market mechanisms also can allocate the cleanup burden more cheaply and quickly than rulemaking procedures. For such reasons, economic incentives could reduce by 400 percent the cost of cutting emissions, according to one estimate.[43]

I published an article in 1983 that suggested that Congress could control air pollution without delegation by using the approach suggested here to tackle the problem of acid rain. Congress did use the essence of this approach in the provisions of the 1990 act on acid rain.[44]

Congress could have made the laws to protect the public from air pollution in less time than it has spent delegating. Legislators would not have had to legislate the terms of the delegation, which can cost more in time and effort, though less in political blame, than enacting the laws themselves. Giving an agency meaningful guidance is difficult without making some goals absolute, and that rarely makes policy sense. The 1970 Clean Air Act tried to deal with this problem by making discretion depend on a multiplicity of variables, such as whether the goal is health or welfare, what sort of threat the pollutant presents, the cost of compliance, and the availability of pollution control devices. Congress could not have attempted to control discretion in a more carefully designed way; yet, as discussed in Chapter 4, the states and EPA found ways to escape that control. Although the 1970 act sailed through with hardly a dissent, half of the sessions of Congress from 1970 to 1990 undertook major efforts to rewrite the act, in addition to the normal business of congressional oversight. The act as amended in 1990 now runs to 718 pages, far longer than the necessary federal laws would run.

Congress Can Make More Time for Lawmaking

Lawmakers in Congress spend far more time promoting themselves than discharging their duty under the Constitution to make law. In particular, they spend more time soliciting contributions, showing themselves to constituents and contributors, and doing casework than enacting statutes and evaluating their implementation. So many legislators spend four days a week in their districts that, according to one senator, "our work [in Washington] is all telescoped into a three-day time frame."[45]

Casework provides members of the public with valuable information and assistance in dealing with the federal bureaucracy, but Congress could arrange for the public to get that help from other sources.

Fourteen countries now provide assistance through national ombuds-men.[46] Alternatively, congressional committees rather than legislators could perform this function. Separating casework from legislators would mean that the level of assistance one got would not depend upon how much one contributed to the legislator's last campaign or the place of the legislator in the congressional pecking order.

Congress also could reorganize in ways that would make the legis-lative process less cumbersome. For example, it could undo the changes made in the 1970s creating so many new subcommittees that over half of the majority party in the House chair something. These chairpersons enjoy the publicity, prestige, extra staff and budget, and perquisites, but they come at the cost of complicating the job of legislating. To illus-trate, seven House committees—Energy and Commerce, Public Works, Ways and Means, Education and Labor, Interior, Merchant Marine, and Science—held hearings on the 1990 Clean Air Act. At the drafting stage, these committees and four others—Small Business, Armed Services, Government Operations, and Banking—claimed a role.[47]

Finally, Congress could reduce the time it spends on the budget. A Congress that no longer delegated legislative power to the executive would have less reason to try to micromanage the executive through the budget.[48]

A Safety Valve

If, contrary to my expectations, Congress could be shown to lack the time to protect the public adequately without some delegation of its legislative powers, delegation might be limited to occasions when it could do the least damage to democratic accountability and liberty. Some concessions to practicality are already built into the traditional conception of legislative powers, as I will show in Chapter 12. Addi-tional concessions are available which would not clash significantly with the purposes of the delegation doctrine. Before approving delega-tion explicitly, courts ruled that Congress could leave "details" to others.[49] Requiring Congress to settle all the controversial questions, leaving only the kinds of "details" unlikely to change many legislators' votes, would go a long way to achieving the purposes of Article I, and simultaneously would save Congress some time.

Besides being unpersuasive, as I have shown in this part of the book, the various theories of why delegation is good for the public bear no discernible relationship to when legislators delegate. If they really delegated because they thought agencies made better decisions for the public, they would delegate as much as they could, but they don't. If they really delegated because they lacked the time to decide the details or the expertise to decide the technical questions, they would decide the big, nontechnical issues and delegate the rest, but they often do exactly the opposite. Instead, they delegate in large part to benefit themselves.

The Courts Should Bar Delegation

All men are created equal in at least one thing: not one of them is to be trusted to rule the rest unless he is restrained by law. And if he is not restrained by it, our discipline teaches us to disobey him and reestablish the rule of law according to the traditions of our native land.
—AUBREY MENON, *Dead Man in the Silver Market*

THE ONLY LAW THAT RESTRAINS OUR ELECTed lawmakers absolutely is the Constitution. They violate the Constitution when they delegate and, according to the traditions of our native land, violations of the Constitution are to be cured by the courts.

The Constitution Prohibits Delegation

CONGRESS AND THE PRESIDENT BENEFIT from both delegation and deficit spending. While the courts cannot stop deficit spending unless the Constitution is amended, they can legitimately stop delegation: the Constitution already prohibits it.

Nonlawyers may wonder why even a short chapter is needed to show that delegation is unconstitutional given that Chapter 2 has already shown that key Framers said it was and early Supreme Court cases agreed. The simple answer is that the legal analysis has a few different wrinkles than the historical one.

Article I Requires Congress to Make Law

The Constitution does not prohibit the delegation of legislative power in so many words, but the Framers probably intended such a prohibition with Article I's opening sentence, which begins: "All legislative Powers herein granted shall be vested in a Congress . . . " John Locke, who influenced many of the Framers, thought that "the legislative cannot transfer the power of making law to any other hands" because "when the people have said, 'We will submit and be governed by laws made by such men, and in such [constitutional] forms,' nobody else can say other men shall make laws for them."[1] Debate at the Constitutional Convention proceeded on the premise that Congress could not delegate its legislative powers to the executive. Moreover, the Framers' claim that Article I protects the people from elected officials would have been inconsistent with a Constitution that permitted officials to make law outside the Article I process. During the debates on the ratification of the Constitution, James Madison read Article I to forbid the exercise of legislative power through delegation.[2]

The debates in Congress over the Bill of Rights, although ambiguous, tend to support the conclusion that Article I was intended to forbid delegation of legislative power. Madison, among others, had proposed a draft of the Bill of Rights that included a provision denying any branch the power to exercise the powers of any other branch. The version recommended by the House committee also included such an amendment. Representative Roger Sherman argued to the House that the amendment was "altogether unnecessary, inasmuch as the constitution assigned the business of each branch of the government to a separate department." Representative James Madison appeared to agree that the amendment was superfluous, but went on to argue that "the people would be gratified with the amendment, as it was admitted, that the powers ought to be separate and distinct, it might also tend to an explanation of some doubts that might arise respecting the construction of the constitution." The House included the amendment in the version of the Bill of Rights sent to the Senate. The Senate, however, deleted the amendment and the House acquiesced, but the record contains no explanation of these actions.[3]

The Supreme Court has always read Article I as implicitly limiting delegation.[4] So the question is not whether, but rather to what extent, Article I prohibits Congress from delegating legislative power. Some early Supreme Court opinions suggest that the prohibition is total. Modern Supreme Court opinions hold that Congress may let others make the laws, as long as Congress describes the goals that those laws should achieve. The early cases were right and the modern cases wrong.

The Constitution's Text

Deciding whether Article I's text allows Congress to delegate the power to make law involves two interrelated questions: (first) is making the law a legislative power? and (second) can Congress delegate the legislative power? Making law was within the ordinary meaning of legislative power at the time of the Constitution's adoption. According to Hobbes, "it belongeth . . . to the Soveraigne . . . to præscribe the Rules of *discerning Good and Evill:* which Rules are Lawes; and therefore in him is the Legislative Power." *Fletcher v. Peck,* decided in 1810, stated that "[i]t is the peculiar province of the legislature to prescribe general rules for the government of society; the application of those rules to individuals in society would seem to be the duty of other departments." *Gibbons v. Ogden,* decided in 1824, stated that "to regulate commerce [which Article I includes in the legislative power] is to prescribe the rule by which commerce is to be governed."[5]

Some modern scholars argue, however, that because the Framers tempered strict separation of powers for practicality's sake, Congress can also temper the Constitution's allocation of duties for practicality's sake.[6] But the Constitution deviates from strict separation of powers partly to protect liberty with a system of checks and balances. For example, the president's veto power, which gives the executive a role in legislating, intentionally makes it harder to legislate. Since the veto power and other aspects of the system of shared and separated powers was designed to protect the people from officials, the Constitution should not be read to allow those officials to rearrange its allocation of powers.

As suggested by the efforts of New Dealers to drape agency lawmaking with the legitimacy of courts, one might argue that the Framers could not have intended to limit delegation of legislative power to agencies because they did accept that unelected judges could make the common law. But, in critical ways, the common law is more like statutory law than agency law. To the considerable extent that common law grows out of community custom, it reflects a popular consensus and so is no less democratic that statutory law. Since custom usually is broadbased, common law based upon it has the supermajoritarian support that Article I uses to deter special interests laws that infringe upon liberty. Even more fundamentally, the Framers saw the common law as inherently protective of liberty.[7] Finally, unlike agency leaders, judges are insulated from day-to-day politics so that the common law is less likely than agency law to follow the dictates of narrow interests.

The Constitution's Purposes

Under the modern Supreme Court's test of proper delegation, Congress need state only an "intelligible principle" and, indeed, need not even do that in cases of necessity.[8] The Supreme Court has tried to justify its "intelligible principle" test by arguing that it is consistent with the delegation doctrine's purposes of making the government democratically accountable and of protecting liberty.[9] These purposes might be served if the intelligible principle test meant that Congress had to take responsibility for the controversial implications of its legislation as clearly as if it had stated the law. But, in the Court's hands, the intelligible principle test has meant that Congress can leave the hard choices to the agency.[10]

The Cases That Wrongly Allowed Delegation Do Not Make It Constitutional

Scholars have suggested that the Supreme Court's decisions allowing delegation, even though they may misinterpret the Constitution, either preclude the Court from giving the Constitution its proper meaning now or have changed its meaning to allow delegation.

Precedent Does Not Preclude Enforcing Article I

The question is whether the precedent allowing broad delegation obliges the Supreme Court to repeat its mistakes in the future. Judges think of themselves as bound by precedent under a doctrine known as *stare decisis*, although they disagree among themselves about the extent to which they are bound, especially on constitutional issues, and have difficulty enunciating a clear test of when they are bound.[11] I do not need to sort out those differences here, because enforcing the delegation doctrine does not thwart any of the three major purposes of *stare decisis*.

One purpose of *stare decisis* is to appraise accurately the intention of those who wrote the text being interpreted. Following precedent tends to serve this purpose because the judges who lived closest in time to those who wrote the constitutional provision in question are most likely to have understood its context and its meaning.[12] This purpose would be served better by preventing delegation rather than by following recent precedents. The justices who were contemporaries of the Framers interpreted the text as preventing Congress from delegating the power to make law. The Supreme Court did not begin to depart from this interpretation until the end of the nineteenth century, more than one hundred years after the Constitution was ratified. Even then, as discussed in Chapter 2, the Court did not explicitly reject its earlier reading of the Constitution, but rather upheld statutes in the mistaken belief that they did not delegate.

The Supreme Court's opinion in *Mistretta* conveys a different impression of the views of the early justices:

> Until 1935, this Court never struck down a challenged statute on delegation grounds. After invalidating in 1935 two statutes as excessive delegations, we have upheld, again without deviation, Congress's ability to delegate power under broad standards.[13]

Although this statement neglects to mention the serious attention that jurists and other authorities paid to delegation before 1935, it is technically correct under *stare decisis* to focus only on decisions that use a doctrine to decide a case.[14] So, decisions that uphold statutes because the courts find that they do not delegate count neither as precedent in favor of the delegation doctrine nor as precedent against it.[15] *Mistretta* is wrong, however, in claiming that no Supreme Court opinions struck down any statute on delegation grounds before 1935. In fact, the Court invoked concerns about delegation to strike down statutes in 1920, 1921, and 1924, as I described in Chapter 2. The judges closest in time to the framing of the Constitution and the earliest holdings read Article I to prohibit delegation.

A second purpose of *stare decisis* is to maintain "public faith in the judiciary as a source of impersonal and reasoned judgments,"[16] because following precedent suggests that justices are not responding to personal preferences or political winds.[17] This purpose would also be furthered by preventing delegation rather than by following recent precedent. What prompted the cases from the later New Deal to reject the longstanding precedent against delegation was intimidation, epitomized by the Court-packing plan, and the appointment of new justices to the Court. Defenders of the New Deal claim that the Supreme Court changed position out of conviction; but a scholar notes, "no matter how insistently [Justices] Hughes and Roberts might later deny that their switch to the liberal wing had been politically motivated, few students of the Court view their move as anything but a recognition of the handwriting on the wall."[18] The Court could give principled reasons for reversing itself to enforce the delegation doctrine today: the cases allowing delegation are inconsistent with the earliest precedents, were prompted by intimidation, and were premised on the mistaken belief that delegation is consistent with democracy and Article I's safeguards of liberty.

A third purpose of *stare decisis* is to protect expectations based upon precedent, so that people can rely on prior judicial decisions.[19] Preventing delegation clashes with this purpose, unless ways can be found to accommodate the pervasive reliance on delegation in modern federal regulation. Chaos would result if the Court announced that all laws issued by agencies under delegations of legislative power were void immediately. However, the Court could legitimately make the transition away from delegation sufficiently gradual and orderly to take account of such reliance, as Chapter 11 will show.

The New Deal Did Not Amend the Constitution to Allow Delegation

Bruce Ackerman, supported by some other leading scholars, contends that the New Deal amended the Constitution to permit otherwise unconstitutional aspects of its program, including the delegation of legislative powers, although no amendment was ratified under the Constitution's explicit procedures.[20] Article V of the Constitution provides that an amendment may be proposed in either of two ways: Congress may propose an amendment by at least a two-thirds vote of both houses, or the legislatures of two-thirds of the states may apply to Congress, which then shall call a constitutional convention to propose amendments. However the process begins, the proposed amendments require ratification by three-quarters of the state legislatures or by conventions in three-quarters of the states, with Congress choosing between these two modes of ratification.

Ackerman dismisses the absence of any attempt to comply with Article V by arguing that what happened during the New Deal was just as good as the Constitution's amendment process. His theory is troubling both because it is inconsistent with the Constitution's text and because he is mistaken in believing that the New Deal was the virtual equivalent of the Constitution's amendment process. He argues that (1) a constitutional amendment was proposed to the public when the Supreme Court rejected the New Deal program on several points of principle during President Roosevelt's first term; (2) the public supported the proposed amendment when it reelected Roosevelt and his Congress in 1936; and (3) the amendment was formally ratified when the Supreme Court changed its position, which meant that conservatives "finally recognize[d] that *the People had spoken*."[21]

Ackerman hears "the People" incorrectly because his account of events overlooks critical parts of the story. The Supreme Court cases, which he sees as proposing a constitutional amendment to the public, give little idea of what amendment was proposed. Nor does Ackerman. The Court had overruled a host of New Deal statutes and actions on a wide variety of constitutional points that included delegation as well as the scope of congressional power to regulate commerce, the president's power to fire officials, and more. Ackerman never says how the public would know which of these points the proposed amendment covered or how the amendment treated each. President Roosevelt let the public know that he was considering the possibility of seeking some unspecified amendments under Article V at some point after the 1936 election. If voters had notice of anything as they went to the polls in 1936, it was that no amendment had been proposed. Moreover, President Roosevelt had not yet decided what amendments, if any, he might seek. One prominent correspondent counseled the President to seek several amendments, including one providing "for an intelligent measure of delegation," whatever that meant.[22] The draft amendments that the Department of Justice offered for the president's consideration said nothing about delegation. One of them did, however, require a seven-justice majority to strike down a federal statute, and another would have allowed Congress to overrule a Supreme Court decision that held a statute unconstitutional. President Roosevelt decided to try to pack the Court rather than amend the Constitution partly because of the difficulties in framing appropriate amendments. Ackerman thus is incorrect in suggesting that the New Deal gave the citizens who went to the polls in 1936 notice of the contents of proposed constitutional amendments equivalent to that which Article V would have provided. Notice of the contents of an amendment is critical because ambiguities in the text of proposed amendments have spurred opposition to their ratification.[23]

Ackerman is also incorrect when he suggests that the election of 1936 was equivalent to a national referendum on constitutional principles. Roosevelt won a landslide victory, but it is far from clear whether his election meant that voters favored amending the Constitution. He found it politically advantageous to maintain a "studied silence" on Court and constitutional issues during the 1936 campaign. He decided not to bring constitutional issues to a head because he thought that a majority of the public disapproved of the National Industrial Recovery Act, which *Schechter* and *Panama Refining* had struck down.[24] Not only did the voters lack notice of a proposed amendment, but they may well have defeated such an amendment overwhelmingly if given a chance to vote on it.

Ackerman asserts that approval by the three branches of the federal government is the equivalent of state ratification. But President Roosevelt decided not to seek amendments partly because he thought he probably could not get three-quarters of the states to ratify, as Article V requires.[25] Furthermore, approval by federal officials differs critically from approval by state officials when the amendments in question add to the power of the federal government, as allowing delegation does. Finally, legislators who supposedly voted to ratify Ackerman's supposed amendment never had actually to vote to amend the Constitution. Article V requires legislators to vote explicitly for an amendment, which gives the public some check on constitutional amendments. Another reason President Roosevelt did not seek a constitutional amendment after his 1936 victory is that, in the words of his press secretary, we "might lose a number of 'our congressmen'" in the 1938 elections.[26] Officials were not required to take a discrete position on the supposed amendment but instead could meld the changes with the election of a president. The 1936 election therefore did not present the public with an opportunity to focus on issues of principle in a way equivalent to the Article V process.

While Ackerman is incorrect in concluding that the New Deal amended the Constitution to allow delegation, I agree with him on the more basic point that the Framer's prohibition of delegation should not inexorably bind all future generations. Rather, we should have an opportunity to consider whether we want to change the Constitution to allow delegation.

We reserve constitutional provisions and amendments for issues that are basic and ought to have enduring answers. Indeed, most constitutional provisions seek to make governmental processes fair, rather than to ordain the substantive results that those processes must produce.[27] On this basis, delegation qualifies for resolution at the constitutional level, as it affects democracy and liberty in the making of all our national law. Delegation is comparable in importance to any of the last six amendments to the Constitution.[28]

But we shall never have an opportunity to reconsider delegation through the Constitution's amendment process unless and until the Supreme Court holds delegation unconstitutional. The first method of amendment, which starts in Congress, would never produce an amendment to prohibit delegation because Congress benefits from it.

The second method, by which the states force Congress to call a convention, has never produced a convention, let alone an amendment. The proposed Balanced Budget Amendment, for instance, which has more intuitive political appeal than prohibiting delegation, stands one state short of the required three-quarters. Moreover, state legislatures would find it far more difficult to support a delegation amendment than a balanced budget amendment because state constitutions, as interpreted, already prohibit budget deficits but generally allow at least some delegation. State legislators delegate for the same reasons as federal ones do and so would not throw stones at congressional delegation from their own glass houses.

The upshot is that even a substantial majority of the public would be insufficient to produce an amendment prohibiting or limiting the delegation of legislative power. However, should the courts hold delegation unconstitutional, Congress could seek an amendment to allow delegation, if the public approves. Although Supreme Court decisions are hardly ever overturned by constitutional amendments, the self-interest of national and state legislators would ensure that an amendment to authorize delegation would get legislators' attention. The overcoming of their usual inertia when a constitutional amendment is involved does not, however, mean that they would succeed in the end. They would still have to get supermajorities within Congress and amongst the states, which might roughly counterbalance their self-interest. Moreover, legislators would have to vote squarely on the principle of whether legislators or bureaucrats should make the laws, an issue now resolved silently as a routine aspect of many statutes. These legislators would have to convince a public already quite skeptical about politicians and political institutions that delegation is not just a matter of self-interest.

I believe that it would be desirable to go through such an amendment process for two quite distinct reasons. First and most important, I view delegation as bad policy. I hope and believe that the constitutional amendment process would reject it for that reason. Polls show longstanding distrust of Congress and support for measures that limit legislators' power, such as the Balanced Budget Amendment and limits on legislative terms.[29]

Second, even if legislators might prevail in the end, I believe that going through the constitutional amendment process would be desirable. Delegation has changed our government in a way that has enhanced the power of both legislators and bureaucrats and reduced the participation of those who are governed. The public should have an opportunity to consider such a fundamental change explicitly. The debate would force legislators to show why delegation is so necessary. They surely would not argue that it is because legislators cannot be trusted. The upshot might be a proposed amendment that partially limits delegation or otherwise curbs the abuses that delegation facilitates.

The Antifederalists, who opposed the Constitution because they believed that it gave our elected national lawmakers too much power, criticized Article V for allowing them to readily block any constitutional amendment that would limit their power.[30] The Antifederalists had a point; Article V makes it much easier for those officials to block such an amendment than to secure an amendment enlarging their powers. So, although I admire Bruce Ackerman's interest in integrating discussions of constitutional principle into our political life, the practical effect of deeming the New Deal to have amended the Constitution to allow delegation would be to shut off discussion before it ever begins. As a result, we would permanently discard the Framers' scheme for making law democratically and with respect for liberty. We would do so not because we had faced the issue of principle but because, in a time of desperation, we wanted a strong leader. Only if the Supreme Court recognizes that the Constitution prohibits delegation can the discussion begin.

Why the Courts Should Stop Delegation (and Nobody Else Can)

CHAPTER 11

THE SUPREME COURT MIGHT BELIEVE THAT delegation is unconstitutional and yet refrain from stopping it because they think judicial enforcement is inappropriate or impractical. The Court claims the discretion to tolerate violations of the Constitution when correcting them would require judges to make policy judgments traditionally left to elected officials. The Court is also concerned with protecting the judiciary's power and legitimacy.[1] Given this concern for the courts' institutional integrity, the Court should think hard about enforcing the delegation doctrine. Its attempt to enforce the doctrine in 1935 was part of a series of decisions that helped to prompt President Roosevelt's attempt to pack the Court. He argued that when

> the Congress has sought to stabilize national agriculture, to improve the conditions of labor, to safeguard business against unfair competition, to protect our national resources, and in many other ways to serve our clearly national needs, the majority of the Court has been assuming the power to pass on the wisdom of these acts of the Congress—and to approve or disapprove the public policy written into these laws . . .

... [W]e must take action to save the Constitution from the Court and the Court from itself.[2]

Enforcing the delegation doctrine today would also bring charges that the Court meddles in policy and requires the impossible. And it would draw heavily upon the Court's time and energy.

The Court's practice of avoiding "political questions" is not an open-ended license to avoid cases that have policy implications or are controversial. After all, constitutional decisions usually interfere with controversial policy decisions of politically accountable officials since the Constitution speaks mainly to how officials act. The courts say that they applied the Constitution rather than made policy. A question is too political for the courts to handle only in very special circumstances, such as when courts lack a judicially manageable test of constitutionality and so have no basis for decision except their own policy preferences.[3] In this chapter I want to show that no special circumstance makes delegation a political question. To the contrary, enforcing the delegation doctrine is an essential part of the Court's job.

Preventing Delegation Is an Essential Part of the Court's Job

John Ely seeks to explain the function served by the evaluation in courts of the constitutionality of government action. He concludes that its function is not to impose policies on society but instead to ensure that the Constitution's system for making policies works as it should:

> Rather than dictate substantive results [constitutional review] intervenes only when ... the political market is systematically malfunctioning. ... Malfunction occurs when the *process* is undeserving of trust, when (1) the ins are choking off the channels of political change to ensure that they will stay in and the outs will stay out, or (2) though no one is actually denied a voice or a vote, representatives beholden to an effective majority are systematically disadvantaging some minority [out of prejudice] and thereby denying that minority the protection afforded other groups by a representative system.
>
> Obviously our elected representatives are the last persons we should trust with identification of either of these situations.[4]

Ely argues that this concept of judicial review of the constitutionality of official action promotes democracy because, first, it "involves tasks that courts, as experts on process and (more important) as political outsiders, can sensibly claim to be better qualified and situated to perform than political officials" and, second, it is consistent with the Constitution:

> Contrary to the standard characterization of the Constitution as "an enduring but evolving statement of general values," . . . the selection and accommodation of substantive values is left almost entirely to the political process and instead the document is overwhelmingly concerned, on the one hand, with procedural fairness in the resolution of individual disputes (process writ small), and on the other, with what might capaciously be designated process writ large—with ensuring broad participation in the processes and distributions of government.[5]

His thesis, positively, urges courts to intervene in either of the two situations he points to and, negatively, tells courts not to intervene otherwise. The negative side of his thesis has proved more controversial than the positive one. I invoke the positive side only.

Ely gives as examples of his first sort of malfunction—choking off the channels of political change—inhibitions on freedom of speech, malapportionment of legislatures, and delegations of legislative power. Delegation belongs on the list because it interferes with democratic accountability. Ely gives as examples of his second sort of malfunction —denial of equal consideration to some minority—discrimination against racial minorities, discrimination against those who have no vote in the forum, and the broad discretion over individuals that results from the delegation of legislative power. Delegation belongs on this list because it interferes with the Constitution's procedural protections of liberty. So Ely's concept of the Court's job plainly puts the delegation of legislative powers on its agenda.[6]

Jesse Choper urges courts not to hear separation of powers cases that involve conflicts between the president and Congress, especially those that involve the president and Congress agreeing to delegate powers between them. The Court has not followed his advice, however, for it does reach the merits on such cases. Indeed, the Supreme Court talks as if vindicating the purposes of the delegation doctrine is part of its job, saying in *Mistretta*, for instance, that Article I "generally" prohibits delegation, and claiming that the "intelligible principle" test achieves the doctrine's purposes.[7]

However, Choper's argument demands consideration because, if correct, it would justify the Court's deferring to political decisions about delegation, as it now does. He argues that courts should avoid such cases because (1) there is no clear standard of constitutionality, (2) each branch will protect its "turf" and so maintain the separation of powers, (3) the Court can contradict democratic decisions only so often and, accordingly, ought to lay its prestige on the line only to prevent violations of rights, and (4) the courts can protect rights without protecting separation of powers.[8] I disagree with each of these four theses.

Thesis 1, the lack of a clear standard of constitutionality, does not distinguish the separation of powers cases from the rights cases that he would have the courts hear; many rights are defined loosely. His conclusion that the Court lacks a judicially manageable test of improper delegation fits the Court's current test but not the test that I will offer in Chapter 12.

Thesis 2, that Congress will keep its powers separate from the president's to protect its turf, fails because individual legislators gain from delegation, even if Congress as an institution loses.[9] Individuals gain power and lose accountability. So legislators willingly delegate, though in complicated ways that maximize their control over agency action, minimize their accountability, and generally complicate administration. Legislators do protect their personal turfs, yet violate the ultimate purpose of separation of powers, which is not to protect Congress and the president from each other but rather to protect the people from each of them.[10]

Thesis 3, that the Court's enforcement of separation of powers would undercut its ability to protect rights, rests upon the premise that the Court can contradict the decisions of the political branches only occasionally. But in separation of powers cases, the Court does not countermand the decision of a majoritarian institution on the basis that it disagrees with the substance of that decision.[11] Moreover, enforcing the delegation doctrine enables the Court to drape itself in the mantle of democracy, because it can insist that a majoritarian institution decide questions of substance. Of course, the decision to delegate is itself a policy decision—although a question of procedure rather than substance—and a policy decision lacking widespread popular appeal.

Thesis 4, that the Court can protect rights without being concerned about separation of powers, rests on the premise that protecting individuals from the majority is the job of the Bill of Rights, while protecting the majority from a self-interested government is the job of separation of powers and the division of authority between the federal government and the states. But, surprisingly, those who wrote and adopted the Bill of Rights were concerned more with protecting the majority from a self-interested government than protecting individuals from the majority.[12] Moreover, the Framers of the original Constitution used separation of powers in an effort to protect values which they described in terms of "rights" and "liberty."[13] Since the enumerated rights in the Bill of Rights cover only some of the abuses of public power that the Framers thought of as violations of rights, as argued earlier, many rights receive protection only through separation of powers or federalism. Even business regulations, such as the marketing order that enriched Sunkist at the expense of smaller organizations and consumers, violate *rights* in the sense that the Framers used that word. A sense of injustice certainly moved a small orange handler, John Crane, who wrote to the Department of Agriculture:

> The large Sunkist houses take my growers from me telling them that . . . they can pick the grower's fruit fast. Obviously I cannot do this [because of the marketing order].
> . . . Sunkist and the large handlers want to keep us from competing, keep us from having an opportunity to grow.[14]

Such outrage was shared by Oleah Wilson, who wrote:

> I have been in the orange business for 55 years. . . .
> . . . Our orange competitors in Florida and Texas are free to ship whatever they wish. Other competitive crops, such as apples, bananas, grapes, and Chilean fruit, are also unregulated.
> I know there are many people in the navel industry that are lazy and enjoy what they perceive as a guarantee to ship a percentage of their crop each year. I find it absurd that the government has a policy to protect the lazy and inefficient at the expense of individuals willing to do a better job.[15]

Unlike the Framers, we would not say that the marketing order violates a "right" because we tend to reserve that term for protecting people through the Bill of Rights and other enumerated rights. We would however call the failure to follow due process in a trial the violation of a "right." Yet both the delegation doctrine (an example of Ely's "process writ large") and due process (an example of his "process writ small") use procedure to protect the same set of values that other portions of the Bill of Rights sought to protect. Functionally, the delegation doctrine is neither less important than rights nor concerned with "mere" process, but rather is designed to protect values of constitutional importance—democracy and liberty—by making the Congress and the president take responsibility for the laws they impose upon us.

Another consideration is that even the rights in the Bill of Rights sometimes go underprotected because of the difficulty that courts have in knowing the motives of the political branches.[16] Indeed, *Kent v. Dulles* and its cousins start from the premise that the Court is unable to find a violation of rights but will try to protect rights nonetheless by insisting upon the use of the Article I legislative process. These cases, however, offer only erratic protection, as *Mistretta* illustrated, in upholding a delegation of the power to make rules about incarceration and capital punishment.

No One Else Can Do the Court's Job

Defenders of delegation argue that the Supreme Court should let Congress and the president decide whether to delegate because voters can hold them accountable for delegating.[17] But the voters cannot do so. They do not even know when Congress delegates. Newspaper accounts of bills in the legislative process give far more attention to their goals than to whether Congress or an agency will make the relevant rules.[18] Voters have more difficulty perceiving the adverse consequences of delegation than those of pay raises, franking privileges, or the like. Everyone intuitively sees what is wrong with trustees taking funds in their care, but delegation does not look like overreaching; it appears as if the trustees are giving their power away for the public good. To understand that legislators actually gain unaccountable power by delegation requires more political sophistication than many voters have. On the rare occasions when the failure of Congress to make the hard choices has become a political problem for Congress, it diffused the problem by enacting new legislation that appeared to make the hard choices without actually doing so. For example, criticism of congressional indecisiveness in the pre–1970 air pollution statutes resulted in the spurious decisiveness of the 1970 Clean Air Act. As I showed in Chapter 4, the 1970 act led professors who specialize in administrative law to believe that Congress had made the hard choices. If Congress can fool the experts, it can fool the voters.

Even if the public understood delegation, Congress would resist public pressure to stop the practice for the same reason that it resists public pressure to stop other incumbent protection strategies—their interest in perpetuating their own careers. When legislators have a large personal stake in a practice, they keep it up unless opposition gets so overwhelming that the practice is no longer worthwhile. Legislators could easily conclude that any prospective electoral gain from opposing delegation would be more than offset by the chance to avoid the electoral cost of having to make hard choices. Halting delegation would produce only one issue with an impact on the public that would be indirect and inchoate, while every tough choice that an end to delegation would force them to face would bring electoral cost.

Congressional self-interest is not the whole problem. On issues that actually require trade-offs, voters continue to accept legislation generating schemes that promise the best of everything to everyone. Incumbents unwilling to vote for such legislation risk defeat by candidates who back inflated promises. What is more, immature public attitudes are perpetuated by delegation. As a consequence, delegation is a kind of a trap from which legislators and voters would have trouble escaping through the electoral process.

The difficulty of controlling delegation through the electoral process exceeds the difficulty of controlling deficit spending through the electoral process. Because the electoral process is inadequate to counter legislators' personal stake in incurring budget deficits, most states have constitutional provisions prohibiting them. In the absence of a federal constitutional prohibition on them, the Balanced Budget and Emergency Deficit Control Act of 1985, commonly known as the Gramm-Rudman-Hollings Act, tried to address the problem at the national level by limiting deficits before legislators decide how to spend the money. Deficits are probably less than they otherwise would have been, but Congress and the president have cooperated in cooking the books to make the deficits look smaller than they really are.

Congress would have even less success curbing delegation than deficit spending. Suppose Congress enacted a "Truth in Legislation Act" modeled on the "Truth in Lending Act" and other "Truth in . . . " statutes that require those in a position to fool the public to disclose information necessary for informed consent. The Truth in Legislation Act might provide that any congressional committee shall, before bringing a bill to the floor, publish a Truth in Legislation Statement specifying:

- each issue that the bill delegates;
- the extent to which the bill does and does not give guidance on how the delegation should be implemented;
- why Congress decided not to make the law itself;
- the kinds of blame that the delegation might shift from legislators to the agency;
- the resources and time needed to carry out delegation in comparison with the resources and time provided in the bill and current appropriations;
- the extent to which legislators may intervene in the implementation of the delegation; and
- the personal advantages that could accrue to legislators from such intervention.

The act also might provide that courts should interpret statutes to delegate no more broadly than the accompanying statement specifies and might subject legislators to sanctions for intervening in the implementation of the delegations except in the ways made public in the statement.

In the unlikely event that Congress passed such an act, it probably nonetheless would enact statutes in violation of the act, just as it repeatedly has ignored the provision in the National Environmental Policy Act requiring agencies to accompany proposals for legislation that affects the environment with an environmental impact statement.[19]

Even if the electoral process were adequate to police delegation, voter acquiescence in it would not reconcile it with democracy. Instead, we would have democratically consented to have a less democratic, unconstitutional government. A statute that undercuts provisions of the Constitution that promote democracy is unconstitutional even if the statute is supported by a majority of the voters. For example, a statute that provided that members of the House of Representatives selected in future elections would serve four-year terms is unconstitutional, quite apart from whatever popular support it might garner. Just as the Supreme Court should strike down that statute, it should strike down statutes that delegate.

Delegation also undercuts Article I's safeguards of individual liberty. The election of Congress and the president does not legitimate delegation's weakening of these safeguards any more than it would legitimate a statute curbing the other protections of liberty, such as those in the Bill of Rights, which also is intended to protect the individual against the majority.

In sum, the Court cannot leave its job to the voters.

The Supposed Necessity of Delegation Does Not Excuse the Court's Failure to Enforce the Constitution

The Court may argue, as it did in *Mistretta*, that enforcing the delegation doctrine would make government unworkable: "Congress simply cannot do its job absent an ability to delegate power under broad general directives."[20] The Court, however, ordinarily treats claims that enforcing the Constitution would be impractical at two levels. At the more abstract level, it roundly proclaims that enforcement of the Constitution must not give way to concerns of practicality. As *Chadha* stated, "that a given law or procedure is efficient, convenient, and useful in facilitating functions of government, standing alone, will not save it if it is contrary to the Constitution. Convenience and efficiency are not the primary objectives—or the hallmarks—of democratic government . . . "[21] At the second and less abstract level, the Court often accommodates concerns for practicality by building them into the test of what is constitutional.[22] The Court does so not just when the Constitution's own text invites consideration of practicality, as in the Fourth Amendment's prohibition of "*unreasonable* searches and seizures," but also when a superficial reading of the text might seem to preclude consideration of practicality, as in the First Amendment's statement that "Congress shall make *no* law . . . abridging the freedom of speech."[23] When the Court builds practicality into the test of constitutionality, the justices themselves decide whether concerns of practicality are sufficiently strong to trump constitutional values. So the courts can prevent greater deviations from constitutional values than are really necessary.

Mistretta and other delegation cases are inconsistent with these customary approaches to claims of practicality. The Court has not only built practicality into the test of improper delegation (specifically, Congress need not state an intelligible principle in the case of necessity[24]), but appeals to practicality to justify the delegation allowed by the intelligible principle test without first finding that Congress needed to delegate in the challenged statute. Through the intelligible principle test, the Court essentially grants blanket permission for wholesale violations of the Constitution without any meaningful judicial review.

Mistretta illustrates this abdication of judicial responsibility. The statement from the case quoted above, that government cannot work without delegation, is backed by neither reasoning nor citation to anything but similarly conclusive statements in earlier opinions. This Court has simply not done its own analysis. Such an analysis should lead the Court to conclude that government could work better without delegation or, if it concludes that some delegation is unavoidable, to confine it to those instances. The Court unheld delegation in the *Mistretta* case on the basis that writing sentencing rules requires expertise and is complicated, given the number of crimes and other factors that ought to be taken into account. But lack of expertise should not be a barrier preventing Congress from prescribing the penalties for crimes; it has done so for centuries. Complication is also no excuse; Congress could have addressed the provision of sentencing rules as it has other codifications: by having a commission propose legislation upon which Congress would vote.

The Court would never take this lackadaisical approach to enforcing constitutional prohibitions that it takes seriously, and the Court has no good reason to take Article I of the Constitution lightly.

The Remedy for Delegation Should Ease the Transition

Courts distinguish between decisions about liability (whether someone did wrong) and decisions about remedy (what to do about the wrong).[25] To illustrate: if Jones regularly walks through Smith's land, Smith can usually get a court to order Jones to stop the trespass immediately. That is, the court provides a remedy that completely protects plaintiff's rightful position. But courts do not always provide such a full remedy. If Jones had built a garage that encroached upon Smith's property by one inch, many courts would let Jones compensate Smith rather than remove the garage if the trespass were accidental and the expense to Jones of removing it were disproportionate to the harm of letting it stand.

If the Supreme Court finds liability in a delegation case—that is, if it finds that an agency law wrongs plaintiff because it was promulgated under an unconstitutional delegation—the remedy that fully puts plaintiff in a rightful position is to void the agency law forthwith. The 1935 Supreme Court provided just such a remedy.

Today's Court should provide a different remedy for two reasons: (1) to provide time for a transition away from delegation, and (2) once that transition is over, to give our elected lawmakers the leading role in curing any new unconstitutional delegations.

A Period of Transition

Panama Refining and *Schechter* presented a different remedial problem than a modern decision holding delegation unconstitutional would because the federal government had not yet in 1935 built a huge regulatory apparatus relying on Court decisions that upheld delegations. Today, suddenly enforcing the delegation doctrine without providing for a period of transition would overload the legislative process with requests to replace agency laws with statutory ones. Before Antonin Scalia became a Supreme Court justice, he suggested applying the doctrine only to statutes enacted after the date the court signals that it will stop delegation.[26] I agree with the essence of his position, but suggest two embellishments upon it.

The first embellishment would phase out existing statutes that unconstitutionally delegate. If agencies were permitted to issue new laws and enforce old ones forever under these statutes, old delegations would continue to do harm. The courts should not let those effects endure any longer than the time by which our elected lawmakers can decide which agency laws to enact, which to replace in some other way, and which to jettison altogether. The Supreme Court might, accordingly, announce that courts would allow agency laws promulgated under statutes enacted before the landmark case to be enforced for some specific time—I would suggest perhaps twelve years—after the landmark case. Twelve years would not be excessive, given our long dependence upon delegation.

The second embellishment would give the legislative process some time to adjust to enforcement of the delegation doctrine. Congress might have trouble ceasing delegation immediately because it would have statutes far along in the legislative pipeline that were drafted in reliance on delegation. More broadly, congressional staffs, agencies' staffs, and legislators themselves would have to change their working relationships and habits of mind. More fundamentally still, legislators would need to assess whether to support a constitutional amendment allowing some delegation and whether such an amendment would pass. The Supreme Court could allow for a period of transition by providing that statutes enacted up to a specified time—perhaps four years—after the landmark case would be treated as if enacted before the landmark case. The period also would give a good idea of the fate of Congress's almost inevitable plea for a constitutional amendment.

The Court legitimately can allow a gradual transition to full enforcement of the delegation doctrine. Concern about causing harm through a sudden change, especially when defendant has a plausible claim that the conduct was legal, prompts courts to delay enjoining the illegal harm. For example, when courts hold that the apportionment of a state legislature violates the Equal Protection Clause's requirement of one person/one vote, they give the state some years to reapportion itself.[27] In the meantime, they allow elections to be held under apportionments that fall short of constitutional requirements.

The same principles of equity that have allowed courts to craft remedies specially for malapportionment and other cases would allow the Supreme Court to craft a remedy suitable to a decision to enforce the delegation doctrine.[28] As discussed above, Congress and the president have relied on delegation, and reasonably so because of the many court decisions that upheld it. Moreover, if the Court invalidated all agency laws at once, the ensuing chaos would undermine the very values that the Constitution seeks to protect. Thus the Court could, to the extent needed, allow unconstitutionally promulgated regulations to have binding effect under traditional equitable principles.[29]

In sum, the Supreme Court legitimately can shape the remedy for unconstitutional delegation to take account of our government's understandable reliance on delegation.

A Remand to Congress and the President

After the transition period, courts still should not immediately strike down all laws derived from unconstitutional delegations, as they did in cases like *Panama Refining* and *Schechter*. Rather, the Supreme Court should instruct lower courts to allow enforcement of the agency law for perhaps three months after the first court declares that any given statute delegates unconstitutionally, provided that the government had a plausible argument that the statute did not delegate in the first place. So, if Congress and the president had really tried not to delegate but inadvertently failed, they would have three months to correct their error. Congress could adopt special procedures that would ensure that such agency laws reach the floor of the House and Senate quickly.

This remand to the legislative process would help prevent any irreparable harm that might arise if Congress had difficulty ascertaining the line that courts draw between permissible legislation and unconstitutional delegation. Such a remedy accords with precedents that sometimes let procedurally defective actions continue while defendants try to repair the defect.[30]

The Court Cannot Do Its Job Simply by Construing Statutes against Delegation

In cases like *Kent v. Dulles* the Court might have thought that it could achieve the purposes of the delegation doctrine by construing ambiguities in statutes to limit agencies' delegated power rather than by declaring delegating statutes unconstitutional.[31] When a statute is susceptible to two meanings, one of which raises a delegation problem, interpreting it to avoid the problem accords with the longstanding judicial preference for avoiding constitutional decisions when narrower grounds are available.[32] But making the delegation doctrine a rule of statutory construction and not a rule of constitutionality has meant that Congress could delegate broadly as long as it does so expressly. Moreover, the statutory interpretation tactic is disingenuous when the statute is not, in fairness, open to an interpretation that it does not delegate. When a court construes a statute to delegate more narrowly than Congress intended, the court essentially rewrites the statute, and so does the very opposite of ensuring that Congress exercises the legislative power.[33]

Fear of Political Attacks Does Not Excuse the Court's Failure to Enforce the Constitution

Enforcing the delegation doctrine would provoke heated criticism. The Court's claim that "the Constitution made us do it" does not always stop criticism in the court of politics and would not do so in the case of delegation. If the intentions of the Framers and the purposes of the text are ignored, the language of the Constitution can be interpretated to allow delegation, and the delegation case law is divided. Most landmark constitutional decisions, however, also involve debatable constitutional texts and uncertain precedents. The questions are why the Court could not make its 1935 delegation decisions stick and whether a modern decision enforcing the doctrine would fall for the same reasons.

The Court had to back down in 1935 for reasons that should not stymie a modern Court. First, the public then believed in agencies as experts working for the public good, but the public of today is far more cynical and for good reason.[34] Since 1935, many liberals—including scholars, judges, and a Supreme Court justice—have voiced concern about delegation.[35] If others from across the ideological spectrum —especially a few elected lawmakers—voiced similar concerns, the fear of political backlash would diminish.

Second, the Court's decisions in 1935 seemed to strike at the government's capacity to respond to a national crisis far more desperate than any since the Civil War.

Third, during the early New Deal, the Court struck down many statutes on a variety of grounds other than delegation, sometimes usurping democratic choice on questions of policy.[36] The willingness of some justices to use their power to act on their well-known dislike of the New Deal gave the Court a reputation for exceeding its authority. Given this context and the apparent inconsistency between *Panama Refining* and *Hampton & Co.*, the delegation doctrine appeared to be just another means for the Court to substitute its views for those of democratically elected officials. In *Schechter*, the Court seemed quite ready to use other means of eradicating the policy if Congress and the president somehow reenacted it without delegation. The Court's suspected political motivation made it possible for its foes to portray it as an enemy of democracy rather than as a disinterested interpreter of the Constitution. In contrast, a modern decision to stop delegation could be defended as necessary to bolster democracy. The Court's opinion would carry no implication that Congress could not enact the invalidated agency law through the Article I lawmaking process. Indeed, the remedy for improper delegation that I proposed in the previous section would give our elected lawmakers time to do just that. By making clear that the objection is to the process through which the law was adopted rather than to its substance, the remedy appropriately would transmute anger at the Court for upsetting a law that some people want into pressure on Congress and the president to enact that law. If Congress and the president enacted the agency law, the delegation case would be moot. If not, they could not castigate the Court for striking down the agency law without sounding hollow.

In the next chapter I will propose a test of unconstitutional delegation that is just as manageable as those the Court has applied to most other constitutional questions. The Court still will have to decide an ongoing series of delegation cases to flesh out the delegation doctrine, just as it has had to decide an ongoing series of cases to flesh out most other constitutional doctrines. Should the Court devote some of its limited time to stopping delegation? For me, the answer is yes. It is, I think, a sufficient reason that delegation undercuts democratic accountability, a most fundamental constitutional value.

I have argued that delegation also threatens another fundamental constitutional value, liberty. Stopping delegation allows the Court to help protect liberty in a wholesale manner, by insisting that laws be made through a process that tends to respect liberty. In contrast, the Court usually has to protect liberty piecemeal, by dealing with individual laws or individual actions taken under those laws. Protecting liberty wholesale is an economical use of the Supreme Court's time. Stopping delegation would not commit the Court to an equally close review of all separation of powers questions. Because the rivalry between Congress and the president does help prevent many breaches of the Constitution's system of separated powers other than delegation, the Court can protect those other aspects of separation of powers through more episodic intervention than prohibiting delegation requires.

Stopping delegation is an economical use of the Court's time for a second reason—because my proposed remedy will prompt our elected lawmakers to moot many delegation cases. It will also take away much of the political incentive to delegate because the hard choices that they try to shunt to an agency will come right back to them.

Finally, and this is a clincher, for the federal courts in general and the Supreme Court in particular, the time they devote to stopping delegation will be offset by saving the time that they now devote to reviewing agency lawmaking under the Administrative Procedure Act. Such reviews tend to be unusually time-consuming and enervating because the records that accompany them are usually immense.

How the Courts Should Define Unconstitutional Delegation

CHAPTER 12

JUSTICE SCALIA STATED IN HIS DISSENT IN *Mistretta* that

while the doctrine of unconstitutional delegation is unquestionably a fundamental element of our constitutional system, it is not an element readily enforceable by the courts. Once it is conceded, as it must be, that no statute can be entirely precise, and that some judgments, even some judgments involving policy considerations, must be left to the officers executing the law and to the judges applying it, the debate over unconstitutional delegation becomes a debate not over a point of principle but over a question of degree.[1]

I agree with Justice Scalia that the Court's present test of improper delegation depends entirely upon questions of degree, which means that the courts lack a judicially manageable test of unconstitutional delegation. Without a judicially manageable test, the decision whether to strike down a statute turns upon policy rather than law. So the court exercises the very legislative power that the delegation doctrine says only Congress may wield. Yet I disagree with Justice Scalia's suggestion that the Court could not develop a judicially manageable test. This chapter proposes one.

The Court requires that a statute say enough about its goals to provide an "intelligible principle" but has never specified how much is enough. Since the Court's test is inherently elastic, justices uphold statutes or strike them down in patterns that bear a striking similarity to their own policy proclivities. Some justices express concern about a statute that lets an agency balance workers' health against costs in regulating pollution in the workplace but uphold statutes that grant executive officials broad scope to arrest people for "contemptuous" use of the American flag or to decide whether resident aliens can be denied civil service jobs.[2] Other justices have exactly the opposite set of concerns.[3] The incoherence of the intelligible principle test and the Court's selective invocation of a tougher test of improper delegation is unprincipled.

The Court's test, furthermore, excuses the lack of an intelligible principle in cases of "necessity." The Court has used "necessity" to justify delegation of decisions on the grounds that they are technical, complicated, or require frequent adjustment,[4] even though Congress itself sometimes decides just such questions. "Necessity," as used by the Court, is therefore a question of degree concerning the allocation of legislative time, a matter about which the Court has shown no inclination to state standards.[5]

My proposed test of improper delegation, briefly outlined in Chapters 1 and 9, forbids Congress from delegating the legislative powers that Article I grants. The essence of such legislative power is the making of laws of private conduct. On the other hand, legislative power includes neither the interpretation nor the application of a legislated law—these are judicial and executive functions—nor the exercise of other executive powers, such as the commander-in-chief power or the management of public enterprises. Unlike the Court's current test, my test depends on differences of kind rather than on differences of degree. In this chapter I will describe each element of my test, show that each accords with the purposes of the Constitution, and finally argue that the test is judicially manageable.

Lawmaking versus Law Interpretation

The premise of my test is that Congress may not delegate any of the legislative power which Article I grants. Early Supreme Court decisions share this premise, and hints of it pop up in a few modern discussions of delegation.[6] But most modern commentators and cases treat this premise as naive.[7] As one noted scholar put it, "every statute is a delegation of lawmaking power to the agency appointed to enforce it" because, even if the legislature tries to settle the outstanding issues, "[l]anguage and experience alike can never be so divinely comprehensive as to make clear provision for all future cases."[8] This attack wrongly equates the legislative function of making laws—that is, rules of conduct—with the judicial and executive function of interpreting them.

The word *rule*, derived from the Latin for straightedge, connotes the even application of a discernible criterion. So a "rule of conduct" or "law" is a statement that prohibits some activity in terms that others can understand.[9] Defining *law* as a meaningful statement prohibiting some conduct fits the delegation doctrine's purposes, since fulfilling those purposes depends upon voters' being able to figure out what a statute does.

A statutory law will always require interpretation. The need for interpretation comes not just from the ambiguity of language but also from the need to read statutes in context.[10] As noted in Chapter 1, a statute that outlawed "unreasonable" pollution would state a law in a society with a clear understanding of what constituted unreasonable pollution, because that shared connotation would provide a basis for interpretation. While statutory laws that require interpretation do not delegate legislative power, Congress would delegate legislative power if it enacted language in the form of a law, but which in fact left an agency or the courts to decide what conduct was prohibited. For example, a statute that prohibited "unreasonable" pollution when that term had no customary meaning would, functionally, require the courts to develop the law case by case.

Distinguishing a statute that enacts a law from one that only purports to do so requires knowing the difference between law interpretation and lawmaking.[11] In legal tradition, an interpreter makes manifest a part of the law that had previously been latent, while a lawmaker creates a new dictate.[12] The traditional account makes laws sound a bit too much like Platonic forms stowed in a freezer, ready for judges to defrost. Interpretation is not that mechanical. A law interpreter looks for evidence of how the legislature that enacted the statute would have clarified the law, if confronted with the present question about its meaning, while a lawmaker looks for evidence of what law would best serve the relevant social goals. In short, a law interpreter looks backwards, to what a past legislature thought, while a lawmaker looks forward to how a proposed law would affect society.[13]

Some people dismiss this distinction between law interpretation and lawmaking as so much snake oil while others, who believe there is a difference, debate how to describe it.[14] Nevertheless, most lawyers would agree on the four following differences between a statute that leaves to an agency or courts the job of interpreting statutory law and a statute that leaves to an agency the job of making a law pursuant to delegation.

First, a person interested in knowing whether the statute prohibits any given conduct will, in most cases, get a clear answer from the statute that states the law, but may well get no answer, for any particular case, from a statute that delegates. For example, back in 1970, none of the thousands of existing factories could tell from the new Clean Air Act whether they would have to reduce their emissions.[15]

Second, by clearly resolving most cases, a statute that states a law implicitly indicates the relative weight the legislature gave to conflicting social goals, but a statute that delegates may well leave such conflicts totally unresolved. So while a law interpreter can use the balance between conflicting social goals that the legislature struck to resolve disputes about the meaning of a statutory law, a statute that delegates often leaves the agency to strike its own balance between conflicting goals.

Third, the relationship between court and agency differs when a statute states a law rather than delegates the power to make laws. Courts have the final say in interpreting statutory laws but must defer to agencies on matters left to them, including their choice of how to formulate their laws.[16]

Fourth, courts generally cannot change their past interpretations of statutory laws, so that changing a statutory law, once interpreted, requires legislation. In contrast, agencies can change the laws they make for any rational reason.[17]

These differences suggest why the interpretation of statutory laws, although it requires the exercise of judgment, is consistent with democratic accountability and Article I's safeguards of liberty. Statutory laws, by providing a clear outcome for most cases, make legislators accountable for at least the major outlines of the laws that they impose on society. In contrast, delegation allows Congress to avoid taking a position on any controversial choice. This is fundamental, because both democratic accountability and Article I's safeguards of liberty depend upon legislators having to take a position on the laws that government imposes. Even in hard cases when the statutory law provides no clear answer, the interpreter's ability to infer legislative priorities from easy cases provides some basis for the belief that interpretation reflects values inherent in the legislation. Moreover, the courts' final say in interpreting statutory laws means legislators cannot exercise power without being accountable, because legislators cannot manipulate judges as they manipulate agency staffs.

A series of examples involving price regulation statutes illustrates the distinction between interpreting laws and making them. Beginning over a century ago, statutes required public utility commissions to set rates that produced "just and reasonable" revenues for public utilities. "Just and reasonable," although initially an unclear term, became a term of art that signified revenues equal to the operating costs of the utility plus a return on capital commensurate with the return on investments of similar size and risk.[18] This "cost-based" approach to utility revenues is a law if the commission knows how to measure the capital on which the utility gets to earn a return. The most obvious way to measure capital is to consider the amount that the utility spent on its plant. If capital is measured in this way, the "just and reasonable" standard provides a benchmark against which to calculate allowable public utility rates: the market value of inputs, including capital, needed to provide the service. The cost-based approach requires more than simple arithmetical calculation[19] but does balance the goals of holding down costs to consumers and attracting capital to build the utility without leaving the commission free to craft its own, unpredictable ways of resolving these conflicting goals.[20]

In an 1898 case dealing with a state public utility rate statute, *Smyth v. Ames*, the Supreme Court decided that state utility rates that failed to provide a "just and reasonable" return are unconstitutional as a taking of property under the Fourteenth Amendment. Many states used *Smyth v. Ames'* definition of "just and reasonable" to give content, as a matter of statutory interpretation, to the term "just and reasonable" in the statutes they enacted. But *Smyth v. Ames* defined the value of the capital of a utility in a way that most definitely is not readily measurable by public utility commissions.[21] The case held that the value of capital should reflect four quite different concepts: (1) the original cost of the utility's plant, (2) the cost of building a similar plant at the time of the hearing, (3) the earning capacity of the plant, and (4) the amount and value of the utility's stocks and bonds. Since each of these four measurements usually produces a different quantity, the commission must meld them, but is given no clear guidance about how to do so. The third and fourth concepts, moreover, are circular because they vary with the rates that can be charged. *Smyth v. Ames* points to the way in which changes in formulation can turn a statutory law into a delegation.

The case of *FPC v. Hope Natural Gas*, decided in 1944, makes the same point in a different context. It deviated from *Smyth v. Ames* in two ways. First, as a matter of constitutional law, the Court freed regulators from valuing capital in *Smyth v. Ames'* terms. Regulators could use original plant cost as the sole measure of capital or could measure capital in some other way. Today, most jurisdictions measure capital by original cost. Rate regulation statutes enacted with this understanding of capital make a law. But, second, *FPC v. Hope Natural Gas* held that neither the Constitution nor the statute in question prohibited the Federal Power Commission from departing from the cost-based approach altogether, provided that the rates set were calculated reasonably to achieve the goals of rate regulation. As so interpreted, the statute delegated the power to make the laws. The Supreme Court did not go on to hold that other statutes must be interpreted to delegate, and many jurisdictions continue to interpret their statutes to require adherence to the cost-based approach.[22]

In contrast to the cost-based rate-making statutes, other statutes have delegated to agencies broad power to regulate prices during times of war or inflation, to prosecute the charging of excessive prices, or to recoup excessive wartime profits. In upholding most of these statutes against delegation challenges, the Court has used traditional public utility rate-making as a precedent to find that these statutes provided a standard of decision.[23] That reliance was misplaced, as these statutes provided no measurable standard—such as the cost of providing services—with which to gauge whether prices or profits were unreasonable or excessive. In *Yakus v. United States*, for instance, the Office of Price Administration was instructed to set prices using the level charged at a given time in the past, adjusted to take account of a wide variety of goals.[24] Since the administrator had no benchmark by which to gauge the size of these adjustments, the statute in *Yakus* failed to state the law.

Executive versus Legislative Powers

Independent Executive Powers

As the Framers understood, legislation does not delegate when it leaves the executive branch with discretion within the scope of the powers granted to the executive by Article II of the Constitution.[25] For instance, Congress does not delegate legislative power to the president when it declares war and provides armed forces for the fighting, without telling the president how to use the forces to accomplish the war's goals. Command of the armed forces is an executive, not a legislative, power under Article II of the Constitution. The president is making war, not law. The scope of the president's discretion is, however, limited by legislative powers because Congress controls whether and against whom war may be declared and how much money is spent on the effort.

Lawyers disagree about the scope of executive power. The Court has broadly construed executive power over war and foreign affairs, but that view has sparked weighty criticism.[26] Whatever the appropriate scope of executive powers in matters of war and foreign affairs, granting such powers can be reconciled with forbidding the delegation to the executive of the power to make rules regulating domestic conduct. The Framers sought to create a government whose efficiency in dealing with foreign powers was sufficient to protect the commonwealth and whose efficiency in dealing with its own citizens was tempered because of concern for their liberty.[27]

In enforcing the delegation doctrine, the Court can uphold statutes leaving the president with the discretion already within executive power, however defined.

Management of Government Property

Congress need not make rules for the management of government property, such as federal lands, monies, and corporations like the Postal Service. Rather, Congress may allow the executive branch to manage the public domain, including making management rules. Congress acts appropriately, for instance, when it allows the Department of Interior to decide how to care for the national parks, what fees should be charged for park admission, and what rules should be imposed on visitors to prevent damage to the park or interference with its use by others.

The text of the Constitution permits such an interpretation. Article II, as already discussed, grants the president executive powers and presumes that there will be various executive departments. The Framers understood that such executive officials would have discretionary powers as well as mandatory duties.[28] In addition, Article IV states, "The Congress shall have Power to dispose of and make all needful Rules and Regulations respecting the . . . Property belonging to the United States . . . " This rulemaking power thus is not listed as one of the legislative powers enumerated in Article I following its injunction that "[a]ll legislative Powers herein granted shall be vested in a Congress . . . " One could read Article I to forbid delegation of legislative powers but read Article IV to permit delegation of the power to make rules concerning the public domain. On the other hand, one could find that rulemaking concerning the public domain is nondelegable by reading Article IV itself to preclude delegation or by reading the "herein" in Article I to refer to all powers granted to Congress throughout the entire Constitution rather than just in Article I itself. Significantly, however, the Public Property Clause is located outside the first three Articles of the Constitution, which focus on separation of powers; this supports the interpretation that Congress may permit agencies to make rules concerning public property.

Precedent also supports this interpretation. When courts still took the delegation doctrine seriously, they nonetheless thought that Congress functioned as a proprietor rather than a lawgiver in managing public property.[29] More recently, the Supreme Court in *National Cable Television Association v. United States* decided that the delegation of the power to impose license fees raised constitutional concerns because the license was for the use of private rather than public property. The Court held that a license fee for cable television companies was a tax rather than a fee. Justice Douglas, writing for the majority, explained: "The backbone of [cable television] is individual enterprise and ingenuity, not governmental largesse. The regulatory regime placed by Congress and the courts over [cable television] was not designed to make entrepreneurs rich but to serve the public interest."[30] In other words, what made them define the "fee" as a "tax" was that cable television companies were not being charged for any special access to *public* property, but rather for the regulation of the use of their *private* property. Rather than tackling the question of whether Congress could delegate the power to tax, the Court interpreted the statute as denying the Federal Communications Commission the power to tax.[31]

Allowing Congress to delegate the management of public property serves a practical purpose quite different from that supposedly derived from allowing Congress to delegate the power to make the laws of private conduct. Laws, even if promulgated by an agency rather than Congress, usually cannot dictate how to act. Most laws that govern private conduct neither tell people how to act nor are addressed to specific persons, but rather tell people in general what they cannot do. In other words, laws of private conduct are negative and general.[32] Such negative, general laws leave a private person—whether managing a home or a business—much scope in selecting personal goals and deciding how to achieve them. For example, even very complex laws such as building codes do not tell a builder how to construct, say, a simple house. The same negative, general laws applied to a manager of public property, such as the post office or public lands, would leave big unanswered questions about what goals to pursue and how. Because neither Congress nor an agency could write negative, general laws that would fully answer those questions, delegating the management of public property serves a practical purpose not served by delegating the power to regulate private affairs.

The arguments I have marshalled so far for permitting the power to manage public property to be delegated still leave me with doubts. The Constitution's text on this point is open to question, precedent is not always binding, and I am suspicious of arguments of practicality as a reason to violate the constitutional requirement of separation of powers. What convinces me to approve delegation of the power to manage public property is that it can be made consistent with the safeguards of liberty in Article I. When government manages public property it affects private citizens in the way that private individuals do when they manage their private property—as a proprietor, not as a lawgiver. For example, the post office's decision to change the oil in its trucks at intervals of three thousand rather than five thousand miles affects me little more than would a similar decision made by the Federal Express Corporation. Such managerial decisions pose no threat to liberty because they do not deploy government's coercive power.

Sometimes, however, government does use its property to induce changes in private conduct. For example, it conditions grants to family planning clinics on their not providing abortion counseling and sometimes to artists on their not producing obscene work. Such grant conditions do not literally coerce anyone, but they do use government property—in truth, *our* property—for essentially regulatory ends.[33] Such regulatory uses of government property should be considered lawmaking, not management.

Judicial versus Legislative Powers

Legislation does not delegate when it leaves the courts with discretion within the scope of the powers granted to the judiciary by Article III of the Constitution. Thus a statute that states a law may leave the court with discretion to decide the remedy for a violation of that law in a particular case. For example, a judge may need to decide whether to grant a plaintiff an injunction or money damages and, if so, on what terms.[34] Although remedial discretion is part of the Article III judicial powers, Congress also has the power to legislate principles that courts must apply in formulating remedies in particular cases.[35] So courts and Congress have concurrent jurisdiction over remedies. If Congress decides not to mandate a particular remedy, it leaves the courts with an Article III power, not with delegated legislative power.

In addition to according with the Constitution, remedial discretion is consistent with the purposes of the prohibition on the delegation of legislative power. The judge can supply a remedy only in response to a violation of a law or to prevent an impending violation; the laws laid down in statutes place an outer boundary on the judge's remedial power.[36] Further, the court's discretion is narrow, as it is circumscribed by precedent that ordinarily requires a judge to place plaintiff in its rightful position and to honor the judgments that the legislature made in enacting the law. Since the court must ordinarily provide an effective remedy, remedial discretion does not blunt our elected lawmakers' political accountability for the laws.[37] In contrast, agency discretion does blunt the accountability of elected lawmakers for agency laws given that the agencies have discretion to decide the extent to which statutory goals will be achieved by their laws. Moreover, judges, it should be noted, also are insulated far more than agency leaders from the influence of elected lawmakers, which lessens any threat to liberty.

Is the Proposed Test Judicially Manageable?

My test rests upon distinctions of kind rather than degree—distinctions with which the courts are already familiar. Specifically, courts distinguish between "rules" and "goals" throughout their work. They distinguish the outer boundaries of the president's Article II powers in many separation of powers cases.[38] They distinguish between government as a proprietor and government as a lawmaker in many different constitutional and common law contexts, and the distinction is manageable when courts are clear about its purpose.[39]

In Chapter 9, I suggested a way to loosen my test of delegation, if that course is really necessary to enable Congress to make the laws needed to protect the public. Specifically, the Court could allow delegation of issues that would not cause a significant controversy in Congress. Such a modification would require the Court to break some new ground but would still yield a test no less clear than the present test of delegation. Indeed, it would be clearer than the tests applicable to most other constitutional doctrines.

To say that my test has substance does not mean that it would make every case an easy one. The rich variety of statutory types and the importance of looking at each statute in context makes this impossible. Rather, the test outlined here purports to provide no more than a sound doctrinal basis for case law development. But that should be enough. As Louis Jaffe wrote in the context of the Court's elastic intelligible principle test: "Nearly every doctrine of constitutional limitation has been attacked as vague. Essentially the charges go to the institution of judicial review as we have it rather than specifically to the delegation doctrine."[40] My remedy for unconstitutional delegations also would give Congress, should it inadvertently delegate, time to ratify agency laws and thereby would reduce the consequences of any uncertainty about what the delegation doctrine requires of Congress.

My test of delegation, no less than constitutional adjudication generally, carries a risk that members of the Court will use constitutional doctrine as a pretext to advance their private policy views. Still, my test provides less opportunity for such judicial intrusion into policy matters than does the current approach to delegation. Because the present test is incoherent, the justices' approach to delegation can vary with their policy proclivities. More important, delegation itself thrusts the courts into a policymaking role when reviewing agency laws: judges must decide whether agencies acted reasonably despite the absence of a clear test of reasonableness.[41] In 1980, as a professor of law, Antonin Scalia observed:

> In fact, the argument may be made that in modern circumstances the unconstitutional delegation doctrine, far from permitting an increase in judicial power, actually reduces it. For now that judicial review of agency action is virtually routine, it is the courts, rather than the agencies, that can ultimately determine the content of standardless legislation. In other words, to a large extent judicial invocation of the unconstitutional delegation doctrine is a *self-denying* ordinance—forbidding the transfer of legislative power not to the agencies, but to the courts themselves.[42]

The Court needs, and can adopt, a judicially manageable test of unconstitutional delegation.

Conclusion

PART VI

America Is No Exception

> We here highly resolve that these dead shall not have died in vain—that this nation shall have a new birth of freedom—and that government of the people, by the people, for the people, shall not perish from the earth.
>
> —ABRAHAM LINCOLN,
> *Gettysburg Address*, 1863

CHAPTER 13

IN THE FIRST CENTURY OF INDEPENDENCE, Americans believed that, as a rule, republics degenerate into tyrannies—that is, states in which the rulers use public power for their own advantage. These early Americans believed, however, that by guaranteeing a government by and for the people the Constitution made their country an exception among nations and a beacon of liberty to the world.[1]

The Framers understood that the selection of rulers by election is no guarantee against tyranny; some tyrants rule behind a smile rather than a sword.[2] The Constitution was designed to thwart smiling tyrants by not only granting the power to make law to elected officials but also requiring them to exercise that power in a way likely to discourage laws intended to serve their own or others' private purposes.

Many Americans no longer believe that they have a government by and for the people. They see the government as unresponsive to their concerns and be-

195

yond their control and view elected officials as a class apart, serving themselves in the guise of serving the public. Many political scientists and thoughtful journalists agree with this assessment. Delegation bears some of the blame. It reduces our participation in lawmaking, our understanding of how government works, and our power to hold legislators to account when the government fails to provide timely, balanced resolutions of regulatory disputes. Delegation also disables the Constitution's safeguards against laws that serve private purposes.

The self-aggrandizing government that we thereby suffer pales in comparison to that suffered by the peoples of Eastern Europe and the former Soviet Union. They risked their lives to free themselves from a ruling class that vowed to govern on their behalf, but then oppressed and beggared them. Nonetheless, their sufferings and their desire to emulate American democracy should make us less, rather than more, patient with our smiling officials, because we have promised ourselves and told the world that our Constitution stops alienation from reaching such heights that we need to revolt. Congress and the president should obey the Constitution voluntarily. If they violate it, the Supreme Court should enjoin their violations.

No one knows what laws would come from a Congress that could not shift blame or whether we would elect different sorts of people to it. We have never dealt with the modern world through a government that used Article I of the Constitution to make all new laws. In that sense, such a government has, as G. K. Chesterton said of Christianity, "not been tried and found wanting. It has been found difficult; and left untried."[3] Ending delegation would require taking the risk that, in the end, we would prefer to live under laws made by those we elect. That is a risk much smaller than the one incurred in Eastern Europe and the former Soviet Union. It should be well worth taking for those who get no privileges from delegation and receive limited comfort from officials' protestations that they truly care for their constituents.

Many elected lawmakers undoubtedly would object that the Supreme Court should not stop delegation because judges have no right to intervene in matters of policy. But that objection stands the issue on its head. The Court's job is to enforce the Constitution's provisions designed to ensure a democratically responsive, liberty-respecting government. The Court should not hesitate to do that job because the people, acting through the Constitution's procedures, would produce different laws than Washington's subgovernments now produce. If members of Congress and the president want to change the Constitution, let them take their case to the people by using their power to initiate the amendment process. I hope that they would lose. They deserve to lose.

It's time for a little *perestroika* on the Potomac.

Notes

Citations of judicial opinions are presented in the following order: case name, volume number of the law report, name of the law report, the page on which the opinion begins, page(s) cited (if any), court (if not clear from the name of the law report), and year. For example: *Riverbend Farms v. Madigan*, 958 F.2d 1479, 1483 (9th Cir. 1992). Book citations are presented in the following order: volume number (if any), author, title, page(s) cited, and year. For example, Theodore J. Lowi, *The End of Liberalism* 15 (2d ed. 1979). Citations of articles in scholarly journals are presented in the following order: author, title of article, volume of publication, name of publication, the page at which the article begins, the page(s), cited, and year. For example: Lawrence Shepard, "Cartelization of the California-Arizona Orange Industry, 1934-1981," 29 *Journal of Law and Economics* 83, 91-92 (1986). Statutes, rules, and most other sources are cited analogously.

1. The Nub of the Argument

1. As a rough measure of the relative quantity of law made by agencies and Con-

gress, the Code of Federal Regulations (containing the regulations issued by agencies, departments, commissions, and boards) occupies twenty feet of library shelving, while the United States Code (containing statutes) occupies six feet. The measure is only rough because many rules are not incorporated into either codification and both contain material other than rules of conduct.

2. Agricultural Adjustment Act, Pub. L. No. 10, 48 Stat. 31 (1933). This act established "agricultural marketing licenses." Under this statute, the secretary also may regulate crop quality or other aspects of agriculture, but the primary original purpose of the statute was to restrict supply. Id. § 8(1) ("To provide for reduction in the acreage or reduction in the production for market, or both, of any basic agricultural commodity . . . "). The 1935 amendments substituted the term *order* for *license*. See Pub. L. No. 320, 49 Stat. 750, 753, § 5 (1935) (amending 48 Stat. 31, 35 § 8(3) (1933)).

The orange marketing order is entitled Navel Oranges Grown in Arizona and Designated Part of California, 7 C.F.R. § 907 (1992).

3. For supply restriction, see 7 C.F.R. § 907.51–.54. The supply restrictions are administered to maximize short-term grower revenue. See General Accounting Office (GAO), *Analysis Of Certain Aspects of the California-Arizona Navel Orange Marketing Order*, Appendix I at 9 (CED-81-129) (July 2, 1981); Lawrence Shepard, "Cartelization of the California-Arizona Orange Industry, 1934-1981," 29 *Journal of Law and Economics* 83, 91–92 (1986). The order also restricts supply indirectly by keeping smaller oranges out of the fresh fruit market. 7 C.F.R. § 907.63; Shepard, 29 *Journal of Law and Economics* at 91. For data on growers, see Department of Justice, *Post-Hearing Memorandum and Proposed Findings of Fact* at 8, in *In re Proposed Amendment of Marketing Agreements and Orders 907 and 908* (Department of Agriculture No. AO-245-A8, AO-250-A6) (Aug. 15, 1983). For a wonderful description of how oranges are grown and sold in Florida, do read John McPhee, *Oranges* (1967).

For effect of quotas, see Shepard, 29 *Journal of Law and Economics* at 94. For increase in grower revenue, see Sheldon Kimmel, *Marketing Orders and Stability: The Case of California-Arizona Oranges* 2–3 (Economic Analysis Group, Anti-trust Division, U.S. Department of Justice No. 87-4, June 16, 1987); Glenn Nelson and Tom H. Robinson, "Retail and Wholesale Demand and Marketing Order Policy for Fresh Navel Oranges," 60 *American Journal of Agricultural Economics* 502, 508 (1978).

Sunkist claimed, in regard to the orange dump described in the opening epigraph, that "after the fruit rots and the juice runs off, the leavings are mashed into cattle feed" (Doug Foster, "Forbidden Fruit," *Inquiry*, May 11, 1981, at 20, 23). The orange dump led to massive, unfavorable publicity for Sunkist and the marketing order. After 1981, oranges were not put in large dumps, but did continue to rot or were otherwise economically wasted.

4. For effect of increase in supply of oranges for processing, see Shepard, 29 *Journal of Law and Economics* at 97, 114, 120. For Department of Justice statement, see *Comments of the Department of Justice* at 19 (Oct. 9, 1990), in the administrative proceeding on weekly volume regulations for the 1990–91 season, proposed at 55 *Federal Register* 36,653 (1990). For effect of abandoning the

quotas, see Shepard, 29 *Journal of Law and Economics* at 121. The effect of lower prices on profits could be offset, however, by increased market share. Marketing orders now cover only about one-half of the fruits and nuts and one-sixth of the vegetables grown in the United States, and most of these orders do not limit sales (GAO, *The Role of Marketing Orders in Establishing and Maintaining Orderly Marketing Conditions* at i [July 31, 1985]). Only five of the marketing orders in force directly limit supply.

5. "Perennial and increasing" is from Shepard, 29 *Journal of Law and Economics* at 121. Sunkist statement is from Charles C. Teague, President, California Fruit Growers Exchange (Sunkist), Department of Agriculture, *Hearings on the California-Arizona Lemon Market Ordering Order*, 1940, at 305, quoted in Shepard, 29 *Journal of Law and Economics* at 83. Information on increased fruit imports can be found in Ellen Paris, "Sunset in the Groves?" *Forbes*, March 23, 1987, at 35, and in a follow-up article in *Forbes*, July 25, 1988, at 10. In addition, the United States limits its ability to export oranges to Canada because the marketing order counts sales to Canada as domestic sales for the purpose of the quota. See 7 C.F.R. § 907.18 (1992). The quality of the oranges is discussed in Thomas M. Lenard and Michael P. Mazur, "Harvest of Waste: The Marketing Order Program," *Regulation*, May/June 1985, at 19, 21, 25. Nicholas J. Powers, Glenn A. Zepp, and Frederic L. Hoff point out that without quotas, growers with higher-quality fruit would get a larger market share. *Assessment of a Marketing Order Prorate Suspension: A Study of California-Arizona Navel Oranges* at 30 (See Department of Agriculture, Agricultural Economic Report No. 557 [1986]).

6. The descriptive quotations are from an undated flyer entitled *Sunkist*. Budget figures are from the 1990 and 1991 annual reports of Sunkist Growers, Inc.

7. Unlike a publicly traded corporation, Sunkist faces no requirement to reveal the compensation of its top management. On decline in Sunkist's membership, see Department of Justice, *Post-Hearing Memorandum and Proposed Findings of Fact* at 9, in *In re Proposed Amendment of Marketing Agreements and Orders 907 and 908* (Department of Agriculture No. AO-245-A8, AO-250-A6) (Aug. 15, 1983).

8. On Sunkist's need for quotas to maintain membership: Charles C. Teague, who essentially founded the modern Sunkist and led the fight to establish the marketing order, thought that quotas were essential to Sunkist's existence (C. C. Teague, *Fifty Years As a Rancher*, chap. 11 [2d ed., 1944]). In addition, Douglas P. Barker, Sunkist's former domestic sales manager, opined that the quotas helped maintain Sunkist's membership. See Testimony of Douglas P. Barker, Tr. at 1306, 1312, in *In re Sequoia*, AMA Dkt. No. 907-6, an administrative case which, after multiple reversals, was decided by the court of appeals in *Riverbend Farms v. Madigan*, 958 F.2d 1479 (9th Cir. 1992).

In regard to the weekly quotas being set to suit Sunkist, according to Douglas Barker, who was also one of its representatives in NOAC, Sunkist's sales staff was told to sell as much as it could, in the expectation that NOAC would set the weekly quotas to accommodate Sunkist's sales (See Testimony of Barker in *In re Sequoia* at 1295, 1301, 1304, 1313, and 1317).

In regard to production costs, Sunkist and the larger handlers get a cost advantage over small, independent handlers because the marketing order limits the amount each handler can sell by week rather than by season. Many small handlers would prefer to operate at full capacity for part of the season rather than at partial capacity for the entire season. With their small weekly quotas, small handlers cannot keep equipment and crews busy full time. They cannot compete for the orders of the large grocery chains. Nor can they compete effectively for the unregulated export business, because much of the crop does not meet the highly selective export standards, so that putting together a large export order would leave them with more leftovers than they could sell as fresh fruit. The marketing order does allow handlers to exceed their quota by the greater of two numbers: 20 percent of the quota, or one carload in any one week, provided that they reduce the next week's shipments accordingly. This degree of flexibility is too slight to reduce the problems for small handlers significantly.

For allegations of misuse of enforcement mechanism, see Carolyn Lochhead, "Fruit Fight: Independent Growers Challenge Agribusiness Giants," *Insight*, July 29, 1991 at 13, 17–18. In 1989, the Department of Agriculture dismissed a number of such charges made in connection with the order's administration, although it found that some cases went unprosecuted for no apparent reason. See Office of Inspector General, *Report of Investigation: Sunkist Growers, Inc. et al.* (Jan. 24, 1989). The department also found that NOACs audit enforcement procedures could be evaded and were insufficient. See Agricultural Marketing Service, *Review of the Auditing and Enforcement Procedures in the Navel and Valencia Orange Marketing Orders* 4-6 (Oct. 19, 1989). Through its influence over NOAC, Sunkist has substantial control over, and knowledge of, these procedures. Independent growers instituted actions under the False Claims Act against alleged violators of the marketing order. Despite the efforts of the Department of Agriculture and Sunkist, the district court has refused on four occasions to dismiss these actions. See *United States ex rel. Sequoia Orange Co. v. Sunland Packing House Co.*, No. CV F-88-566 EDP (E.D. Cal. July 7, 1989); *United States ex rel. Sequoia Orange Co. v. San Joaquin Citrus*, No. CV F-89-002 EDP (E.D. Cal. July 25, 1990); *United States ex rel. Sequoia Orange Co. v. Oxnard Lemon Co.*, No. CV-F-91-194 OWW (E.D. Cal. May 4, 1992); and *United States ex rel. Sequoia Orange Co. v. Stark Packing Co. and Sunkist Growers. Inc.*, No. CV-F-89-058 OWW (E.D. Cal. Dec. 18, 1992). The United States Attorney has granted immunity to some of the alleged violators, including important Sunkist officials. (See, e.g., Letter to Gerald Vinnard from George L. O'Connell, July 6, 1992, on file with author). Subsequently, Secretary Madigan reported that his staff advised him that there was "significant 'cheating'" under the navel orange quotas (Declaration of Edward Madigan, Dec. 23, 1992 at 6, *Leavens v. Madigan*, No. 92-2832 [D.D.C.]).

The House passed an amendment to the False Claims Act to exclude actions brought for violations of agricultural marketing orders. See H.R. 4563, § 4, 102d Cong., 2d Sess. (1992) (amending 31 U.S.C. § 3729(e) (1988)); 138 *Cong. Rec.* H7978 (1992) (passed by the House). For a report linking that action with

Sunkist donations to members of the House Judiciary Committee, see Michael Doyle, "Sunkist Seeks Legal Shield," *Fresno Bee*, Sept. 29, 1992.

9. The agricultural economists' study is *A Review of Federal Marketing Orders for Fruits, Vegetables and Specialty Crops: Economic Efficiency and Welfare Implications* 34 (Department of Agriculture, Agricultural Economic Report No. 477) (1981). For handlers' opposition, see letter from Mark Heywood, Acting Chief of Advocacy, Small Business Administration, to Dan Haley, Administrator, Agricultural Marketing Service, Oct. 5, 1990, at 5–6 (on file with author). For opposition within Sunkist, see discussion of June 1991 referendum in Chapter 3. Editorials include *New York Times*, April 11, 1981, and Aug. 21, 1985; *Wall Street Journal*, Aug. 20, 1985, and Jan. 2, 1991; *Los Angeles Times*, June 14, 1981; and *San Francisco Examiner*, March 13, 1981 and July 1, 1981. Quotas were suspended by 57 *Fed. Reg.* 5,975 (1992), reinstated by 57 *Fed. Reg.* 54,169 (1992), and suspended again on December 14, 1992, as noted in 57 *Fed. Reg.* 62,153 (1992). For statements by judge in case to enjoin suspension, see Transcript of Preliminary Injunction Hearing, Dec. 29, 1992 at 2, 7 in *Leavens v. Madigan*, CA 92-2832GAG (D.D.C.). Letter from Dianne Feinstein to Secretary of Agriculture Edward R. Madigan, Dec. 11, 1992; letter from Patrick Leahy to Madigan; and letter from Barbara Boxer to Madigan, Dec. 17, 1992 (all on file with the author). For the cost of retaining marketing orders, see Editorial, "End of the Citrus Cartel," *Wall Street Journal*, Dec. 15, 1992, at A18.

10. On Sunkist's lawyers, see Kim I. Eisler, "Attack of the Killer Lawyers," *Regardie's: The Business of Washington*, April, 1990, at 96.

On James Lake, see e.g., *Who's Who in American Politics,1989–90*, at 1665 (12th ed.); Eisler, "Attack of the Killer Lawyers," at 101-04; Coelho quote is from "The Bitter Struggle of a Non-Lawyer Lobbyist," *National Journal*, Sept. 17, 1983, at 1901; "Defending California's Agricultural Turf," *National Journal*, Sept. 1, 1990, at 2058.

The FEC reports that Sunkist's PAC gave a total of $393,010 to political candidates from 1979 to 1992, split almost evenly between Democrats and Republicans. Figures for Bodine donations are from *Los Angeles Times*, Jan. 25, 1989, at 3; and *Washington Post*, Nov. 17, 1988, at A20. Coelho's Valley Education Fund, a conduit for funding various political campaigns, received contributions from Julian Heron and others with ties to Sunkist (Eisler, "Attack of the Killer Lawyers" at 104). Sunkist donated $14,000 to Pete Wilson's successful senatorial campaign; later, they donated $6,000 and raised an additional $28,200 from state fruit growers for his successful gubernatorial campaign. (*Los Angeles Times*, Oct. 24, 1990, at A1).

11. 7 U.S.C. § 602 (1988).

12. Even a law clamping a numerical limit on pollution raises questions, such as how to measure pollution. See, for example, *Natural Resources Defense Council v. Ruckelshaus*, 359 F. Supp. 1028 (D.D.C. 1972).

13. Former EPA deputy administrator John Quarles, quoted in H.R. Rep. No. 410, 96th Cong., 1st Sess., pt. 2, at 71 (1979) (dissenting view of Rep. Corcoran).

14. Commission on Executive, Legislative, and Judicial Salaries, Pub. L.

No. 90-206, 81 Stat. 642 (1967) (codified as amended at 2 U.S.C. § 351 (1988)). The 1988 incident is described in Michael K. Frisby and Michael Kranish, "Congressional Raise: The Hedge," *Boston Globe*, Jan. 31, 1989; Elaine S. Povich, "House Sets Pay Hike Vote, 50% Raise Probably Doomed, Wright Admits," *Chicago Tribune*, Feb. 7, 1989; and "Congress Rejects Pay Raise; Public Outrage Overwhelms Lawmakers," *Facts on File*, Feb. 10, 1989.

15. Chapter 4 uses the Clean Air Act to illustrate these conclusions. Other scholars reach similar conclusions about a wide range of environmental statutes. See, e.g., Richard J. Lazarus, "The Tragedy of Distrust in the Implementation of Federal Environmental Law," 54 *Law and Contemporary Problems* 311, 323-28 (Autumn 1991).

16. See Robert Pear, "U.S. Laws Delayed by Complex Rules and Partisanship," *New York Times*, March 31, 1991, A1. One can get a whiff of the problem as experienced on the inside by reading the lament of former EPA Administrator Douglas M. Costle, "Brave New Chemical: The Future Regulatory History of Phlogisten," 33 *Administrative Law Review* 195 (1981).

17. For many of the arguments in favor of delegation, see Attorney General's Committee on Administrative Procedure, *Administrative Procedure in Government Agencies*, S. Doc. No. 8, 77th Cong., 1st Sess. (1941); and Jerry L. Mashaw, "Prodelegation: Why Administrators Should Make Political Decisions," 1 *Journal of Law, Economics and Organization* 81 (1985).

18. See, for example, Professor Richard B. Stewart's article, "The Reformation of American Administrative Law," 88 *Harvard Law Review* 1669 (1975), which begins with the explicit premise that delegation is necessary. In *The End of Liberalism* (2d ed. 1979), Theodore J. Lowi indicts delegation but does not address the question whether government would work better without it, nor does he consider how we might abolish it.

19. E.g., *Yakus v. United States*, 321 U.S. 414, 426 (1944).

20. See text accompanying note 24 in Chapter 6.

21. Public Health Service Act, Title X, 84 Stat. 1506, as amended, 42 U.S.C. §§ 300–300a-41 (1970); § 1008 forbids use of federal funds in programs where abortion is practiced. Amendments are at 53 *Fed. Reg.* 2923-25 (1988) (codified at 42 C.F.R. § 59 (1989)).

22. Eight justices considered the constitutional question in *Rust v. Sullivan*, 111 S. Ct. 1759 (1991).

23. Adam Clymer, "Abortion Ruling Is Focus of Panel," *New York Times*, June 7, 1991, at A16.

24. James M. Landis, *The Administrative Process* 76 (1938).

25. 42 U.S.C. § 7412(d)(3)(A) (Supp. II 1990). If Congress had stopped there, it would have made the law. However, the statute allows EPA to make the standards stronger than this baseline. Id. §7412(d)(3).

26. 42 U.S.C. § 2000e-2 (1988). See Charles A. Sullivan, Michael J. Zimmer, and Richard F. Richards, *Employment Discrimination* §3.6 (2d ed.,1988).

27. The Department of Energy recognizes that its regulations could have anticompetitive effects as standards that require substantial redesign and retooling have a disproportionate effect on smaller competitors. 56 *Fed. Reg.*

22, 250; 22, 254–55; 22, 269 (1991). While the department has an obligation to take such anticompetitive effects into account, persuading it not to recognize them could help large manufacturers eliminate smaller competitors, discourage new competitors, and raise prices to consumers. Other regulatory programs have been used to impose costs on competitors. See, e.g., William A. Jordan, "Producer Protection, Prior Market Structure and the Effects of Government Regulation," 15 *Journal of Law and Economics* 151 (1972).

28. R. Douglas Arnold, *The Logic of Congressional Action* 73 (1990).

29. See, e.g., Mary Ann Glendon, *Rights Talk: The Impoverishment of Political Discourse* (1991).

30. Quote is from Benjamin Ginsberg and Martin Shefter, *Politics by Other Means: The Declining Importance of Elections in America* 26, 171–75 (1990). See also E. J. Dionne, Jr., *Why Americans Hate Politics* (1991).

31. The *locus classicus* for many of these arguments is Theodore Lowi's *The End of Liberalism.*

32. Quotes from the Kettering Foundation, *Citizens and Politics: A View from Main Street America* at iv (1991). See also Alan Ehrenhalt, *The United States of Ambition: Politicians, Power, and the Pursuit of Office* (1991).

2. The Vain Search for Virtuous Lawmakers

1. Virtual representation is discussed in Gordon S. Wood, *The Creation of the American Republic, 1776–1787,* at 173-76 (1969). My account relies on this work.

2. "No interest of their own . . . " and "but one interest . . . " are from Wood, *American Republic* at 59 (quoting *Boston Independent Chronicle,* July 10, 1777). The statutes which inflicted harm to minorities are described id. at 403-13 and 502-03.

3. "The members of the various state assemblies were 'everywhere observed to lose sight of the aggregate interests of the Community, and even to sacrifice them to the interests or prejudices of their respective constituents.'" Wood, *American Republic* at 195. See also id. at 475; and *The Federalist* No. 51, at 351 (J. Madison) (Jacob E. Cooke ed. 1961). "Natural aristocracy" in Forrest McDonald, *Novus Ordo Seclorum: The Intellectual Origins of the Constitution* 165 (1985); "an *aristocracy* of experience . . . " in Wood, *American Republic* at 509 (emphasis in original), and discussion at 508-18. Washington is described in McDonald, *Novus Ordo Seclorum* at 193-98. John Adams is quoted in Wood, *American Republic* at 569-70, 571, 572. On fear of reverting to a monarchy, see id. at 393-98.

4. On accountability, see *Federalist* No. 46 (J. Madison); on meeting national needs, see *Federalist* No. 11 (A. Hamilton); and on protecting individual liberty, see *Federalist* No. 10 (J. Madison).

5. On the identity of interest groups and factions, see Daniel A. Farber and Philip P. Frickey, *Law and Public Choice: A Critical Introduction* 10 (1991). Madison quote is in *Federalist* No. 10, at 57. The new concern with individual liberty was somewhat antithetical to the self-denial implicit in the concept of public virtue. Wood, *American Republic* at 610-12.

6. *Federalist* No. 10, at 58.

7. For Madison's acknowledgment of failure to produce virtuous leaders, see Jack N. Rakove, "The Structure of Politics at the Accession of George Washington," in *Beyond Confederation: Origins of the Constitution and American National Identity* 286-89 (Richard Beeman et al. eds. 1976).

8. Madison was concerned, however, that a legislature with too many members would devolve real power upon a few individuals. See *Federalist* No. 58, at 395-96.

9. "Even for bad men . . . " in Wood, *American Republic* at 611 (quoting James Wilson). See James Roland Pennock, *Democratic Political Theory* 310 (1979); Hanna Pitkin, *The Concept of Representation* 195-96 (1972).

10. See Leonard W. Levy, "The Original Constitution as a Bill of Rights," 9 *Constitutional Commentary* 163 (1992). Another rationalization for the lack of a bill of rights was that the national government was delegating only limited powers, thereby reducing the risk of having rights infringed. Wood, *American Republic* at 539-40.

11. *Massachusetts, Colony to Commonwealth: Documents on the Formation of Its Constitution, 1775-1780*, at 131 (Robert J. Taylor ed. 1961) (citing Massachusetts Constitution of 1780, Part I, art. XXX).

12. Quote from *Ludecke v. Watkins*, 335 U.S. 160, 171 n.18 (1947). The act was denounced in state resolutions; the Virginia Resolutions, which James Madison wrote, declared that it "exercise[d] a power nowhere delegated to the Federal Government; and which by uniting legislative and judicial powers to those of executive, subvert[ed] the general principles of free government, as well as the particular organization and positive provisions of the federal Constitution . . . " *The Virginia Report of 1799-1800. Touching the Alien and Sedition Laws. Together with the Virginia Resolutions of December 21, 1798*, at xv, 23 (Leonard W. Levy ed. 1970).

13. 11 U.S. (7 Cranch) 382, 388-89 (1813). The president's decision that France had revoked its decree required some difficult statutory interpretation. As Sotirios Barber shows, Napoleon did not revoke the embargo decree forthwith, but rather announced that the decree would cease to operate in four months to allow time for Britain to revoke its decree. President Madison then had to decide whether France had revoked its decree within the meaning of the statute. Sotirios A. Barber, *The Constitution and the Delegation of Congressional Power* 53-59 (1975).

14. In *Wayman v. Southard*, decided in 1825, the Supreme Court said that the prohibition on delegating legislative powers did not mean that Congress could not let others "fill up the details," but did not make clear whether "the details" consisted of more than interpreting and applying legislated laws. 23 U.S. (10 Wheat.) 1, 43 (1825). "[T]he maker of the law may commit something to the discretion of the other departments, and the precise boundary of this power is a subject of delicate and difficult inquiry, into which a court will not enter unnecessarily." Id. at 46.

15. 1 Alexis de Tocqueville, *Democracy in America*, 57-58 (Phillips Bradley ed. 1946).

16. Quotes are from William Nelson, *The Roots of American Bureaucracy, 1830–1900*, at 62, 87 (1982). I understand that Progressivism had many faces; I am using the term *Progressive* to refer to those who shared the old mugwumps' belief in expert, scientific administration.

17. See id. at 73-81; and Robert H. Wiebe, *The Search for Order, 1877–1920*, at 6 (1967).

18. For importance of science, see, e.g., Wiebe, *Search for Order* at 147, 170. "Scientific morality" and "science of justice" are from Nelson, *Roots of Bureaucracy* at 6, 82-112, 140-44. For bureaucracy, see both of these sources and also Stephen Skowronek, *Building a New American State: The Expansion of National Administrative Capacities 1877–1920*, at 42-43 (1982).

19. E.g., Samuel Freeman Miller, *Lectures on the Constitution of the United States* 25, 86, 89, 449 (1893).

20. For economic mugwumps, see Skowronek, *Building a New American State* at 133. For Wilson's proposal to amend the Constitution, see, e.g., John A. Rohr, *To Run a Constitution: The Legitimacy of the Administrative State* ch. 5 (1986). Wilson proposed allowing the president to appoint legislators to the cabinet and lengthening the terms of the president and legislators. He aimed to make American government more like that of the United Kingdom. For administrators making better public policy, see William T. Gormley, Jr., *Taming the Bureaucracy: Muscles, Prayers, and Other Strategies* 7-8 (1989); and Wiebe, *Search for Order* at 169-70. For independent agencies, see id. at 200, 222.

21. Wiebe, *Search for Order* at 149.

22. Theodore Lowi, *The End of Liberalism* 94-105 (2d ed. 1979); Richard B. Stewart, "The Reformation of American Administrative Law," 88 *Harvard Law Review* 1667, 1672-76 (1975); Mark Seidenfeld, "A Civic Republican Justification for the Bureaucratic State," 105 *Harvard Law Review* 1511, 1517 n.22 (1992).

23. On the Court's interpretation of ICA, see, e.g., *ICC v. Cincinnati, New Orleans & Texas Pac. Ry. Co.*, 167 U.S. 479,505,511 (1897), Skowronek, *Building a New American State* at 148-58; Robert L. Rabin, "Federal Regulation in Historical Perspective," 38 *Stanford Law Review* 1189, 1212-15 (1986). On the ambiguity of the ICA, see id. at 1206-08. Judges understood the common law as "neutral and prepolitical." Cass R. Sunstein, *After the Rights Revolution: Reconceiving the Regulatory State* 18 (1990).

24. See Skowronek, *Building a New American State* at 16, 22, 46.

25. See *Field v. Clark*, 143 U.S. 649, 692 (1892). Louis Jaffe concludes that the statute left the President "a wide and uncertain area of judgement." Jaffe, "An Essay on Delegation of Legislative Power" (pts. I and II), 47 *Columbia Law Review* 359 and 561, 566 (1947).

26. The Court stated that it is "essential for the protection of the interests of our people, against the unfriendly or discriminating regulations established by foreign governments, in the interests of their people, to invest the President with large discretion in matters arising out of the execution of statutes relating to trade and commerce with other nations." *Field v. Clark*, 143 U.S. at 691. See also Jaffe, 47 *Columbia Law Review* at 566.

27. For opinions of political leaders, see Skowronek, *Building a New American State* at 165-76, 248-84.

For Supreme Court decisions, see Rabin, 38 *Stanford Law Review* at 1235-36. For example, the Federal Trade Commission Act as originally enacted prohibited "unfair methods of competition." Ch. 311, Pub. L. No. 203, § 5, 38 Stat. 717, 719 (1914). The Court held that the act allowed the Federal Trade Commission (FTC) only to interpret and enforce an existing common-law cause of action. *FTC v. Gratz*, 253 U.S. 421, 427 (1920). Brandeis argued in dissent (id. at 436-37) that problems of unfair competition necessitated broad regulatory power. Then, in 1938, the act was amended to give the FTC authority to move against "unfair or deceptive acts or practices," terms unconfined by common law or customary standards. Ch. 49, Pub. L. No. 447, § 3, 52 Stat. 111 (1938). Subsequent judicial interpretation gave the commission a more open-ended mandate to pursue the goals of the act, unconfined by common-law standards. See Ernest Gellhorn and Glen O. Robinson, "Perspectives on Administrative Law," 75 *Columbia Law Review* 771, 776 (1975). The act as now amended and interpreted delegates legislative power.

In *Mahler v. Eby*, 264 U.S. 32 (1924), the Court upheld a statute that empowered the secretary of labor to deport immigrants convicted of crimes and certain other categories of immigrants that were found to be "undesirable." The Court found the "declared policy of Congress to exclude aliens classified in great detail by their undesirable qualities" in various statutes and asserted that administrative usage in the field of immigration and naturalization "has created a common understanding of the words 'undesirable residents' which gives them the quality of a recognized standard." Id. at 40.

In the 1911 case *United States v. Grimaud*, 220 U.S. 506 (1911), the Court reached the right result for the wrong reason. It upheld a statute that authorized the secretary of interior to promulgate regulations for the use of federal lands in furtherance of vaguely stated goals and made violation of the regulations a crime. A rancher found to have violated a regulation forbidding grazing of animals on federal land without a permit challenged the statute. At first, a divided Court affirmed a lower court decision that had found the statute to be an unconstitutional delegation, but, on reargument after new justices were appointed, including one familiar with federal land management, the result was changed to a unanimous reversal of the lower court. See Jaffe, 47 *Columbia Law Review* at 567. The Court noted in passing that the secretary's regulations "[did] not declare general rules with reference to rights of persons and property" —presumably private property—but instead managed public property. 220 U.S. at 516. The Court could have stopped there because, as I will discuss in Chapter 12, courts have not considered making policy for the management of public property an exercise of legislative power. Instead, the Court went on to repeat the error of *Field v. Clark*, by holding that a statute that authorized an official to make rules of conduct required the secretary to do no more than apply the statute to the facts, ignoring the broad discretion that the statute vested in the secretary.

See also *Buttfield v. Stranahan*, 192 U.S. 470 (1904), which upheld a statute that ordered an agency, acting upon the advice of a board of experts, to set standards for the exclusion of imported tea of inferior quality. Jaffe argues that the ostensibly vague standard of inferior-quality tea was anchored in "the settled judgment of the trade." Louis L. Jaffe, *Judicial Control of Administrative Action* 57 (1965).

28. 255 U.S. 81 (1921). Quotes in 255 U.S. at 87, 92. Modern discussions of delegation usually omit mentioning *Cohen Grocery*. An exception, *Fahey v. Mallonee*, 332 U.S. 245 (1947), cited *Cohen Grocery* and distinguished it as concerning criminal sanctions. Id. at 250.

29. 253 U.S. 149 (1920) and 264 U.S. 219 (1924).

30. 276 U.S. 394 (1928). Quote in 276 U.S. at 401. For weakness of argument, see Jaffe, 47 *Columbia Law Review* at 569. ("[A]n analysis of the Act and even more the history of its administration shows a tremendous scope for manipulation.").

31. 276 U.S. at 406.

32. "With Our Readers," 13 *Constitutional Review* 98, 100 (1929) (citing President-elect Hoover's speech of Oct. 15, 1928).

33. Id. at 101 (J.S. Cotton).

34. The first case mentioned was *United States v. Shreveport Grain & Elevator Co.*, 287 U.S. 77, 85 (1932) ("That the legislative power of Congress cannot be delegated is, of course, clear."). The second was *Norwegian Nitrogen Products Co. v. United States*, 288 U.S. 294, 305 (1933). After *Hampton & Co.* and before *Norwegian Nitrogen*, a prominent law review article argued that the Constitution allowed some delegation. Patrick W. Duff and Horace E. Whiteside, "Delegata Potestas Non Potest Delegari: A Maxim of American Constitutional Law," 14 *Cornell Law Quarterly* 168 (1929).

35. Laurence H. Tribe, *American Constitutional Law* §§ 8-1 to 8-4 (2d ed. 1988).

36. See the discussion of Charles A. Beard's *An Economic Interpretation of the Constitution of the United States* (1913) in *Fame and the Founding Fathers: Essays by Douglass Adair* 86-88 (Trevor Colbourn ed. 1974). See also Arthur Meier Schlesinger, *New Viewpoints in American History* ch. VIII (1922).

37. For rebuttal of class warfare theory of Article I, see John Phillip Reid, "The Apparatus of Constitutional Advocacy and the American Revolution: A Review of Five Books," 42 *New York University Law Review* 187, 188-89 (1967); Wood, *American Republic* at 483-84. "Jejune abstraction" in Felix Frankfurter and James M. Landis, "Power of Congress over Procedure in Criminal Contempts in 'Inferior' Federal Courts—A Study in Separation of Powers," 37 *Harvard Law Review* 1010, 1013 n.11 (1924). Even some recent accounts of how the Constitution seeks to protect individual liberty leave out separation of powers. E.g., McDonald, *Novus Ordo Seclorum* at 165-66.

38. For an account of the position that appointed experts should make law, see Edward A. Purcell, Jr., *The Crisis of Democratic Theory: Scientific Naturalism and the Problem of Value* 98-109 (1973). For Landis, see James M. Landis, *The Administrative Process* 1, 98–101 (1938).

39. For legal realism, see, e.g., Thurman Arnold, *The Symbols of Government* (1935); and Jerome Frank, *Law and the Modern Mind* (1930).

40. For New Deal belief in science as guiding policy, see Attorney General's Committee on Administrative Procedure, *Administrative Procedure in Government Agencies*, S. Doc. No. 8, 77th Cong., 1st Sess. 19 (1941). For New Deal delegations to dependent agencies, see Gormley, *Taming the Bureaucracy* at 8.

41. "I am prepared under my constitutional duty to recommend the measures that a stricken nation in the midst of a stricken world may require. . . . I shall ask the Congress for . . . broad Executive power to wage a war against the emergency, as great as the power that would be given to me if we were in fact invaded by a foreign foe." 2 *The Public Papers and Addresses of Franklin D. Roosevelt* 11, 15 (S. Rosenman ed. 1938).

42. Ch. 25, Pub. L. No. 10, 48 Stat. 31 (1933).

43. Ch. 90, Pub. L. No. 67, 48 Stat. 195 (1933).

44. "To supporters and critics . . . " is from James Q. Whitman, "Of Corporatism, Fascism, and the First New Deal," 39 *American Journal of Comparative Law* 747, 748 (1991). *Fortune* quote is from "The Corporative State," 10 *Fortune* 57 (July 1934). Roosevelt is quoted in Whitman, 39 *American Journal of Comparative Law* at 747; Mussolini in id. at 766. On public concern, see 1 Dr. George H. Gallup, *The Gallup Poll: Public Opinion 1935–1971*, at 30 (1972) (45%).

45. See Wayne Gard, "Hot Oil from Texas," 35 *American Mercury* 71 73 (May 1935).

46. On industrial self-regulation, see Morton J. Horwitz, *The Transformation of American Law, 1870–1960: The Crisis of Legal Orthodoxy* 208 (1992). The mackerel comment is from Ellis W. Hawley, *The New Deal and the Problem of Monopoly: A Study in Economic Ambivalence* 115 (1966).

47. 295 U.S. 495, 553 (1935).

48. Quoted in Arthur Schlesinger, Jr., *The Politics of Upheaval* 280 (1960).

49. 293 U.S. 388 (1935). The provision superficially resembled those struck down in *Knickerbocker* and *Washington v. W. C. Dawson*, which made federal law incorporate state law. But the provision prohibiting interstate shipment of oil produced in violation of state law gave the president a choice about whether to incorporate state law into federal law.

Significantly, Justice Cardozo disagreed not with the doctrinal assumptions of the Court but with their application to the provision under review. See Note, "Rethinking the Nondelegation Doctrine," 62 *Boston University Law Review* 257, 277 n.93 (1982). He found that the statute's declared policy and structure provided standards sufficient to support the delegation. 293 U.S. at 435.

50. Ch. 641, Pub. L. No. 320, 49 Stat. 750 (1935); ch. 296, Pub. L. No. 137, 50 Stat. 246 (1937).

51. See Chapter 11.

52. The fate of the delegation doctrine in the post–New Deal era prompted one commentator to note that the "intelligible principle" test had become "all but a vestigial euphemism, virtually shorn of practical meaning." Bernard Schwartz, "Of Administrators and Philosopher-Kings: The Republic, the Laws, and Delegations of Power," 72 *Northwestern University Law Review* 443, 446 (1977). The cases support the observation. See, e.g., *Fahey v. Mallonee*, 332 U.S. 245 (1947); and *Yakus v. United States*, 321 U.S. 414 (1944). *United States v. Rock*

Royal Co-operative Inc., 307 U.S. 533, 574-78 (1939) upheld the delegation to the secretary of agriculture.

53. Tribe, *American Constitutional Law* §§ 8-5 to 8-7.

54. For example, *Lichter v. United States*, 334 U.S. 742, 785 (1948), and *Yakus*, 321 U.S. at 419-23, cite the war more as motive for delegation than as constitutional justification. More recent cases do appear to indicate that, in the war and foreign affairs contexts, legislation may leave the president broader powers than would be permissible in domestic matters. See, e.g., *Federal Energy Administration v. Algonquin SNG Inc.*, 426 U.S. 548, 559-60 and n.10 (1976); *United States v. Mazurie*, 419 U.S. 544, 556-57 (1975); *Zemel v. Rusk*, 381 U.S. 1, 17 (1965). See also Michal R. Belknap, "The New Deal and the Emergency Powers Doctrine," 62 *Texas Law Review* 67 (1983).

55. See, e.g., *Amalqamated Meat Cutters v. Connally*, 337 F. Supp. 737 (D.D.C. 1971) (three-judge panel); *Goldstein v. Clifford*, 290 F. Supp. 275 (D.N.J. 1968) (three-judge panel). As Clinton Rossiter said, "The Court has had little success in preventing the precedents of war from becoming precedents of peace." Clinton Rossiter, *The Supreme Court and the Commander in Chief* 129 (1951, and reprint 1970). Justice Roberts warned in 1944 that this would happen. *Yakus*, 321 U.S. at 459-60 (Roberts, J., dissenting).

56. Quoted in *New York Times*, June 12, 1962, at 1. Kennedy's book *Profiles in Courage* celebrated public virtue, as did his much-quoted exhortation, "Ask not what your country can do for you; ask what you can do for your country."

57. This point of view is described in William A. Niskanen, Jr., *Bureaucracy and Representative Government* vi (1971).

58. For established areas, see, e.g., *Fahey v. Mallonee*, 332 U.S. at 250. For new areas, see, e.g., *United States v. Southwestern Cable Co.*, 392 U.S. 157, 172-73 (1968), holding that the Federal Communications Commission (FCC) had authority to regulate cable television even though that technology did not exist at the time the FCC's enabling legislation was enacted.

59. On democracy, see *Yakus*, 321 U.S. at 426. On liberty, see *Amalgamated Meat Cutters*, 337 F. Supp. at 759-62.

60. 1 Kenneth Culp Davis, *Administrative Law Treatise* 75 (1958).

61. 357 U.S. 116, 129 (1958).

62. Justice Brennan offered an alternative distinction in a later case, namely, that courts should scrutinize delegations more carefully in statutes that impose criminal sanctions. *United States v. Robel*, 389 U.S. 258, 275 (1967) (Brennan, J., concurring). But many statutes that delegate the power to regulate business impose criminal sanctions for violations of agency laws. See, e.g., *Yakus*, 321 U.S. at 444-46; *Currin v. Wallace*, 306 U.S. 1, 7 (1939); *United States v. Curtiss-Wright Export Corp.*, 299 U.S. 304, 311-12 (1936). A recent delegation case, *Touby v. United States*, acknowledged that earlier decisions "are not entirely clear as to whether or not more specific guidance is in fact required" in the criminal context but did not resolve the issue. 111 S. Ct. 1752, 1756 (1991). Justice Brennan also has argued that the "[f]ormulation of policy is a legislature's primary responsibility, entrusted to it by the electorate, and to the extent Congress delegates authority under indefinite standards, this policy-making

function is passed on to other agencies, often not answerable or responsive in the same degree to the people." *Robel*, 389 U.S. at 276. This is true of all delegations.

63. See, e.g., Bernard Schwartz, *Administrative Law* 47-48 (1976); and *Robel*, 389 U.S. at 275 (Brennan, J., concurring).

64. See Tribe, *American Constitutional Law* § 12-38.

65. See, e.g., *Smith v. Goquen*, 415 U.S. 566, 575 (1974); *Papachristou v. City of Jacksonville*, 405 U.S. 156, 168-70 (1972). These "void for vagueness" cases make it clear that vague criminal laws are invalid both because they delegate and because they fail to give notice of what is illegal.

66. *Hampton v. Mow Sun Wong*, 426 U.S. 88, 116 (1976).

67. In *Hampton v. Mow Sun Wong*, Justice Rehnquist argued in dissent that the Court was using the phrase *due process* to obscure the application of a special standard pertaining to delegation in that case, a charge which the Court did not address. 426 U.S. at 122 (Rehnquist, J., dissenting).

68. 373 U.S. 546, 626 (1963) (Harlan, J., dissenting in part).

69. The literature is summarized in Daniel J. Gifford, "The New Deal Regulatory Model; A History of Criticisms and Refinements," 68 *Minnesota Law Review* 299, 309-19 (1983). See, e.g., Ralph Nader, *Unsafe at Any Speed: The Designed-in Dangers of the American Automobile* (1965); Mark J. Green, *The Closed Enterprise System: Ralph Nader's Study Group Report on Antitrust Enforcement* (1972). For gridlock, see, e.g., Louis L. Jaffe, *Judicial Control of Administrative Action* 48-51 (1965); Lowi, *End of Liberalism* at ch. 5. Other critiques include J. Skelly Wright, "Beyond Discretionary Justice" (Book Review), 81 *Yale Law Journal* 575, 582 (1972); John Hart Ely, *Democracy and Distrust* 131-34 (1980); William O. Douglas, *Go East, Young Man: The Early Years* 217 (1974); James O. Freedman, *Crisis and Legitimacy: The Administrative Process and American Government* 78-94 (1978); Stephen Koslow, "Standardless Administrative Adjudication," 22 *Administrative Law Review* 407 (1970); and Jeffrey Rosen, "Danny and Zoë," *New Republic*, February 1, 1993, at 28, 29. (noting Zoë Baird's doubt's about the consitutionality of delegation).

70. See, e.g., Sunstein, *After the Rights Revolution* at 29-30. Quote from *Calvert Cliffs' Coordinating Committee v. Atomic Energy Commission*, 449 F.2d 1109, 1111 (D.C. Cir. 1971).

71. 415 U.S. 336 (1974). *National Cable* was distinguished in *Skinner v. Mid-America Pipeline Co.*, 490 U.S. 212, 223-24 (1989).

72. 448 U.S. 607 (1980).

73. *American Textile Manufacturers Institute v. Donovan*, 452 U.S. 490, 543 (1981) (Rehnquist, J., dissenting).

74. The case is 462 U.S. 919 (1983). Standards are discussed at 953 n.16. Justice White argued in dissent that the Court had not distinguished the legislative veto from delegation. *Id.* at 986-87. Laurence Tribe concluded that the most plausible explanation of *Chadha* is as a transition to "a significant judicial tightening of the limits within which Congress may entrust *anyone* with lawmaking power." Tribe, "The Legislative Veto Decision: A Law by Any Other Name?" 21 *Harvard Journal on Legislation* 1, 17 (1984) (emphasis in original).

75. For permissive approach, see *Lichter v. United States*, 334 U.S. 742, 774-78 (1948). For concurrences and dissents, see, e.g. *Textile Manufacturers*, 452 U.S. at 543-48 (Rehnquist, J., dissenting); *Industrial Union Department AFL-CIO v. American Petroleum Institute*, 448 U.S. 607, 671-88 (1980) (Rehnquist, J., concurring); *California Bankers Association v. Shultz*, 416 U.S. 21, 91-93 (1974) (Brennan, J., dissenting); *McGautha v. California*, 402 U.S. 183, 271-87 (1971) (Brennan, J., dissenting); *Arizona v. California*, 373 U.S. 546, 624-27 (1963) (Harlan, J., dissenting in part).

76. 488 U.S. 361 (1989). "Congress generally . . ." is in 488 U.S. at 372 (citing *Field v. Clark*, 143 U.S. 649, 692 (1892)). See Justice Scalia's dissent at 413.

77. Replying to a concerned railroad president in 1892, Attorney General Richard Olney wrote, "The Commission, as its functions have now been limited by the courts, is, or can be made, of great use to the railroads. It satisfies the popular clamor for a government supervision of railroads, at the same time that the supervision is almost entirely nominal. Further, the older such a commission gets to be, the more inclined it will be found to take the business and railroad view of things. It thus becomes a sort of barrier between the railroad corporations and the people and a sort of protection against hasty and crude legislation hostile to railroad interests. . . . The part of wisdom is not to destroy the Commission, but to utilize it." Quoted in Jaffe, *Judicial Control of Administrative Action* at 12 n.6. See also Wiebe, *Search for Order* at 53.

78. Paul T. Homan, "The Pattern of the New Deal," 51 *Political Science Quarterly* 161, 170 (1936).

79. As *Mistretta* stated, "Until 1935, this Court never struck down a challenged statute on delegation grounds." 488 U.S. at 373. See also *Chadha*, 462 U.S. at 985 (White, J., dissenting); and *Federal Power Commission v. New England Power Co.*, 415 U.S. 345, 352-53 (1974) (Marshall, J., concurring).

80. In addition, the architects of the Rules Enabling Act, including Chief Justice Taft, were concerned to avoid improper delegation. See Stephen B. Burbank, "The Rules Enabling Act of 1934," 130 *University of Pennsylvania Law Review* 1015, 1073-75, 1106-07 (1982). Leading jurists took the delegation doctrine seriously. See, e.g., Ernst Freund, *Administrative Powers over Persons and Property* 218 (1928).

81. For example, Hamilton asked rhetorically, "[Do] momentary passions and immediate interests have a more active and imperious controul over human conduct than general or remote considerations of policy, utility or justice?" *Federalist* No. 6, at 31. The quote is from Madison, cited in Wood, *American Republic* at 473.

82. Many scholars have commented upon the unrealistic hope of finding public officials who would steadily steer toward the long-term public good. See Schwartz, 72 *Northwestern University Law Review* at 449-53 (collecting comments).

Part III. Delegation in Practice

1. See, e.g., James Q. Wilson, *Political Organizations* 330-37 (1973); and James Q. Wilson, *American Government*, 422-47 (4th ed. 1989).

2. For discussion of public-interest groups as concentrated interests, see *Environmental Politics: Public Costs, Private Rewards* (Michael S. Greve and Fred L. Smith, Jr., eds. 1992).

3. Broad Delegation: Regulating Navel Oranges

1. E.g., James M. Landis, *The Administrative Process* ch. 1 (1938).

2. The direction appears in 7 U.S.C. § 602 (1988). "Euphemism" in Frank H. Easterbrook, "The Supreme Court, 1983 Term—Foreword: The Court and The Economic System," 98 *Harvard Law Review* 4, 50 n.117 (1984). On the broad discretion left to the secretary, see *Pescosolido v. Block*, 765 F.2d 827 (9th Cir. 1985).

3. 7 U.S.C. § 608c(7)(C) (1988). Although recommending quotas is not specifically mentioned in the statute, that power can be implied from the power to recommend amendments to the order, which may include quotas.

4. The provisions cited in this paragraph are from 7 U.S.C. § 608c (17), (19), (4), (9), (16) (1988).

5. For phone line, see Testimony of Douglas P. Barker, Tr. at 1314, in *In re Sequoia*, AMA Dkt. No. 907-6. For pension plan, see Office of Inspector General, *Report of Investigation: Sunkist Growers. Inc. et al.* 4-6 (January 24, 1989).

6. Lawrence Shepard, "Cartelization of the California-Arizona Orange Industry, 1934–1981," 29 *Journal of Law and Economics* 83, 89 (1986). See also General Accounting Office, *Analysis of Certain Aspects of The California-Arizona Navel Orange Marketing Order,* Appendix I, at 3 (CED-81-129) (July 2, 1981).

7. 5 U.S.C. § 553 (b), (c) (1988). Each year, NOAC invited handlers to a meeting to consider its tentative schedule of quotas for the coming marketing year. It also published notices of the meeting in newspapers read by growers. After the meeting NOAC sent its recommendations to the secretary, who adopted a tentative schedule of weekly quotas. Notice in the *Federal Register* and invitation of written comments from the public were not employed, on the theory that this policy for the year was not a binding rule.

During each week of the selling season, NOAC held meetings to consider a quota for the coming week. Handlers and growers usually were notified. Again, NOAC sent recommendations to the secretary and the secretary promulgated the weekly quotas without first publishing notice in the *Federal Register* or inviting written comments, on the theory that the schedule for the coming week had to be issued immediately.

In 1990 a federal court agreed that final weekly quotas could not be set far enough in advance to allow full notice and comment but nonetheless found that the secretary had departed further from the statutory requirements than good cause justified. See *Riverbend Farms, Inc. v. Yeutter,* No. CV-88-0098-EDP (E.D. Cal. March 22, 1990), affirmed in part and reversed in part in *Riverbend*

Farms v. Madigan, 958 F.2d. 1479 (9th Cir. 1992). While the litigation was pending, the secretary decided to treat the tentative schedule of weekly quotas for the coming year as a rulemaking. 55 *Federal Register* 50,157 (1990).

8. The Cost of Living Council is discussed in Glenn Nelson and Tom H. Robinson, "Retail and Wholesale Demand and Marketing Order Policy for Fresh Navel Oranges," 60 *American Journal of Agricultural Economics* 502, 502 (1978). "Went up to the Hill" quote in Kim Isaac Eisler, "Attack of the Killer Lawyers," *Regardie's: The Business of Washington*, April 1990, at 97, 101. See Federal Trade Commission Improvements Act of 1980, Pub. L. No. 96-252, § 20, 94 Stat. 374, 393 (1980), for restriction of FTC authority over agricultural cooperatives. Sunkist's lawyer worked through two California congressmen on the House Agriculture Committee with whom he had close ties, Tony Coelho and Charles Pashayan. Eisler, "Attack of the Killer Lawyers" at 104; telephone interview with Larry Adams, Administrative Assistant to Congressman Pashayan (November 6, 1990).

9. Breakfast meeting discussed in Greg Critser, "The Oranges of Wrath," *California Business*, June 1984, at 71, 79; quote is in Robert Lindsey, "Citrus Farmers Hold Off Reagan Plans," *New York Times*, December 12, 1983, at A24, col. 1.

10. For the role of Sunkist, see Critser, "The Oranges of Wrath" at 77-79. The bill was Pub. L. No. 98-151, § 575, 97 Stat. 964, 973 (1983) (incorporating by reference H.R. 4139, 98th Cong., 1st Sess. § 514, 129 *Cong. Rec.* H8717 (daily ed. Oct. 27, 1983)). The rider has been inserted in subsequent appropriations bills. See letter from Rep. George Miller to Secretary of Agriculture Edward Madigan, August 10, 1992 (on file with author). Miller, unlike some of his co-signers, has consistently opposed marketing orders.

11. Declaration of John Ford at 4, *Sequoia Orange Co. v. Yeutter*, No. CV-89-F-632-EDP (E.D. Cal.).

12. For the procedural history, see *Sequoia Orange Co. v. Yeutter*, 973 F.2d 752 (9th Cir. 1992). For Hanlin statement, see Declaration of John Ford at 12; for Ford quotation, see id. at 16. See also John Johnson, "Block Drops Citrus Plan; Sunkist Claims a Victory," *Sacramento Bee*, July 28, 1984, at A8; and David Hoffman, "White House Considers Scrapping a Longtime Crop Restriction," *Washington Post*, April 18, 1983, at A3.

13. The "right to review" quotation is from Press Release, "California-Arizona Navel and Valencia Orange Growers To Vote on Continuing Marketing Orders," at 5, 6 (Agricultural Marketing Service, Department of Agriculture) (March 29, 1991). The case was *Ivanhoe Citrus Association v. Handley*, 612 F. Supp. 1560 (D.D.C. 1985).

14. Pub. L. No. 100-460, § 630, 102 Stat. 2229, 2262 (1988). In addition, at Sunkist's behest, Congress requires that no such information can be released without ten days' notice to the agriculture committees in Congress, thereby giving them time to prevent its release. 7 U.S.C. § 608d (2) (1988).

15. *Cal-Almond, Inc. v. United States Department of Agriculture*, 960 F.2d 105 (9th Cir. 1992).

16. 7 C.F.R. § 907.83 (c) (1992). Alternatively, support representing two-thirds of the oranges grown by those voting is also considered sufficient.

17. For 1982 policy statement, see Department of Agriculture, *Guidelines for Fruit, Vegetable, and Specialty Crop Marketing Orders* Appendix V at 7-8 (January 25, 1982). For Sunkist's actions, see "Sunkist Affirms Grower Support for Federal Orange Marketing Order," Sunkist News Release, undated (on file with author). See Letter to Sunkist Growers from Its Chairman and President, March 26, 1991 (on file with author). For votes, see Carolyn Lochhead, "Fruit Fight: Independent Growers Challenge Agribusiness Giants," *Insight*, July 29, 1991, at 13, 19.

18. For vote, see Press Release, "California and Arizona Navel and Valencia Orange Growers Vote To Continue Their Federal Marketing Orders," at 2 (Agricultural Marketing Service, Department of Agriculture) (Aug. 21, 1991).

19. It would be a mistake to dismiss the navel orange example as unrepresentative of broad delegation to federal agencies on the theory that Congress really delegated to Sunkist. Congress did not delegate to Sunkist; the secretaries of agriculture did so as a practical matter.

20. Robert James Bidinotto, "Standing Up to the Citrus Squeeze," *Oasis*, July 27, 1987, at 34, 35.

21. Declaration of John Ford at 5.

22. See 129 *Cong. Rec.* H8719 (daily ed. Oct. 27, 1983) for remarks of Representative Roybal explaining why the Appropriations Committee had inserted the rider that prevented OMB from reviewing marketing orders.

23. Telephone interview with Larry Adams, who had been an aide to former Representative Charles Pashayan (November 6, 1990).

24. See General Accounting Office, *The Role of Marketing Orders in Establishing and Maintaining Orderly Marketing Conditions* 55-61 (RCED-85-57) (July 31, 1985); and 55 *Federal Register* 50,157 (1990).

25. The official is quoted in Ann Crittenden, "Growers' Power in Marketing under Attack," *New York Times*, March 25, 1981, at A1, col. 1. See also Editorial, "Rotten Oranges, Crude Pricing," *New York Times*, April 11, 1981, at 22, col. 1. The marketing order titularly exempts oranges given to charity at 7 C.F.R. § 907.67 (1992), but the department deemed that Pescosolido's donation did not qualify because the charity in question, the West Oakland Food Coop, paid the cost of transporting the oranges and sold them at eight cents a pound to cover its costs.

26. Shepard, 29 *Journal of Law and Economics* at 85.

4. Narrow Delegation: Regulating Air Pollution

1. The federal role was limited, for the most part, to research and to encouraging the states to regulate. The Air Pollution Control Act of 1955, Pub. L. No. 84-159, 69 Stat. 322, confined the federal role to giving advice to the states. A later statute, the Clean Air Act of 1963, Pub. L. No. 88-206, 77 Stat. 392, gave the states federal grants and also authorized the Department of Health, Education, and Welfare (HEW) to control pollution sources, albeit in narrowly defined circumstances. Automotive emissions first received federal attention in Pub. L. No. 86-493, 74 Stat. 162 (1960), which required the surgeon general to study such emissions and report the findings to Congress.

2. E. Donald Elliott, Bruce A. Ackerman, and John C. Millian, "Toward a Theory of Statutory Evolution: The Federalization of Environmental Law," 1 *Journal of Law, Economics, and Organization* 313, 330-31 (1985). The 1965 statute was the Motor Vehicle Air Pollution Control Act, Pub. L. No. 89-272, 79 Stat. 992 (1965). This statute did not preempt state regulation of auto emissions, but a 1967 statute (mentioned in the next sentence of the text) did.

3. Elliott, Ackerman, and Millian, 1 *Journal of Law, Economics, and Organization* at 331-33. Air Quality Act of 1967, Pub. L. No. 90-148, § 208, 81 Stat. 485, 501 (amending the Clean Air Act).

4. The pollution control standards promulgated by HEW required modifications in new cars that were expected to add between $18 and $45 to their cost. David R. Jones, "U.S. Sets Limits on the Amount of Car Exhaust Permissible, Effective with '68 Models," *New York Times*, March 30, 1966, at A20, col. 2. For 1967 statute, see William H. Rodgers, Jr., *Handbook on Environmental Law* 213 (1977).

5. 116 *Cong. Rec.* 42,381-82 (1970) (remarks of Sen. Muskie).

6. Ralph Nader, "Foreword" to John C. Esposito, *Vanishing Air*, at vii-ix (1970).

7. See Elliott, Ackerman, and Millian, 1 *Journal of Law, Economics, and Organization* at 333-38.

8. Clean Air Act Amendments of 1970, Pub. L. No. 91-604, 84 Stat. 1676 (hereafter, "CAA 1970"). Because of the many changes in the act since 1970, and for the sake of convenience, I will give a parallel citation, when there is one, to the United States Code. Until 1990 this was codified in the 1988 edition of Title 42; the 1990 amendments are codified in the 1990 Supplement II.

9. Citizen suits in CAA 1970 § 304 (current version at 42 U.S.C. § 7604). "Federal and State agencies would pursue" is from S. Rep. No. 1196, 91st Cong., 2d Sess. 3 (1970) (hereafter, "1970 Senate Report"). Muskie quoted in 116 *Cong. Rec.* 42,381 (1970).

10. CAA 1970 § 108(a)(1) (current version at 42 U.S.C. § 7408 (a)(1)). The five pollutants identified before enactment were sulfur oxides, particulates, carbon monoxide, hydrocarbons, and photochemical oxidants. The five mentioned in the Senate Report were fluorides, nitrogen oxides, polynuclear organic matter, lead, and odors. 1970 Senate Report at 9.

11. CAA 1970 § 109 (current version at 42 U.S.C. § 7409). The administrator was required to set two national ambient air quality standards for each pollutant: a *primary standard* to protect human health, CAA 1970 § 109(b)(1) (current version at 42 U.S.C. § 7409(b)(1)), and a *secondary standard* to protect welfare, which included impact on buildings, forests, and visibility, CAA 1970 §§ 109(b)(2), 302(h) (current versions at 42 U.S.C. §§ 7409(b)(2), 7602(h)). In referring to the national ambient air quality standards, I mean the primary standards unless I indicate otherwise.

12. CAA 1970 § 110(a)(1) (current version at 42 U.S.C. § 7410 (a)(1)).

13. The deadline specified was actually three years. CAA 1970 § 110(a)(2)(A)(i). But, when submitting the state plan, a governor might seek a two-year extension if necessary technology was not yet available and reasonable alter-

natives were used. CAA 1970 § 110(e)(1). An additional one-year extension was available after approval if, *inter alia*, the required technology was not available despite good-faith efforts. CAA 1970 § 110(f)(1). The 1970 Act provided no further extension.

14. 1970 Senate Report at 20, 4.

15. For authority to issue new source performance standards, see CAA 1970 § 111(a)-(b) (current version at 42 U.S.C. § 7411 (a)–(b)). For authority to regulate new mobile sources, see CAA 1970 § 202(a) (current version at 42 U.S.C. § 7521(a)). The administrator might also regulate fuels and their refiners. CAA 1970 § 211 (current version at 42 U.S.C. § 7545). The three pollutants specified by Congress were carbon monoxide, hydrocarbons and nitrogen oxides. CAA 1970 § 202(b)(1) (current version at 42 U.S.C. § 7521(b)(1)). See H.R. Rep. No. 490, 101st Cong., 2d Sess., pt. 1, at 280 (1990).

16. On one-year extension, see CAA 1970 § 202(b)(5), 84 Stat. 1691; 116 *Cong. Rec.* 32,904 (1970) (remarks of Sen. Muskie). On establishing ambient standards, see *Lead Industries Association Inc. v. EPA*, 647 F.2d 1130, 1150 (D.C. Cir. 1980); *Train v. Natural Resources Defense Council*, 421 U.S. 60, 64-67 (1975).

17. See, e.g., *Train v. Natural Resources Defense Council*, 421 U.S. 60 (1975).

18. 116 *Cong. Rec.* 42,386 (1970).

19. The House version passed with a lone dissenting vote, 375 to 1. 116 *Cong. Rec.* 19,244 (1970). The Senate version of the act passed unanimously, 73 to 0. Id. at 33,120. Both Senate and House agreed to the conference bill unanimously. Id. at 42,524 (House), 42,395 (Senate).

20. Quote from 1970 Senate Report at 2. See also discussion at 2-3.

21. See, e.g., *Train v. Natural Resources Defense Council*, 421 U.S. at 90-91.

22. For expectations about standards, see 1970 Senate Report at 23-25. For Los Angeles, see 38 *Federal Register* 2194, 2195 (1973). For Manhattan, see *Friends of the Earth v. EPA*, 499 F.2d 1118, 1124 (2d Cir. 1974).

23. See John Quarles, *Cleaning Up America* 200-02 (1976) (gas rationing); "Cabbies Prevent Queens Bus Test," *New York Times*, April 15, 1975, at 39, col. 1 (New York drivers), and "Express Car-Pool and Bus Test Disrupts Los Angeles Freeways," *New York Times*, March 16, 1976, at 14, col. 4 (Los Angeles drivers).

24. David Schoenbrod, "Goals Statutes or Rules Statutes: The Case of the Clean Air Act," 30 *UCLA Law Review* 740, 763-65, 770 (1983).

25. States "shall . . . adopt . . . " in CAA 1970 § 110(a)(1) (current version at 42 U.S.C. § 7410 (a)(1)). Supreme Court quote from *Train v. Natural Resources Defense Council*, 421 U.S. at 64. Statutory remedy in CAA 1970 § 110(c) (current version at 42 U.S.C. § 7410(c)).

26. For interpretation of act, see *Maryland v. EPA*, 530 F.2d 215 (4th Cir. 1975), vacated as moot sub nom. *EPA v. Brown*, 431 U.S. 99 (1977); *District of Columbia v. Train*, 521 F.2d 971 (D.C. Cir. 1975), vacated as moot sub nom. *EPA v. Brown*, 431 U.S. 99 (1977); *Brown v. EPA*, 521 F.2d 827 (9th Cir. 1975), vacated as moot, 431 U.S. 99 (1977). See also *United States v. Ohio Department of Highway Safety*, 635 F.2d 1195 (6th Cir. 1980), cert. denied, 451 U.S. 949 (1981). Contra *Pennsylvania v. EPA*, 500 F.2d 246 (3d Cir. 1974). For EPA's lack of political mandate and resources, see Quarles, *Cleaning Up America* at 252.

27. Quote is from CAA 1970 § 109(b)(1) (current version at 42 U.S.C. § 7409(b)(1)). For chemicals in food, see *Toxic Hazards in Food* 14-16 (D.M. Conning and A.B.G. Lansdown eds. 1983). Some level of pollution is, after all, absolutely inevitable, because *pollution* is only a loaded word for emissions to the air. It is physically impossible to cook a meal or heat a home without generating some emissions, directly or indirectly.

The D.C. Circuit found that the administrator may consider cost in deciding what margin of safety should be built into the emission standards for hazardous air pollutants. *Natural Resources Defense Council v. U.S.E.P.A.*, 824 F.2d 1146 (D.C. Cir. 1987).

28. *Clean Air Act Amendments of 1977: Hearing Before the Subcommittee on Environmental Pollution of the Senate Committee on Environment and Public Works*, 95th Cong., 1st Sess., pt. 3, at 8 (1977).

29. Quotes from CAA 1970 § 110(a)(2)(E), 84 Stat. 1681. For silence on dividing cleanup burden, see Statement of Richard E. Ayres, Senior Attorney, Natural Resources Defense Council, and Chairman, National Clean Air Coalition, in *Clean Air Act Reauthorization: Hearing on H.R. 144, 1470, 2586, 2909, 3030, and 3211 Before the Subcommittee on Energy and Power of the House Committee on Energy and Commerce*, 101st Cong., 1st Sess., pt. 1, at 471 (1989).

30. See letter from Russell E. Train, EPA Administrator, to Carl T. Albert, Speaker of the House of Representatives, March 22, 1974, H.R. Rep. No. 1013, 93d Cong., 2d Sess. 33, reprinted in 1974 *U.S. Code Congressional and Administrative News* 3281, 3300. See also D. Bruce La Pierre, "Technology-Forcing and Federal Environmental Protection Statutes," 62 *Iowa Law Review* 771, 774 (1977). In Chapter 8 I discuss how the 1990 Clean Air Act approaches this problem in its acid rain provisions.

31. See generally Richard J. Lazarus, "The Neglected Question of Congressional Oversight of EPA: *Ouis Custodiet Ipsos Custodes* (Who Shall Watch the Watchers Themselves)?" 54 *Law and Contemporary Problems* 205 (Autumn 1991); and David Clarke, "Point of Darkness," 9 *Environmental Forum* 28, 33 (Jan./Feb. 1992).

32. Joint Appendix, at 2717-21, *Lead Industries Association v. EPA*, 647 F.2d 1130 (D.C. Cir. 1980).

33. Only one legislator expressed any support for enforcing the state's strategy; Representative Jonathan Bingham endorsed tolls on all bridges, except those connected to his district. Letter to the Editor, *New York Times*, March 8, 1977, at L30, col. 3.

34. Quarles, in *Cleaning Up America*, documents the importance of White House pressure on EPA. There were instances during the Carter administration as well of the White House apparently requiring EPA personnel to put political loyalty above statutory duty.

35. CAA 1970 § 113(a)(4) (current version at 42 U.S.C. § 7413(a)(4)). See *Union Electric Co. v. EPA*, 427 U.S. 246, 264-69 (1976).

36. Citizens could petition for a revision of the state implementation plan on the basis that subsequent events had made it inadequate to attain the ambient air standards, CAA 1970 § 110(a)(2)(H) (current version at 42 U.S.C. §

7410(a)(2)(H)), but this remedy was worth little in practice because of the difficulties of proving an existing plan's inadequacy and the years required to produce results.

37. CAA 1970 § 304 (current version at 42 U.S.C. § 7604).

38. The gas rationing plan had been affirmed by the court of appeals. See *City of Santa Rosa v. United States EPA*, 534 F.2d 150 (9th Cir. 1976). The EPA acknowledged that its withdrawal of the regulations was without statutory authority. 41 *Federal Register* 45,565 (1976). However, to avoid making their cause look silly, environmental groups did not try to force EPA to implement the plan. For refusal to block the building of new sources, see 44 *Federal Register* 3274 (1979). One example of congressional interference with EPA is the Energy Supply and Environmental Coordination Act of 1974, Pub. L. No. 93-319, § 4, 88 Stat. 246, 256-58 (current version at 42 U.S.C. § 7410(c)(2)) which, among other things, forbids the administrator from imposing parking surcharges and allowed the suspension of limits on parking supply.

39. S. Rep. No. 228, 101st Cong., 1st Sess. 62-63 (1989) (hereafter, "1989 Senate Report").

40. "EPA Internal Memorandum from Robert Kenney to Richard G. Kozlowski on Lead Ambient Air Quality," reported in *Washington Post*, July 11, 1982, at A6, col. 1, noted that ambient lead levels often were underestimated because monitors were located too high, too far or upwind from roadways, or in areas with little traffic. See also Deirdre Carmody, "City's Air Cleaner Than in 1960's but Pollution Level Is Unknown," *New York Times*, May 26, 1981, at Al, col. 1; and *National Commission on Air Quality, To Breathe Clean Air* 74, 94 (1981) (hereafter, "*National Commission*").

41. William F. Pedersen, Jr., "Why the Clean Air Act Works Badly," 129 *University of Pennsylvania Law Review* 1059, 1080 n.70 (1981).

42. A commission-sponsored analysis answered the question of how much of a particular state plan's emission reductions was likely to be achieved as follows: "about one-third is a definite yes; another one-third is a definite no; and the final third is possible." Quoted in Schechter and Plakins, "South Coast Air Quality Management Plan: Implementation and Enforcement Issues" in 3 *National Commission on Air Quality Los Angeles Regional Study—SIP Process Review* 4-53 (Energy and Environmental Analysis, Inc. 1980), which suggested that only half the predicted reduction would be realized. See also *National Commission* at 117.

43. Muskie quoted in 123 *Cong. Rec.* 18,463 (1977); H.R. Rep. No. 294, 95th Cong., 1st Sess. 106-10 (1977). For presidential directives, see e.g., Executive Order No. 12,044, 3 C.F.R. 152 (1979) (President Carter); and Executive Order No. 12,291, 3 C.F.R. 127 (1982) (President Reagan).

44. List requirement in 1970 CAA § 112 (current version at 42 U.S.C. § 7412). For knowledge of harmful pollutants, see testimony of David D. Doniger, Senior Attorney, Natural Resources Defense Council, on behalf of the National Clean Air Coalition, in *Clean Air Act Amendments of 1989: Hearing on S. 816 and S. 196 before the Subcommittee on Environmental Protection of the Senate Committee on Environment and Public Works*, 101st Cong., 1st Sess. 182 (1989). The

Clean Air Amendments of 1990, Pub. L. No. 101–549, 104 Stat. 2399 (hereafter, "CAA 1990"), require that 189 hazardous pollutants be listed. CAA 1990 § 112 (b)(l) (current version at 42 U.S.C. § 7412 (b)(l)). See H.R. Rep. No. 490, 101st Cong., 2d Sess., pt. 1, at 317 and n.5 (1990), citing EPA, Office of Air Radiation, "Updated Source-Specific Cancer Risk Information," Air Toxics Exposure and Risk Information System (ATERIS). In a February 6, 1990 letter to the House Committee on Energy and Commerce, EPA emphasized that these data had "weaknesses" and cautioned against "misinterpretation."

45. Clean Air Act Amendments of 1977, Pub. L. No. 95-95, § 172, 91 Stat. 685, 746 (hereafter, "CAA 1977").

46. An example of the legislative claims: "The committee intends to demonstrate its adherence to the primary goal of reaching healthful levels of air quality by a date certain." H.R. Rep. No. 294, 95th Cong., 1st Sess. 64 (1977). If a state did not submit a plan that EPA approved, no major stationary source could be located in the part of the state to which the plan applied, CAA 1977 § 172(a)(1), 91 Stat. 746, and the state could become ineligible for certain federal grants, CAA 1977 § 176(a), 91 Stat. 749. On limiting sanction authority, see, e.g., "EPA Outlines Policy To Avert Sanctions for Nonapproval of SIPs," 10 *Environment Reporter* (Bureau of National Affairs) (hereafter, "BNA") 225 (June 15, 1979); "EPA To Interpret Liberally Policy for 1982 State Implementation Plans," 12 *Environment Reporter* (BNA) 575, 575-76 (Sept. 11, 1981). See also R. Shep Melnick, "Pollution Deadlines and the Coalition for Failure," in *Environmental Politics: Public Costs, Private Rewards* ch. 5 (Michael S. Greve and Fred L. Smith, Jr., eds. 1992).

47. Quote from *National Commission* at 17. Methods to avoid sanctioning are discussed id. at 16-17.

48. See Philip Shabecoff, "Mrs. Gorsuch as a Crusading Tiger? Critics Wonder Why," *New York Times*, December 26, 1982, sec. 4, at 14, col. 1.

49. 1989 Senate Report at 11.

50. For example, Congress prescribed deadlines for ozone ranging from three to twenty years from the date of the plan's adoption, CAA 1990 § 181(a)(1) (current version at 42 U.S.C. § 7511(a)(1)).

51. CAA 1990 §§ 171-192 (current version at 42 U.S.C. §§ 7501- 7514a).

52. CAA 1990 § 202 (current version at 42 U.S.C. § 7521).

53. There were no challenges to the primary standards and only one to the secondary standards. See *Kennecott Copper Corp. v. EPA*, 462 F.2d 846 (D.C. Cir. 1972).

54. Determining the rules of conduct on the basis of this act would have required interpolating the complex requirements laid out in the text of the act with information such as the levels at which EPA was expected to set ambient air standards, the ambient air levels in various locales, the options for reducing emissions, and predictions about the options the states would choose. See Elliott, Ackerman, and Millian, 1 *Journal of Law, Economics, and Organization* at 320.

55. Louis L. Jaffe, "The Illusion of the Ideal Administration," 86 *Harvard Law Review* 1183, 1198 (1973). The sponsors of the 1970 act expressed similar views. See 116 *Cong. Rec.* 32,901 and 42,381 (1970) (remarks of Sen. Muskie);

and 1970 Senate Report at 3, 12. Some other legal experts shared Jaffe's view. See, e.g., Colin S. Diver, "Policymaking Paradigms in Administrative Law," 95 *Harvard Law Review* 393, 413 (1981).

56. 1970 Senate Report at 1-3 and 9-11.

57. See, e.g., 116 *Cong. Rec.* 33,073-96 (1970). The only close votes on the act involved two proposed amendments regarding a one-year extension to the deadline for reaching the 90-percent reduction. Id. at 33,088 (on Sen. Gurney's amendment, for: 22, against: 57); id. at 33,089 (on Sen. Dole's amendment, for: 32, against: 43).

58. William H. Rodgers, Jr., "The Lesson of the Red Squirrel: Consensus and Betrayal in the Environmental Statutes," 5 *Journal of Contemporary Health Law and Policy* 161, 166-69 (1989). On the general propensity of Congress to salve the public's environmental concerns by placing impossible demands on EPA, see Richard J. Lazarus, "The Tragedy of Distrust in the Implementation of Federal Environmental Law," 54 *Law and Contemporary Problems* 311 (Autumn 1991); John P. Dwyer, "The Pathology of Symbolic Legislation," 17 *Ecology Law Quarterly* 233 (1990); and James A. Henderson, Jr., and Richard N. Pearson, "Implementing Federal Environmental Policies: The Limits of Aspirational Commands," 78 *Columbia Law Review* 1429 (1978).

59. Bruce A. Ackerman and William T. Hassler, "Beyond the New Deal: Coal and the Clean Air Act," 89 *Yale Law Journal* 1466, 1568 (1980).

60. Ackerman and Hassler themselves acknowledge that EPA "would have found a way to have its computers declare that its policies had saved far more" lives than required in the formula. Id. at 1569. They argue that their approach is correct because Congress would have to face the right question—not whether to protect health, welfare, and other values, but what priority to put on those goals. Id. at 1569-70. Unfortunately, the numerical component of their approach leaves Congress with no way to provide a coherent response to that question. On exposure to saccharin, see William D. Ruckelshaus, "Risk in a Free Society," 14 *Environmental Law Reporter* 10,190 (May 1984).

61. *National Commission* at 10.

62. A New York Times/CBS News poll in 1990 reported that 74 percent of the 1,515 adults questioned believed that requirements and standards for protecting the environment cannot be too high, and that environmental improvement must be made without regard to cost; in 1981, only 45 percent had held that opinion. Richard L. Berke, "Oratory of Environmentalism Becomes the Sound of Politics," *New York Times*, April 17, 1990, at A1, col. 1.

63. On blaming others for pollution, see 116 *Cong. Rec.* 32,901 (1970) (remarks of Sen. Muskie). For Mitchell's remarks, see *Environmental Policy Weekly Bulletin*, Jan. 29, 1990, at A3.

64. Congress did of course enact one law in the 1970 and 1977 acts, the limit on emissions from new cars. Some economists argue that less strict limits would have produced nearly the same benefits at far less cost. See, e.g., Robert W. Crandall et al., *Regulating the Automobile* 109-16 (1986). But the public's general perception that Congress refused to make the hard choices may have galvanized legislators to make the one law they enacted unnecessarily tough.

Being tough on new-car emissions was politically easier than being tough on other sources because the public tends to perceive the costs as falling on the auto manufacturers rather than on consumers. On California referendum, see Jessica Mathews, "The Big, the Green, the Political," *Washington Post*, November 16, 1990, at A19. On cost of CAA 1990, see, e.g., Arnold W. Reitze, Jr., "Overview and Critique: A Century of Air Pollution Control Law: What's Worked; What's Failed; What Might Work," 21 *Environmental Law* 1549, 1550 (1991).

65. E.g., *National Commission* at 15.

66. Schoenbrod, 30 *UCLA Law Review* at 745; see also Elliott, Ackerman and Millian, 1 *Journal of Law, Economics, and Organization* at 332.

67. *Air Pollution—1970, part I: Hearings before the Subcommittee on Air and Water Pollution of the Senate Committee on Public Works*, 91st Cong., 2d Sess. 129-30 (1970).

68. See, e.g., "Markup of Toxic Substances Bill Starts in House Commerce Committee," 7 *Environment Reporter* (BNA) 196, 196-97 (June 4, 1976); "Chemical Company Announces Support of Toxic Substances Control Measure," 5 *Environment Reporter* (BNA) 1730, 1730-31 (March 7, 1975); Doug Bandow, *The Politics of Plunder* 213–15 (1990).

69. *National Commission* at 4.

70. Proposals: 47 *Federal Register* 7812 (1982); 47 *Federal Register* 7814 (1982); 47 *Federal Register* 38,078 (1982); 48 *Federal Register* 13,428 (1983); 49 *Federal Register* 31,032 (1984); 50 *Federal Register* 718 (1985); 51 *Federal Register* 25,253 (1986). Promulgated amendments: 41 *Federal Register* 42,675 (1976); 44 *Federal Register* 46,275 (1979); 44 *Federal Register* 53,144 (1979); 45 *Federal Register* 55,134 (1980); 47 *Federal Register* 49,322 (1982); 48 *Federal Register* 5724 (1983); 48 *Federal Register* 50,482 (1983); 50 *Federal Register* 9386 (1985); 50 *Federal Register* 13,116 (1985); 50 *Federal Register* 25,710 (1985).

71. Quote is from statement of Dr. Roger Cortesi, in a transcript of a meeting of the Science Advisory Board panel on photo-chemical oxidants, at 1-135 (contained in EPA docket on ozone standard).

72. "A huge number" is from Douglas Costle, EPA Administrator, "Remarks at the Meeting of the Air Pollution Control Association" in Montreal, Canada at 19 (June 23, 1980). "Really silly" is from Deirdre Carmody, "City's Air Cleaner Than in 1960's but Pollution Level Is Unknown," *New York Times*, May 26, 1981, at A1, col. 1 (quoting Dr. Edward Ferrand). "Modeling is becoming elevated" is from Costle, "Remarks" at 10. Uncertainty is present at each of the many steps in setting the ambient air quality standards. For example, determining the health effects of lead at given ambient concentrations depends upon a number of factors, such as how much lead a person breathes in or ingests at given ambient concentrations, how much of that lead is excreted or exhaled versus being absorbed into the body, what portion of that lead is taken into the blood, the dose-response relationship between lead in the blood and certain changes in body chemistry, the dose-response relationship between these changes in body chemistry and the ability of the individual to function normally, and so on.

73. For Massachusetts, see 46 *Federal Register* 40,190 (1981).

74. The EPA did the same—stating many different limits—when it imposed a plan on a state, because its power was limited to ensuring compliance with the ambient standard. Schoenbrod, 30 *UCLA Law Review* at 764-65.

75. Pedersen, 129 *University of Pennsylvania Law Review* at 1078-79 and n.66.

76. As of 1981, Florida had been waiting since 1974 for EPA action on nineteen proposed revisions. *National Commission* at 101-02. For prosecution, see *General Motors Corp. v. United States*, 496 U.S. 530 (1990).

77. *United States v. Apache Powder Co.*, Civ. No. 78-058 (D. Ariz. November 21, 1978).

78. See Elliott, Ackerman, and Millian, 1 *Journal of Law, Economics, and Organization* at 336; Melnick, "Pollution Deadlines and the Coalition for Failure," in *Environmental Politics* at 94.

79. For additional instructions, see, e.g., CAA 1977 §§ 109(d), 111(f), 122 (current versions at 42 U.S.C. §§ 7409(d), 7411(f), 7422). Requirement to publish is in CAA 1977 § 110(g)(1) (current version at 42 U.S.C. § 7410(h)). For characterization of the 1979 plan revision as unworkable, see Pedersen, 129 *University of Pennsylvania Law Review* at 1082. *National Commission* quote is in *National Commission* at 14.

80. Lazarus, "The Tragedy of Distrust," 54 *Law and Contemporary Problems* at 325.

81. Amended complaint in *Waxman v. Reilly*, Civ. No. 92-1320 HHG (D.D.C.).

82. Terry M. Moe, "The Politics of Bureaucratic Structure" in *Can the Government Govern?* 267 (John E. Chubb and Paul E. Peterson eds. 1989).

5. How Delegation Changes the Politics of Lawmaking

1. For capture, see e.g., *The Monopoly Makers* (Mark J. Green ed. 1973). The capture theories have been criticized as simplistic. E.g., Kay Lehman Schlozman and John T. Tierney, *Organized Interests and American Democracy* 276-78, 339-46 (1986). For subcommittees, see, e.g., David R. Mayhew, *Congress: The Electoral Connection* 135 (1974). Mayhew argues that Congress has considerable influence over how agencies use their delegated power. Barry R. Weingast and Mark J. Moran, among others, have pressed the notion of congressional dominance in more absolute terms. See, e.g., Weingast and Moran, "Bureaucratic Discretion or Congressional Control? Regulatory Policymaking by the Federal Trade Commission," 91 *Journal of Political Economy* 765, 768-70 (1983). In turn, their work has received extensive criticism. E.g., James Q. Wilson, *Bureaucracy: What Government Agencies Do and Why They Do It* 254-56 (1989); Terry M. Moe, "An Assessment of the Positive Theory of 'Congressional Dominance,'" 12 *Legislative Studies Quarterly* 475 (1987). D. Roderick Kiewiet and Mathew D. McCubbins have shown that in delegating Congress does not abdicate power, but rather controls the exercise of power in indirect ways. Kiewiet and McCubbins, *The Logic of Delegation: Congressional Parties and the Appropriations Process* 3, 235-37 (1991). For agencies as interest groups, see, e.g., Robert A. Dahl, *Democracy and Its Critics* 338 (1989).

2. See, e.g., *The Politics of Regulation* (James Q. Wilson ed. 1980); and Robert B. Reich, Review of *The Politics of Regulation* in *New Republic* at 36, 37 (June 14, 1980).

3. Morris P. Fiorina, *Congress: Keystone of the Washington Establishment* 65-66 (1977). Fiorina attributes the term *subgovernment* to Douglas Cater.

4. See, e.g., John Herbers, "Government Power Poised for a Grand Re-alignment," *New York Times*, June 26, 1983, sec. 4, at 1, col. 4.

5. Jonathan Rauch, "Hidden in the Grocery Bag," 19 *National Journal* 2479, 2482 (October 3, 1987).

6. For interests of citizens' groups, see *Environmental Politics: Public Costs, Private Rewards* ch. 1, 4, 5, 6 (Michael S. Greve and Fred L. Smith, Jr., eds. 1992). For alliances, see, e.g., id. at ch. 2, 3, 4, 8; and Bruce A. Ackerman and William T. Hassler, "Beyond the New Deal: Coal and the Clean Air Act," 89 *Yale Law Journal* 1466 (1980). For new metaphors, see Hugo Heclo, *A Government of Strangers: Executive Politics in Washington* 110–12 (1977).

7. Mayhew, *Congress: The Electoral Connection* at 132, 134-35. Mayhew is seeking to explain symbolic legislative action, in which category he includes delegation.

8. For a recent discussion of the literature, see R. Douglas Arnold, *The Logic of Congressional Action* (1990).

9. Jerry Mashaw at one point contended that there is little evidence that legislators act in a self-serving way. See Mashaw, "Prodelegation: Why Administrators Should Make Political Decisions," 1 *Journal of Law, Economics, and Organization* 81, 89 (1985). I disagree, and marshall some of the available evidence in this section. Mashaw since has taken a more agnostic position about self-interest on the part of legislators. Mashaw, "The Economics of Politics and the Understanding of Public Law," 65 *Chicago-Kent Law Review* 123, 143-49 (1989).

10. Alan Ehrenhalt, *The United States of Ambition: Politicians, Power, and the Pursuit of Office* 230-31 (1991). See also, Chuck Alston, "If Money Talks, Mr. Smith Won't Go to Washington," 48 *Congressional Quarterly* 3756 (November 3, 1990).

11. Hedrick Smith, *The Power Game: How Washington Works* 131 (1988). See also, e.g., Ehrenhalt, *United States of Ambition* at 235.

12. See Walter Gellhorn, *When Americans Complain: Governmental Grievance Procedures* 77-86 (1966).

13. Even under the amendment prohibiting retention of campaign funds, until 1993 legislators in office as of January 8, 1980, could still convert accrued campaign contributions to their personal use upon retirement. Ethics Reform Act of 1989, Pub. L. No. 101-194, § 504(b), 103 Stat. 1716, 1755 (codified at 2 U.S.C. § 439a (1989 Supp. I)). Honoraria are disallowed by § 1101(b), 103 Stat. 1782 (codified at 2 U.S.C. § 31-1 (1989 Supp. I)) (senators); and § 601(a), 103 Stat. 1760 (codified at 5 U.S.C. app. § 501(b) (1989 Supp. I)) (representatives). For use of campaign funds for personal expenses, see Sara Fritz and Dwight Morris, *Handbook of Campaign Spending: Money in the 1990 Congressional Races* ch. 3 (1992); and Brooks Jackson, "Congressmen Charge All Kinds

of Things to Campaign Chests," *Wall Street Journal*, December 3, 1985, at 1. They also may accept trips paid for by corporations and other private interests; House members take two thousand such trips per year. Karen De Witt, "Consumer Group Criticizes Travel by House Members," *New York Times*, September 13, 1991, at A16, col. 5.

14. Cranston quote is from Jill Abramson, "Keating Five Hearings Depict a Senate Marred by Money, Staff Power and a Lack of Courtesy," *Wall Street Journal*, November 27, 1990, at A18, col. 1. His fundraiser's statement is from Richard L. Berke, "Aide Defends Cranston but Talks of 'Link' to Gifts from Keating," *New York Times*, December 4, 1990, at B14, col. 2. Proxmire is quoted in Editorial, *Wall Street Journal*, December 6, 1990, at A18, col. 1

15. My assumption that legislators care significantly about looking good is a less restrictive variation upon the assumption of many "public-choice" theorists that legislators' only goal is reelection. Public-choice theory is controversial, but my approach differs from it in ways that should skirt much of that controversy. See note 23 infra.

16. Mayhew, *Congress: The Electoral Connection* at 32-37.

17. Ehrenhalt, *United States of Ambition* at 242; Richardson quoted in Smith, *Power Game* at 95.

18. Thomas Maeder, "Wounded Healers," *Atlantic Monthly*, January 1989, at 37. Harold Lasswell said much the same of "political types" who seek power out of "private motives displaced on public objects rationalized in terms of public interest." Harold D. Lasswell, *Power and Personality* 38 (1948).

19. Smith, *Power Game* at 107-13. The Founding Fathers were plainly right to see the desire of politicians for fame and a good reputation as a passion rather than a virtue. Douglass Adair, "Fame and the Founding Fathers" in the book of the same name (Trevor Colbourn ed. 1974).

20. Veronica Geng, *Partners* (1984).

21. Julie Johnson, "Harried Lawmakers Find Congress 'Too Chaotic,'" *New York Times*, January 13, 1988, at A15, col. 1.

22. Judith Martin, "No One Stays Clean in Washington," *New York Times* (Book Review), January 1, 1989, sec. 7, at 1, col. 1; Ward Just, *Jack Gance* 183 (1989).

23. Morris P. Fiorina, "Legislative Choice of Regulatory Forms: Legal Process or Administrative Process?" 39 *Public Choice* 33 (1982); Fiorina, "Group Concentration and the Delegation of Legislative Authority," in *Regulatory Policy and the Social Sciences* 175 (Roger G. Noll ed. 1985). Michael T. Hayes, *Lobbyists and Legislators: A Theory of Political Markets* (1981) reaches similar results.

Fiorina's model employs standard assumptions of public-choice theory, which uses the techniques of economics to analyze political decisions. See, e.g., James M. Buchanan and Gordon Tullock, *The Calculus of Consent: Logical Foundations of Constitutional Democracy* (1962). For helping to launch public-choice theory, James Buchanan received a Nobel Prize in economics. The theory assumes that legislators care only about reelection. Some scholars argue that it is incorrect to assume that legislators care about reelection only, that they clearly have other objectives. See, e.g., Steven Kelman, "'Public Choice' and Public Spirit," 87 *Public Interest* 80 (Spring 1987); Daniel A. Farber, "Democracy and Disgust: Reflections on Public Choice," 65 *Chicago-Kent Law Review* 161 (1989). Although sophisticated public-choice theorists acknowledge that their assumption simplifies reality, they argue that it leads to important theoretical hypotheses, which can then be tested empirically. Mayhew, *Congress: The Electoral Connection* at 5-6.

Two thoughtful critics of public-choice theory, Daniel A. Farber and Philip P. Frickey, conclude that it is useful if applied in a qualified way. Farber and Frickey, *Law and Public Choice: A Critical Introduction* 33 (1991). My adaption of Fiorina's model accordingly qualifies the theory's assumptions in a number of ways. Fiorina assumes that the typical legislator has only one goal, reelection, and to that end seeks to make constituents think that he has maximized their economic interests. I modify Fiorina's assumption, stipulating instead that legislators tend to care about looking good to their constituents. I also modify Fiorina's definition of benefits and costs to constituents, encompassing their noneconomic as well as economic interests.

My assumptions are consistent with a more rounded view of legislators' objectives. Richard F. Fenno, Jr., contends, I think correctly, that legislators care about power and prestige within Congress, making good public policy, and moving into higher political office as well as getting reelected. Fenno, *Congressmen in Committees* (1973). Looking good to the public is important to some of these other goals. Achieving influence within Congress, for example, can require building a home base safe enough that one can concentrate on successfully helping other legislators look good and on national affairs. Ehrenhalt, *United States of Ambition* at 243. Attaining higher office requires keeping up appearances with a broader constituency.

Steven Kelman cites instances in which he believes that legislators opted for the public's interest over what was politically expedient at the time. Kelman, 87 *Public Interest* at 86-87. Such examples would not contradict my assumption, although they would contradict the assumption that reelection is the only goal of politicians. R. Douglas Arnold argues convincingly, however, that such supposed instances of altruistic legislative behavior are explicable in terms of the legislator's self-interest, because legislators are concerned not only with current public opinion but also future public opinion and, in particular, worry that a future campaign opponent could blame them for a public-policy disaster. Arnold, *Logic of Congressional Action* at 10-11.

Kelman maintains that it is not only inaccurate but also morally objectionable to assume that lawmakers are entirely self-interested: "The cynicism of journalists—and even the writings of professors—can decrease public spirit simply by describing what they claim to be its absence. Cynics are therefore in the business of making prophecies that threaten to become self-fulfilling." Kelman, 87 *Public Interest* at 94. But to blame journalists and professors for public cynicism about government is to blame the messenger for the bad news, old as officialdom itself, that officials are not entirely virtuous and also to fail to take that bad news into account. Cf. Mashaw, 65 *Chicago-Kent Law Review* at 141.

24. A mathematical description, simplified from that presented in Fiorina, "Group Concentration," in *Regulatory Policy* at 178–80, is this: The legislator will vote for the project if $pb > qc$, where b is the benefit of the project, c is its cost, p is the probability that constituents will perceive the government as the source of the benefits, and q is the probability that constituents will perceive the government as the source of the costs.

25. Id. at 180-81.

26. Id. at 188-89. He actually compares his categories of broad delegation and narrow delegation. He could as well have talked of delegation and no delegation, depending on how one defines delegation.

27. Arnold, *Logic of Congressional Action* at 101 (emphasis in original). See also Peter H. Aranson, Ernest Gellhorn, and Glen O. Robinson, "A Theory of Legislative Delegation," 68 *Cornell Law Review* 1, 55-62 (1982).

28. Fiorina, "Group Concentration," in *Regulatory Policy* at 188. Again, to simplify Fiorina's formula, the legislator will prefer to delegate if $a_d pb - s_d qc > a_n pb - s_n qc$ where a_d is the probability that constituents will credit the legislator for benefits under a statute that delegates, s_d is the probability that constituents will blame the legislator for costs under a statute that delegates, a_n is the probability that constituents will credit the legislator for benefits under a statute that does not delegate, and s_n is the probability that constituents will blame the legislator for costs under a statute that does not delegate.

29. Id. at 189.

30. E. Donald Elliott, Bruce A. Ackerman, and John C. Millian, "Toward a Theory of Statutory Evolution: The Federalization of Environmental Law," 1 *Journal of Law, Economics, and Organization* 313, 330 (1985). Elmer E. Schattschneider, in *Politics, Pressures and the Tariff: A Study of Free Private Enterprise in Pressure Politics, as Shown in the 1929–1930 Revision of the Tariff* 159–60 (1935), offered a similar explanation of why New York importers proved so impotent in trying to stop the disastrous Smoot-Hawley Tariff. This explanation also accords with the 1989 legislation to prohibit smoking on airline flights. Permanent Prohibition Against Smoking on Scheduled Airline Flights, Pub. L. 101-164, § 335, 103 Stat. 1098 (1989) (codified at 49 U.S.C. § 1374(d) (1990 Supp. II)).

31. That is, if $a_n - a_d$ is large, or if $s_n - s_d$ is small.

32. Without delegation, that is, s_n and q are small. With delegation, $a_n - a_d$ is large.

33. Elliott, Ackerman, and Millian raise this as a possibility. 1 *Journal of Law, Economics, and Organization* at 320.

34. Fiorina, "Group Concentration," in *Regulatory Policy* at 187.

35. Mayhew, *Congress: The Electoral Connection* at 127-30, quote at 134.

36. Quoted in Janet Bass, "Florio: Congress Is a Frustrating Place to Work," *UPI*, November 29, 1989.

37. Fiorina assumes a different set of probabilities for each legislator, but he does not discuss the legislators' capacity to affect those probabilities.

38. In Fiorina's mathematical notation, a legislator will seek to increase a_d and s_d if $pb - qc$ is positive and decrease them if it is negative. In identifying

themselves with a beneficial agency action, legislators increase a_d and s_d. In detaching themselves from harmful actions, legislators decrease a_d and s_d.

39. Here, the legislator tries to have a positive a_d and a negative s_d.

40. In these cases, delegation allows the legislator to vary the a_d and s_d to suit the constituent. For letters to constituents, see Smith, *Power Game* at 146-50. Quote is from Aranson, Gellhorn, and Robinson, 68 *Cornell Law Review* at 58.

41. Quoted in Richard J. Lazarus, "The Neglected Question of Congressional Oversight of EPA: *Quis Custodiet Ipsos Custodes* (Who Shall Watch the Watchers Themselves)?" 54 *Law and Contemporary Problems* 205, 214 n.47 (Autumn 1991).

42. Fiorina shows that delegation is more likely to allow Congress to avoid a sin of omission (that is, avoid neglecting to enact a beneficial law) than to prompt it to commit a sin of commission (that is, prompt it to enact a harmful law) *if* delegation shifts blame for costs and credit for benefits proportionally, without changing anything else. However, delegation is likely to shift costs that concentrated interests perceive less than proportionally because such interests tend to be sophisticated. Moreover, delegation is likely to do more than shift blame and credit (that is, it is likely to change the action that government takes), as I have shown.

43. These theories will be discussed in Chapters 7, 8, and 9.

44. Mayhew, *Congress: The Electoral Connection* at 5.

45. Bruce Cain, John Ferejohn, and Morris Fiorina, *The Personal Vote: Constituency Service and Electoral Independence* 206 (1987). The authors, however, note a trend for British legislators to emulate techniques used in the United States Congress that weaken the link between their personal electoral fates and those of their party.

46. For benefits of doing casework, see Mayhew, *Congress: The Electoral Connection* at 54-55, 57-58; and John R. Johannes, *To Serve the People: Congress and Constituency Service* (1984). Pattison is quoted in John H. Fund, "Perot Voters Can Still Vote to Fix the System," *Wall Street Journal*, July 21, 1992, at A12, col. 3. In order to get campaign contributions or other contributions in exchange for interceding with an agency, the legislator need not even wait for the constituent to ask for help: "Congressmen can also threaten adverse agency actions against 'uncooperative' constituents. Imposing costs . . . by threatened agency action is certainly far easier than doing so by statute." Aranson, Gellhorn, and Robinson, 68 *Cornell Law Review* at 58-59. See also Fred S. McChesney, "Regulation, Taxes, and Political Extortion," in *Regulation and the Reagan Era: Politics, Bureaucracy and the Public Interest* 223 (Roger E. Meiners and Bruce Yandle eds. 1989).

47. Richard L. Doernberg and Fred S. McChesney, "On the Accelerating Rate and Decreasing Durability of Tax Reform," 71 *Minnesota Law Review* 913, 933-34 (1987) ("Legislators can and do propose legislation, sometimes referred to as 'milker bills' or 'juice bills,' intended to squeeze payments from the potentially affected parties, rather than actually to be enacted into law.").

48. See, e.g., Chuck Alston, "As Clean-Air Bill Took Off, So Did PAC Donations," 48 *Congressional Quarterly* 811 (March 17, 1990).

49. "Memorandum for Certain Department and Agency Heads," 28 *Weekly Compilation of Presidential Documents* 232 (Jan. 28, 1992; extended April 29, 1992); and Kirk Victor, "Regulatory Diet," *Government Executive*, April, 1992.

50. In response to a request for instances of President Bush's asserting concern for separation of powers by opposing delegation of legislative powers, I received a stack of statements made by the president in signing legislation, all of which opposed congressional encroachments on executive powers. Letter from Nelson Lund, Associate Counsel to the President, to David Schoenbrod, Nov. 19, 1990 (on file with author). As for President Reagan, see Schoenbrod, "How the Reagan Administration Trivialized Separation of Powers (and Shot Itself in the Foot)," 57 *George Washington Law Review* 459, 460-61 (1989).

6. Delegation Weakens Democracy

1. Of course, supermajorities in Congress can override a presidential veto.

2. Robert A. Dahl, *Democracy and Its Critics* 337 (1989). Dahl was speaking of delegation as well as of other means by which policy elites get power.

3. 276 U.S. 394, 409 (1928).

4. Richard B. Stewart, "The Reformation of American Administrative Law," 88 *Harvard Law Review* 1667, 1684 (1975).

5. For a "standard," see, e.g., *United States v. Rock Royal Co-operative, Inc.*, 307 U.S. 533, 574 (1939); and *A.L.A. Schechter Poultry Corp. v. United States*, 295 U.S. 495, 530 (1935). For a "rule of conduct," see, e.g., *Amalgamated Meat Cutters v. Connally*, 337 F. Supp. 737, 746 (D.D.C. 1971) (three-judge panel). For the possible implication that the statute must state the law, see *Yakus v. United States*, 321 U.S. 414, 424-25 (1944); and *Panama Refining Co. v. Ryan*, 293 U.S. 388, 421 (1935).

6. E.g., *National Broadcasting Co. v. United States*, 319 U.S. 190, 216-17 (1943); *New York Central Securities Corp. v. United States*, 287 U.S. 12, 24-25 (1932).

7. *Mistretta v. United States*, 488 U.S. 361 (1989).

8. Robert B. Reich, Book Review of *The Politics of Regulation* (James Q. Wilson ed., 1980), in *New Republic* at 36, 37 (June 14, 1980).

9. E.g., *Yakus*, 321 U.S. at 425-26. See also *Amalgamated Meat Cutters*, 337 F. Supp. at 759; Louis L. Jaffe, "An Essay on Delegation of Legislative Power" (pts. I and II), 47 *Columbia Law Review* 359 and 561, at 360, 580 (1947).

10. Agencies have less political capacity: See Louis L. Jaffe, "The Illusion of the Ideal Administration," 86 *Harvard Law Review* 1183, 1188-91 (1973); Paul Gewirtz, "The Courts, Congress, and Executive Policy-making: Notes on Three Doctrines," 40 *Law and Contemporary Problems* 46, 58-59 (Summer 1976); William T. Mayton, "The Possibilities of Collective Choice: Arrow's Theorem, Article I, and the Delegation of Legislative Power to Administrative Agencies," 1986 *Duke Law Journal* 948, 962.

11. Morris P. Fiorina, *Congress: Keystone of the Washington Establishment* 66 (1977) (citing Randall Ripley, *Congress: Process and Policy* (1975)).

12. Jonathan Rauch, "Hidden in the Grocery Bag," 19 *National Journal* 2479, 2482 (October 3, 1987).

13. *Zuber v. Allen*, 396 U.S. 168, 185 (1969). See also *Schweiker v. Chilicky*, 487 U.S. 412, 440 (1988) ("Inaction, we have repeatedly stated, is a notoriously poor indication of congressional intent . . .") (Brennan, J., dissenting); and *Immigration and Naturalization Service v. Chadha*, 462 U.S. 919, 958 n.23 (1983) ("To allow Congress to evade the strictures of the Constitution and in effect enact Executive proposals into law by mere silence cannot be squared with Art. I.").

14. Fifty-five of the bills are listed at the end of Justice White's dissent in *Chadha*, 462 U.S. at 1003-13.

15. Id. at 944-59.

16. Id. at 966 (Powell, J., concurring).

17. U.S. Constitution art. I, § 5, cl. 3.

18. Congress, of course, does not delegate most key budgetary decisions, but, from the perspective of any particular legislator, most appropriations items are not hard choices, as Chapter 5 explained. Deciding how to pay for the total spending package would be a hard choice if deficit spending were not allowed. But it is.

19. Jerry L. Mashaw, "Prodelegation: Why Administrators Should Make Political Decisions," 1 *Journal of Law, Economics, and Organization* 81, 87 (1985).

20. E.E. Schattschneider, *The Semisovereign People: A Realist's View of Democracy in America* 1-2 (1975).

21. Surprisingly, some political scientists claim that there is no evidence that constituents' policy preferences influence how legislators vote or affect their chances of reelection. E.g., Robert A. Bernstein, *Elections, Representation, and Congressional Voting Behavior: The Myth of Constituency Control* 104 (1989). However, most legislators do seem carefully to adjust their votes to avoid taking positions that might anger their constituents, in the apparent belief that their votes do affect chances of reelection. John W. Kingdon, *Congressmen's Voting Decisions* 60-67 (2d ed. 1981) ; Richard F. Fenno, Jr., *Home Style: House Members in Their Districts* 10-18 (1978). R. Douglas Arnold, in *The Logic of Congressional Action* (1990), explains the lack of evidence that constituents' preferences matter in this way: researchers do not find much evidence that voting contrary to the policy preferences of constituents makes a difference because legislators so consistently and skillfully try to please their constituencies. Id. at 9. Arnold also argues that researchers do not find a close correlation between legislators' votes and the policy preferences of their constituents at the time of the votes because legislators are concerned with constituents' future preferences as well as those of the present: "legislators regularly attempt to *anticipate* how specific roll-call votes might be used against them [by a future challenger] and regularly adjust their votes in ways designed to forestall electoral problems." Id.

22. Fiorina, *Congress: Keystone* at 36-37.

23. The 97-percent figure was based on election results reported in *Congres-*

sional Ouarterly's Guide to Congress 705 (4th ed. 1991); and in "Departing House Members," 50 *Congressional Ouarterly* 3579 (November 7, 1992). Quote is from Rhodes Cook, "Is Competition in Elections Becoming Obsolete?" 47 *Congressional Ouarterly* 1060, 1064 (May 6, 1989).

24. The 93-percent figure is from Dave Kaplan and Charles Mahtesian, "Election's Wave of Diversity Spares Many Incumbents," 50 *Congressional Ouarterly* 3570, 3576 (November 7, 1992). For reasons for not running in 1992, see Rhodes Cook, "Incumbency Proves Liability in '92," 50 *Congressional Ouarterly* 2774 (September 12, 1992); and Phil Kuntz, "Overdrafts Were a Potent Charge," 50 *Congressional Ouarterly* 3575 (November 7, 1992).

25. For 3-to-5-percent figure, see Fiorina, *Congress: Keystone* at 53. Gary C. Jacobson, in "The Marginals Never Vanished: Incumbency and Competition in Elections to the U.S. House of Representatives, 1952-82," 31 *American Journal of Political Science* 126 (1987), disagrees that legislators are more secure in recent decades, although incumbency may be an advantage. Casework does help to secure reelection, although some political scientists disagree. Certainly legislators think casework helps them. John R. Johannes, in *To Serve the People: Congress and Constituency Service* ch. 8 (1984), notes that, contrary to the belief held by most legislators that casework helps, "casework per se . . . does not seem to provide any particularly strong electoral advantage." Id. at 206. Gary Jacobson collects the literature disagreeing with Johannes and argues that the lack of a close correlation between casework and election margins may reflect the possibility that those incumbents in the greatest danger of defeat do the most casework. Jacobson, "Running Scared: Elections and Congressional Politics in the 1980s" in *Congress: Structure and Policy* 39, 43-44 (Mathew D. McCubbins and Terry Sullivan eds., 1987).

26. 467 U.S. 837, 865-66 (1984). The holding in *Chevron* did not address the propriety of delegation, but the quoted language is cited as a rejoinder to the delegation doctrine. See, e.g., Richard J. Pierce, Jr., "The Role of Constitutional and Political Theory in Administrative Law," 64 *Texas Law Review* 469, 506 (1985).

27. *The Federalist* No. 73, at 494-96 (A. Hamilton) (J. Cooke ed., 1961).

7. Delegation Endangers Liberty

1. " . . . nor shall private property be taken for public use, without just compensation." U.S. Constitution amendment V. However, if just compensation is paid, private property can be taken and conveyed to other private owners when doing so supposedly serves a public purpose. See, e.g., *Hawaii Housing Authority v. Midkiff*, 467 U.S. 229 (1984).

2. On takings, see Laurence H. Tribe, *American Constitutional Law* 595-99 (2d ed. 1988). On public purpose, see id. at 587-95.

3. "Inquiries into congressional motives or purposes are a hazardous matter." *United States v. O'Brien*, 391 U.S. 367, 383 (1968). See also John Hart Ely, "Legislative and Administrative Motivation in Constitutional Law," 79 *Yale Law Journal* 1205 (1970). Cass R. Sunstein comprehensively demonstrates the

difficulty of determining whether statutes serve the public purpose by showing the wide array of conceivable public purposes and the difficulty of determining what purpose a statute serves. Sunstein, *After the Rights Revolution: Reconceiving the Regulatory State* ch. 2 (1990). For example, in the orange case, even if a court found that making markets orderly is not a public purpose, Congress hypothetically could assert instead that it seeks to increase Sunkist's profits because they are unjustly low. Whether the public interest includes redistributing income to Sunkist is, again, a question that would be left to elected officials.

4. Government cannot intrude on the areas of life mentioned on the basis of ordinary public purposes, but super-exceptional purposes may suffice. See *Schenck v. United States*, 249 U.S. 47, 52 (1919), for the "clear and present danger" doctrine.

5. For balancing private rights against public purposes, see Nadine Strossen, "The Fourth Amendment in the Balance: Accurately Setting the Scales through the Least Intrusive Alternative Analysis," 63 *New York University Law Review* 1173 (1988); T. Alexander Aleinikoff, "Constitutional Law in the Age of Balancing," 96 *Yale Law Journal* 943 (1987). Expanding the scope of judicial review would not help, as Einer R. Elhauge shows. Elhauge, "Does Interest Group Theory Justify More Intrusive Judicial Review?," 101 *Yale Law Journal* 31 (1991).

6. John Hart Ely, *Democracy and Distrust: A Theory of Judicial Review* 133-34 (1980).

7. See Richard B. Stewart, "The Reformation of American Administrative Law," 88 *Harvard Law Review* 1667, 1713-15 (1975).

8. Quote from *The Federalist* No. 62, at 417 (J. Madison) (J. Cooke ed. 1961).

9. See, e.g., David R. Mayhew, *Divided We Govern: Party Control, Lawmaking, and Investigations, 1946–1990* at 131-35 (1991); James M. Buchanan and Gordon Tullock, *The Calculus of Consent: Logical Foundations of Constitutional Democracy* 233-48 (1962). See also, Jonathan R. Macey, "Promoting Public-Regarding Legislation through Statutory Interpretation: An Interest Group Model," 86 *Columbia Law Review* 223, 247-49 (1986).

Einer Elhauge argues that public choice theory does not justify more expansive judicial review as an antidote for the influence of concentrated interests in the political process. He believes that the same arguments militate against using the delegation doctrine as an antidote for the influence of concentrated interests in the administrative process. Elhauge, 101 *Yale Law Journal* at 88 n.214. While I am sympathetic to his conclusion about judicial review, I disagree with his extension of the argument to the delegation doctrine. He maintains that "if more intrusive judicial review does increase the transaction costs of capture, that can perversely encourage interest group activity by making successful capture harder to undo." Id. at 88. Nonetheless, requiring that laws be enacted through the Article I process would be useful because the supermajoritarian requirement would tend to prevent concentrated interests from securing the passage of laws in the first place. Even without the supermajoritarian requirement, it will be tough to repeal laws that they back successfully, as the navel orange marketing order illustrates.

Elhauge also argues that "because increasing transaction costs [through increased judicial review] also increases the costs facing large diffuse groups, it may increase the *relative* advantage of small intense groups and thus increase their success." Id. This argument against expanded judicial review is inapplicable to the delegation doctrine because concentrated interests tend to have a relative advantage in the administrative process. John E. Chubb, *Interest Groups and the Bureaucracy: The Politics of Energy* 37-41 (1983). Finally, Elhauge argues that "any increase in transaction costs will affect not only legal changes favoring organized interest groups but all legal changes, a result that interest group theory does not justify because it provides no grounds for finding the status quo preferable to the mix of likely legal changes." 101 *Yale Law Journal* at 88. But, while public choice theory does not justify that result, Article I does, because it serves to discourage concentrated interests from securing laws that hurt the majority and majorities from securing laws that unjustly hurt minorities.

10. This argument depends upon there being a difference between lawmaking and law enforcing. See Thomas O. Sargentich, "The Contemporary Debate about Legislative-Executive Separation of Powers," 72 *Cornell Law Review* 430, 458-59 (1987). I discuss the difference in Chapter 12.

11. See Frederich A. von Hayek, *The Constitution of Liberty* 154-55 (1960); Peter H. Aranson, Ernest Gellhorn and Glen O. Robinson, "A Theory of Legislative Delegation," 68 *Cornell Law Review* 1, 65 (1982).

12. Compare, e.g., *United States v. Lovett*, 328 U.S. 303 (1946), with *Nixon v. Administrator of General Services*, 433 U.S. 425 (1977). See also, e.g., Tribe, *American Constitutional Law* 641–63; John Hart Ely, "*United States v. Lovett:* Litigating the Separation of Powers," 10 *Harvard Civil Rights-Civil Liberties Law Review* 1 (1975).

13. *The Federalist* No. 47, at 324 (J. Madison).

14. E.g., Sunstein, *After the Rights Revolution* at 22-23.

15. E.g., James M. Landis, *The Administrative Process* 23-29, 55-60 (1938); Attorney General's Committee on Administrative Procedure, *Administrative Procedure in Government Agencies*, S. Doc. No. 8, 77th Cong., 1st Sess. 104-20 (1941) (rulemaking procedures and judicial review).

16. Robert A. Dahl, *Democracy and Its Critics* 338 (1989).

17. For benefit to agencies, see James V. DeLong, "How to Convince an Agency: A Handbook for Policy Advocates," 6 *Regulation* 27, 28 (September/October 1982).

18. For an appraisal of the literature on incentives, see Susan Rose-Ackerman, "Reforming Public Bureaucracy through Economic Incentives?" 2 *Journal of Law, Economics, and Organization* 131 (1986).

19. Stewart, 88 *Harvard Law Review* at 1677–78.

20. Id. at 1684-85. Kay Lehman Schlozman and John T. Tierney argue that

the relative inhospitality of pressure politics to the interests of the less advantaged and broad publics does not imply that such interests are completely ignored in American politics. . . .

... broad publics and the disadvantaged sometimes achieve vicarious representation in our political system, benefiting from the efforts of narrower interests working on their own behalf in the political process ...

The interests of the less advantaged and broad publics achieve representation through other avenues of citizen politics—namely, electoral politics and protest activity. Observers of American politics have argued ... that the interests of the less advantaged fare better in electoral politics than in pressure politics. ...

... At various times and under various circumstances, various governmental institutions and actors have adopted the causes of the less advantaged and broad publics. Sometimes, especially in periods of social ferment and unusual party polarization, Congress takes on this role. Sometimes it is the President who carries the banner.

Organized Interests and American Democracy 401-03 (1986). This analysis suggests that delegation, by distancing Congress and the president from lawmaking, reduces the influence of diffuse interests.

21. For lack of representation for diffuse interests, see Stewart, 88 *Harvard Law Review* at 1762-70. For participation by narrower spectrum of interests, see Chubb, *Interest Groups and the Bureaucracy* at 37-41, 259–60. For "the poor and the weak" quotation, see Philip B. Heymann, *The Politics of Public Management* 22 (1987). My argument that delegation fails to overcome the influence of concentrated interests on legislation parallels Einer Elhauge's argument that expanded judicial review would fail to overcome the same problem. He argues that concentrated interests are likely to have even more influence over judicial review than over legislation, that judicial review is not entirely exogenous from the political process, and that judges have interests of their own. Elhauge, 101 *Yale Law Journal* at 77-87.

22. Schlozman and Tierney, *Organized Interests and American Democracy* at 251.

23. E.g., Jerry L. Mashaw, "Prodelegation: Why Administrators Should Make Political Decisions," 1 *Journal of Law, Economics, and Organization* 81, 99 (1985).

24. 5 U.S.C. § 553(c) (rulemaking); §§ 701-706 (judicial review) (1988).

25. Landis, *Administrative Process* at 99-101.

26. See, e.g., *Chevron U.S.A. v. Natural Resources Defense Council*, 467 U.S. 837, 865 (1984) ("an agency to which Congress has delegated policymaking responsibilities may, within the limits of that delegation, properly rely upon the incumbent administration's views of wise policy to inform its judgments"). See also Marianne Koral Smythe, "Judicial Review of Rule Rescissions," 84 *Columbia Law Review* 1928, 1934-35 (1984).

27. Richard A. Posner, *Economic Analysis of Law* 572 (3rd ed. 1986) ("We can describe the administrative agencies as a form of 'dependent' judiciary designed to promote the operation of interest group politics rather than allocative efficiency").

28. 5 U.S.C. § 706(2)(A), (C) (1988). Section 706 includes additional bases

for setting aside agency laws, but the ones mentioned are the most important in the present context.

29. See, e.g., *Riverbend Farms v. Madigan*, 958 F.2d 1479 (9th Cir. 1992).

30. Martin Shapiro, *Who Guards the Guardians? Judicial Control of Administration* ch. 7 (1988).

31. See, e.g., *Citizens To Preserve Overton Park v. Volpe*, 401 U.S. 402, 420 (1971); *Ethyl Corp. v. EPA*, 541 F.2d 1, 34 (D.C. Cir.) (en banc), cert. denied, 426 U.S. 941 (1976); 3 Kenneth Davis, *Administrative Law Treatise* 298 (2d ed. 1980).

32. See, e.g. *Overton Park*, 401 U.S. at 416-17. Peter H. Schuck and E. Donald Elliott, "To the *Chevron* Station: An Empirical Study of Federal Administrative Law," 1990 *Duke Law Journal* 984, 1059-60.

33. See Bruff, 63 *Texas Law Review* at 239. According to Cass Sunstein, judicial review is "highly unlikely" to "accomplish a great deal" in making agencies truly deliberative. Sunstein, "Interest Groups In American Public Law," 38 *Stanford Law Review* 29, 68 (1985). Martin Shapiro agrees. Shapiro, *Who Guards the Guardians?* 151-55.

34. *Ethyl Corp. v. EPA*, 541 F.2d 1, 68 (D.C. Cir. 1976) (en banc) (Leventhal, J., concurring) (footnote omitted).

35. 401 U.S. at 412-13 (footnote omitted).

36. Richard B. Stewart and James E. Krier, *Environmental Law and Policy* 679 (2d ed. 1978) (footnote omitted).

37. E.g., *Chevron U.S.A. v. Natural Resources Defense Council*, 467 U.S. 837 (1984).

38. *Ethyl Corp. v. EPA*, 541 F.2d at 66 (Bazelon, C.J., concurring); but see Leventhal, J., concurring, id. at 68-69.

39. E.g., William A. Jordan, "Producer Protection, Prior Market Structure and the Effects of Government Regulation," 15 *Journal of Law and Economics* 151, 174-76 (1972).

40. For another example, the flap over the breach of Vice President Gore's campaign pledge to stop an Ohio incinerator helped prompt a moratorium on EPA's even considering other new incinerators. Keith Schneider, "Administration to Freeze Growth of Hazardous Waste Incinerators," *New York Times*, May 17, 1993, at A1.

41. E.g., *Mistretta v. United States*, 488 U.S. 361 (1989). See also Richard B. Stewart, "Beyond Delegation Doctrine," 36 *American University Law Review* 323 (1987).

42. Schlozman and Tierney, *Organized Interests* at 66-87, 107-19.

43. Charles Murray, *In Pursuit: Of Happiness and Good Government* 164, 298 (1988).

8. Delegation Makes Law Less Reasonable

1. E.g., Stephen Breyer and Richard Stewart, *Administrative Law and Regulatory Policy* 140 (3d ed. 1992).

2. Robert A. Dahl, *Democracy and Its Critics* 337 (1989); and id. 68–70.

3. For administrators, I counted both of William Ruckleshaus's tenures

because they were not consecutive. For assistant administrator for air pollution, I counted all of the assistant administrators in charge of implementing the Clean Air Act, although their titles changed through various reorganizations of the agency.

4. Thomas O. McGarity, "The Internal Structure of EPA Rulemaking," 54 *Law and Contemporary Problems* 57, 59 (Autumn, 1991).

5. Little study has been done of how legislatures use social science research. See Richard Lempert, "'Between Cup and Lip': Social Science Influences on Law and Policy," 10 *Law & Policy* 167, 179 (1988). Alex Tanford has compared the extent to which courts, state legislatures, and state commissions take account of new studies in making rules about jury instructions. He found courts totally unresponsive and legislatures and commissions only slowly responsive, with commissions responding somewhat faster than legislatures. Several anecdotes supplied by Tanford suggest that commission members were more aware than legislators that they were responding to new studies; legislators receiving recommendations from a state commission were unaware that those recommendations were based in part on new studies. J. Alexander Tanford, "Law Reform by Courts, Legislatures, and Commissions Following Empirical Research on Jury Instructions," 25 *Law and Society Review* 155 (1991).

6. Committee on the Constitutional System, *A Bicentennial Analysis of the American Political Structure* 15-16 (Jan. 1987).

7. Id. Also see Woodrow Wilson, "Committee or Cabinet Government," *Overland Monthly*, Jan. 1884, at 3.

8. Robert Pear, "U.S. Laws Delayed by Complex Rules and Partisanship," *New York Times*, March 31, 1991, at A1, col. 6.

9. 5 U.S.C. § 553(b), (d) (1988).

10. Learned Hand, "The Speech of Justice," in *Spirit of Liberty* 15-16 (2d ed. 1953).

11. William F. Pederson, Jr., "Why the Clean Air Act Works Badly," 129 *University of Pennsylvania Law Review* 1059, 1073-78 (1981). For lessening of voluntary compliance, see Robert Rickles, "Environmental Rules Mess," *New York Times*, July 22, 1978, at A19, col. 3.

12. Lon L. Fuller, in *The Morality of Law* 77-79 (2d ed. 1969), treats a minimum degree of "constancy through time" as a prerequisite of an effective law.

13. See Terry M. Moe, "The Politics of Bureaucratic Structure," in *Can the Government Govern?* 267, 278 (John E. Chubb and Paul E. Peterson eds., 1989).

14. Leopold J. Pospisil, in *Anthropology of Law* 78-81 (1971), includes as one of the attributes of law an "intention of universal application." When law is not applied universally, those in authority rule by power rather than by law. "Authoritarian law . . . is not internalized by a majority of the members of a group . . . " Id. at 196. Harry H. Wellington has argued that duties based upon principle, which he calls "strong duties," tend to be enforced more vigorously than duties based only on policy, which he calls "weak duties." Wellington, "Common Law Rules and Constitutional Double Standards: Some Notes on Adjudication," 83 *Yale Law Journal* 221, 229-35 (1973).

15. Bruce A. Ackerman and William T. Hassler, "Beyond the New Deal:

Coal and the Clean Air Act," 89 *Yale Law Journal* 1466 (1980). A fuller version of this article is published as *Clean Coal/Dirty Air: or, How the Clean Air Act Became a Multibillion-Dollar Bail-Out for High-Sulfur Coal Producers and What Should Be Done about It* (1981).

16. CAA 1970 § 111(a)(1) (current version at 42 U.S.C. § 7411(a)(1)).

17. See Ackerman and Hassler, 89 *Yale Law Journal* at 1485, 1500.

18. Pub. L. No. 95-95, § 109 (c)(I)(A), 91 Stat. 685, 699–700 (1977).

19. 44 *Federal Register* 33,580-624 (1979); Ackerman and Hassler, 89 *Yale Law Journal* at 1547-56.

20. For their criticism of the power plant ruling, see Ackerman and Hassler, 89 *Yale Law Journal* at 1469. For a rebuttal, see Lowell Smith and Russell Randle, "Comment on 'Beyond the New Deal,'" 90 *Yale Law Journal* 1398 (1981). For endorsement of delegation, see Ackerman and Hassler, 89 *Yale Law Journal* at 1566-71.

21. Ackerman and Hassler, 89 *Yale Law Journal* at 1508-11, 1552–53, 1560. At the time, both the chair of the Senate Committee on Public Works and the Senate majority leader came from West Virginia.

22. 42 U.S.C. § 7411(a)(1) (1988): "taking into account the cost of achieving such reduction . . . "

23. 1990 Clean Air Amendments § 403 (Repeal of Percent Reduction) 104 Stat. 2399, 2631. On concern for ratepayers, see, e.g., 136 *Cong. Rec.* S13,404 (1990) (statement of Sen. Dixon). The 1990 amendments also provide funds for the retraining of unemployed eastern coal miners. See Clean Air Employment Transition Assistance, 1990 CAA § 1101, 104 Stat. 2399, 2709 codified as amended in the Job Training Partnership Act, 29 U.S.C. § 1662e (1990 Supp. II); Damon Chappie et al., "Record of 101st Congress Marked by Progress on Clean Air, Inaction on Hazardous Waste, Cabinet-Level EPA Legislation," 21 *Environment Reporter* (BNA) 1370 (November 16, 1990).

24. Alan Watts, *Psychotherapy East and West* 121 (1975) (emphasis in original).

25. John E. Chubb, "U.S. Energy Policy: A Problem of Delegation" in *Can the Government Govern?* 47, 92 (John E. Chubb and Paul E. Peterson eds. 1989).

26. *Illinois v. Costle*, 12 *Environment Reporter Cases* (Bureau of National Affairs) 1597, 1599 (D.D.C. 1979) (Gesell, J.).

27. Martin Shapiro, *Who Guards the Guardians? Judicial Control of Administration* ch. 7 (1988); quote at 151-52.

28. Id. at 169-170.

29. Benjamin Ginsberg and Martin Shefter, *Politics by Other Means: The Declining Importance of Elections in America* 26 (1990).

30. James Tobin, "Deposit Insurance Must Go," *Wall Street Journal*, November 22, 1989 at A12; see also, Philip T. Sudo, "'Don't Protect Big Banks from Failing,' Bankers Trust Chief Tells Regulators," *American Banker*, March 26, 1987, at 1; and Jonathan R. Macey and Geoffrey P. Miller, "Bank Failures, Risk Monitoring, and the Market for Bank Control," 88 *Columbia Law Review* 1153 (1988). Others oppose curtailing deposit insurance. E.g., William L. Seidman, "The Facts About the FDIC," *Wall Street Journal*, June 5, 1991, at A12.

31. James Smalhout, "The Coming Pension Bailout," *Wall Street Journal*, June 10, 1992, at A14; Editorial, Wall Street Journal, Sept. 10, 1992, at A14. Albert R. Karr, "Risk to Retirees Rises as Firms Fail To Fund Pensions They Offer," *Wall Street Journal*, February 4, 1993 at Al.

32. Charles Murray, *In Pursuit: Of Happiness and Good Government* 94-95 (1988) (emphasis in original).

33. Murray, *In Pursuit of Happiness* at 102-03.

34. Richard H. Pildes and Elizabeth Anderson, "Slinging Arrows at Democracy: Social Choice Theory, Value Pluralism, and Democratic Politics," 90 *Columbia Law Review* 2121, 2194-95 (1990).

35. Jerry Mashaw, "Prodelegation: Why Administrators Should Make Political Decisions," 1 *Journal of Law, Economics and Organization* 81, 98-99 (1985). For a more extended discussion of social choice theory's critique of democracy than can be offered here, see Pildes and Anderson, 90 *Columbia Law Review* 2121 and Einer R. Elhauge, "Does Interest Group Theory Justify More Intrusive Judicial Review?," 101 *Yale Law Journal* 31, 101-09 (1991).

36. Daniel A. Farber and Philip P. Frickey, "The Jurisprudence of Public Choice," 65 *Texas Law Review* 873, 901 n.170, n.172 (1987).

37. Mashaw, 1 *Journal of Law, Economics, and Organization* at 98-99.

38. The research on absence of cycling in Congress, is collected and discussed in Daniel A. Farber and Philip P. Frickey, *Law and Public Choice: A Critical Introduction* 48-49 (1991). For policy changes by agencies, see William T. Mayton, "The Possibilities of Collective Choice: Arrow's Theorem, Article I, and the Delegation of Legislative Power to Administrative Agencies," 1986 *Duke Law Journal* 948, 962. For Arrow's assumptions and Congress, see, e.g., Dahl, *Democracy* at 153-54; Herbert Hovenkamp, "Legislation, Well-Being, and Public Choice," 57 *University of Chicago Law Review* 63, 89-94 (1990); and Mayton, 1986 *Duke Law Journal* at 953–58.

39. Andrew Caplin and Barry Nalebuff, "On 64%-Majority Rule," 56 *Econometrica* 787 (1988).

40. Mashaw, 1 *Journal of Law, Economics, and Organization* at 98-99.

41. Id. Pildes and Anderson point out that the legislative process is criticized as arbitrary because its outcome depends on the agenda (90 *Columbia Law Review* at 2136-37), but argue that such dependence is inevitable and desirable (id. at 2193-96).

42. See Elhauge, 101 *Yale Law Journal* at 104. Elhauge points out that the argument that interest groups disproportionately influence the selection of agenda setters in Congress is susceptible to the counterargument that interest groups may disproportionately influence the selection of agenda setters in alternatives to the legislative process.

43. According to Pildes and Anderson, the reforms of the 1970s regarding the selection of committee chairs "reveal the ways in which the appropriate distribution of agenda-setting powers can itself be subject to political debate, criticism, and change in the name of democratic ideals." 90 *Columbia Law Review* at 2196–97.

44. Jerry L. Mashaw, in "The Economics of Politics and the Understanding

of Public Law," 65 *Chicago-Kent Law Review* 123, 127 (1989), summarizes a charge made against all methods of collective choice, including various forms of democracy. For a summary of such critiques, see Pildes and Anderson, 90 *Columbia Law Review* at 2138-39.

9. Congress Has Enough Time To Make the Laws

1. E.g., *Mistretta v. United States*, 488 U.S. 361 (1989). Similarly, the New Deal architects of delegation believed that Congress lacked the time to protect the public without delegation. Attorney General's Committee on Administrative Procedure, *Administrative Procedure in Government Agencies*, S. Doc. No. 8, 77th Cong., 1st Sess. 14 (1941).

2. E.g., Jerry Mashaw, "Prodelegation: Why Administrators Should Make Political Decisions," 1 *Journal of Law, Economics, and Organization* 1, 97-98 (1985); Richard J. Pierce, Jr., "Political Accountability and Delegated Power: A Response to Professor Lowi," 36 *American University Law Review* 391, 404 (1987).

3. See Clean Air Act, Pub. L. No. 88-206, § 1(a), 77 Stat. 392, 392-93 (1963) (current version at 42 U.S.C. § 7401(a)(1) (1990 Supp. II)).

4. Robert V. Percival, Alan S. Miller, Christopher H. Schroeder, and James P. Leape, *Environmental Regulation: Law, Science, and Policy* 818 (1992). Congress did deal with one important interstate air pollution problem, acid rain, in the 1990 act.

The Clean Water Act fails to provide an adequate remedy for a state which believes that another state harms it by permitting too much pollution. See *Milwaukee v. Illinois*, 451 U.S. 304, 332–53 (1981) (Blackmun, J., dissenting); and Daniel A. Farber and Philip P. Frickey, "In the Shadow of the Legislature: The Common Law in the Age of the New Public Law," 89 *Michigan Law Review* 875, 890-95 (1991).

5. See C. K. Rowland and Roger Marz, "Gresham's Law: The Regulatory Analogy," 1 *Policy Studies Review* 572 (Feb. 1982).

6. *Train v. Natural Resources Defense Council*, 421 U.S. 60, 64 (1975).

7. E. Donald Elliott, Bruce A. Ackerman, and John C. Millian, "Toward a Theory of Statutory Evolution: The Federalization of Environmental Law," 1 *Journal of Law, Economics, and Organization* 313, 326-33 (1985). For sulfur reductions, see David Schoenbrod, "Goals Statutes or Rules Statutes: The Case of the Clean Air Act," 30 *UCLA Law Review* 740, 778 (1983). For state vs. federal methods in the 1980s, see Matthew L. Wald, "Recharting War on Smog: States Like California Are Taking the Lead over Washington in Pollution-Control Law," *New York Times*, October 10, 1989, at A1, col. 5. Crandall is quoted in Peter Brimelow and Leslie Spencer, "You Can't Get There from Here," *Forbes*, July 6, 1992, at 59, 60.

8. For health effects, see "Ruckelshaus Said To Face 'Tough' Choice on Risk from Asarco Smelter in Washington," 14 *Environment Reporter* (BNA) (Bureau of National Affairs) 97 (May 20, 1983); "Arsenic Standards for Tacoma Smelter Said To Be Tighter Than Those Proposed," 15 *Environment Report* (BNA) 297 (June 22, 1984). Children a mile away were found to have arsenic

levels in their blood twice as high as those of children living fifty miles away. Laura Parker, "Tacoma Must Weigh Clean Air against Jobs," *Washinqton Post*, December 11, 1983, at A6. For economic effects, see "EPA Proposes Controls on Arsenic Emissions, Seeks Comment on Smelter Posing High Risks," 14 *Environment Reporter* (BNA) 395 (July 15, 1983).

9. William D. Ruckelshaus, Letter to the Editor, "On Tacoma's Air; How EPA Faces the Arsenic Risk," *New York Times*, July 23, 1983, sec. 1, at 22.

10. E.g., Philip Shabecoff, "Higher Risks Seen in New EPA Rules," *New York Times*, September 18, 1983, sec. 1, at 1.

11. The local authorities were aware of both the arsenic problem and the likely consequences to the economy. Cass Peterson, "High-Pollution Smelter To Close within a Year; Asarco Cites Environmental Regulations," *Washington Post*, June 29, 1984, at A2.

12. Irvin Molotsky, "Koch Tells Fellow Mayors Reasons To Beware of Mandated Programs," *New York Times*, January 25, 1980, at B3. See also Michael deCourcy Hinds, "U.S. Adds Programs with Little Review of Local Burdens," *New York Times*, March 24, 1992, at A1.

13. The program requires states to pay only 10 percent of the cleanup cost. CERCLA, 42 U.S.C. § 9604(c) (3) (1988).

14. Senate Report No. 228, 101st Cong., 1st Sess. 3 (1989).

15. Asbestos Hazard Emergency Response Act, 15 U.S.C. §§ 2641-55 (1988).

16. "Mikulski Raps EPA for Failure to Request Asbestos in Schools Funds," 13 *Chemical Regulation Reporter* (BNA) 35 (April 14, 1989).

17. See Charles Morris, *The Cost of Good Intentions* 35 (1980) ("Programs developed 'vertical autocracies' of their own, a chain of officials stretching from the local government through the state and regional federal bureaucracies to Washington and the halls of Congress. Elected officials rarely could afford the time or trouble to master the complex laws and regulations and were increasingly the captives of their program-oriented bureaucracies").

18. See, e.g., Robert C. Ellickson, "Alternatives to Zoning: Covenants, Nuisance Rules, and Fines as Land Use Controls," 40 *University of Chicago Law Review* 681, 780-81 (1973).

19. Quote from Nicholas Kaldor, *Essays on Value and Distribution* 4 (1960), discussing Joan Robinson, *The Economics of Imperfect Competition* (1933). See also Edward H. Chamberlin, *The Theory of Monopolistic Competition* (1933). For Landis, see James Landis, *The Administrative Process* 7-14 (1938).

20. For *Schechter*, see Ellis W. Hawley, *The New Deal and the Problem of Monopoly: A Study in Economic Ambivalence* 132 (1966). For diminished support for industrial codes, see id. at 122-30. For antitrust, see id. at 130, 281-379.

21. Editorial, "Too Little Deregulation," *New York Times*, June 11, 1990, at A18.

22. Willard W. Cochrane, *Farm Prices: Myth and Reality* ch. 2 (1958).

23. Quote from Robert J. Samuelson, "The Economics of Nostalgia," *Newsweek*, March 25, 1985, at 76.

24. For perishability argument, see General Accounting Office, *The Role of Marketing Orders in Establishing and Maintaining Orderly Marketing Condi-*

tions ii (1985). For raspberries and oysters, see Thomas M. Lenard and Michael P. Mazur, "Harvest of Waste: The Marketing Order Program," *Regulation,* May/ June 1985, at 19, 22. On stability of unregulated crops: "disinterested analysts have questioned whether stabilization schemes designed to mitigate fluctuations in supply rather than demand have any advantage for consumers." Lawrence Shepard, "Cartelization of the California-Arizona Orange Industry, 1934-1981," 29 *Journal of Law and Economics* 83, 92 (1986), citing studies.

25. For Department of Agriculture rationale, see 55 *Federal Reqister* 50,157 (1990). Those concluding that the market can be stable without regulation include Nicholas J. Powers, Glenn A. Zepp, and Frederic L. Hoff, *Assessment of a Marketing Order Prorate Suspension: A Study of California-Arizona Navel Oranges* (Department of Agriculture, Agricultural Economic Report No. 557) (1986); Sheldon Kimmel, *Marketing Orders and Stability: The Case of California-Arizona Oranges* 10 (Economic Analysis Group, Anti-trust Division, U.S. Department of Justice No. 87-4, June 16, 1987).

26. *Comments of J. Kent Burt on 1990 Marketinq Order,* September 13, 1990, at 1. A Department of Justice study rejects another argument for the orange marketing order—that it reduces the risk to growers—because, inter alia, "the orange industry is a small enough part of the total economy that we should expect that most of the risks . . . can be diversified away." Kimmel, *Marketing Orders* at 7.

27. For Brookings study, see Clifford Winston et al., *The Economic Effects of Surface Freight Deregulation* 5 (1990). See also, e.g., Editorial, "Re-regulate? Not on Your Life; Triumphs on the Road, on the Phone, in the Air," *New York Times,* June 10, 1990, sec. 4, at 22; Thomas Gale Moore, "Unfinished Business in Motor Carrier Deregulation," *Regulation,* Summer 1991, at 49.

28. John E. Chubb, "U.S. Energy Policy: A Problem in Delegation," in *Can the Government Govern?* 47, 96 (John E. Chubb and Paul E. Peterson eds. 1989).

29. James Q. Wilson, *Bureaucracy: What Government Agencies Do and Why They Do It* 342-44 (1989).

30. Cass R. Sunstein, *After the Rights Revolution: Reconceiving the Regulatory State* 109 (1990).

31. E.g., Matthew L. Spitzer, "The Constitutionality of Licensing Broad-casters," 64 *New York University Law Review* 990 (1989). Private business, in effect, auctions frequencies when a licensee sells its license or when an applicant for a license buys out competing applicants. Henry Geller, former FCC general counsel and now head of Duke University's Washington Center for Public Policy Research, has said that because the money for the publicly owned airwaves goes to private businesses rather than the government, Congress and the FCC look like "jackasses." "Commission Approves Outside Party Buyout in New Station Comparative Proceedings," *Broadcasting,* January 9, 1989 at 68.

32. "FCC Chairman Outlines Plan To Award Radio Spectrum Licenses through Auctions," *BNA Daily Report for Executives,* October 2, 1986 at A2. For lotteries, see "Winners and Losers in the Great Cellular Giveway," *Time,* November 5, 1990 at 146; Thomas W. Hazlett, "Making Money Out of the Air," *New York Times,* December 2, 1987 at A35.

33. Attorney General's Committee, *Administrative Procedure* at 14.

34. Internal Revenue Code, 26 U.S.C. §§ 1-9602 (1988) (generally not delegating). The Budget for Fiscal Year 1991, Department of Agriculture, A-444.

35. For prohibition on employment discrimination, see 42 U.S.C. § 2000e-2 (1988). For tendency of Congress to enact entitlements rules, see Peter Simon, "Liberty and Property in the Supreme Court: A Defense of *Roth* and *Perry*," 71 *California Law Review* 146, 190-91 (1983).

36. Quote from Landis, *Administrative Process* at 76.

37. Paul A. Samuelson, *Economics: An Introductory Analysis* 494–96 (5th ed. 1961).

38. See statement of Hon. Ross Sandler, Commissioner of Transportation, City of New York, in *Clean Air Act Amendments of 1989: Hearings on S. 1630 Before the Subcommittee on Environmental Protection of the Senate Committee on Environment and Public Works*, 101st Cong., 1st Sess., pt. 4, at 63 (1989).

39. 42 U.S.C. § 11023 (1988). This provision does delegate in part but could be rewritten to avoid delegation.

40. Sulfur dioxide emissions from power plants alone were estimated in 1970 at 20 million tons out of a total of 37 million tons. *Air Pollution—1970: Hearings before the Subcommittee on Air and Water Pollution of the Senate Committee on Public Works*, 91st Cong., 2d Sess. (1970), reprinted in Senate Committee on Public Works, 93d Cong., 2d Sess., *Legislative History of the Clean Air Amendments of 1970*, pt.2, at 1012 (Committee Print 1974). The other large categories were smelting of metallic ores (four million tons) and petroleum refinery operations (less than three million tons). Id. For figures on nitrogen oxides, etc., see EPA, *National Air Quality, Monitoring, and Emission Trends Report* 5-11 (1978); EPA, *Air Quality Criteria for Lead* 1-3 (1977).

41. 42 U.S.C. § 7410 (1990 Supp. II).

42. See statement of Daniel J. Dudek, Senior Economist, Environmental Defense Fund, in *Clean Air Act Amendments of 1989: Hearings on Acid Rain before the Subcommittee on Environmental Protection of the Senate Committee on Environment and Public Works*, 101st Cong., 1st Sess., pt. 5, at 195 (1989).

43. For an overview of the debate on economic incentives, see Bruce Ackerman and Richard Stewart, "Reforming Environmental Laws," 37 *Stanford Law Review* 1333 (1985). The 400-percent figure is from Sunstein, *After the Rights Revolution* at 81-82. Except for the new acid rain program, current law provides only limited opportunities for emissions trading. Emission trading requires a determination that the trade would not cause a violation of the ambient air standard. This would be unnecessary under a statute that enacted rules rather than mandatory goals, such as the ambient standards. The risk that trading would result in excessive emissions in one area could be minimized by requiring the trades to be between firms within a specified distance of each other or by allowing states to set emission limits more stringent than those in federal law. Another problem with emissions trading under current law is that ownership of saleable emissions is based upon the somewhat arbitrary allocation of emissions limits in the the state plans. Those firms which most successfully fought bureaucratic battles to avoid stringent emission lim-

its could now cash in their success by finally installing better pollution-control equipment and selling their valuable emission rights. With a statute that legislated broadly applicable emission limits, a firm would get tradeable emission rights only by emitting less than those limits.

44. 1990 Clean Air Act Amendments, Subchapter IV, Acid Deposition Control, §§ 401-416 (codified at 42 U.S.C. §§ 7651- 76510 (1990 Supp. I)); see also David Schoenbrod, "Goals Statutes or Rules Statutes: The Case of the Clean Air Act," 30 *UCLA Law Review*, 804-16, 825 (1983).

45. Senator Thomas Eagleton quoted in Hedrick Smith, *The Power Game: How Washington Works* 159 (1988).

46. John R. Johannes, *To Serve the People: Congress and Constituency Service* 213 (1984). Johannes notes both that ombudsman have worked effectively in many countries and that surveys show that members of Congress prefer, predictably, the present system.

47. H.R. Conference Report No. 952, 101st Cong., 2d Sess. 350-55 (1990), reprinted in 1990 U.S.C.C.A.N. 3882-87; *CIS/Annual 1990: Legislative Histories of U.S. Public Laws* 409-83 (1991). Some committees participated through more than one subcommittee.

48. A recently adopted practice is to limit most appropriations, even for long-term programs, to one year. Wilson, *Bureaucracy* at 243-44. These one-year appropriations give Congress somewhat more control over the executive, but at the price of a considerable increase in legislative workload.

49. *Wayman v. Southard*, 23 U.S. (10 Wheat.) 1, 43 (1825).

10. The Constitution Prohibits Delegation

1. John Locke, *The Second Treatise on Government* 79 (Prometheus Books, 1986). Moreover, the Framers thought Congress was likely to try to exceed its constitutional powers, not to delegate them. Sotirios A. Barber, *The Constitution and the Delegation of Congressional Power* 39 (1975).

2. For Constitutional Convention, see John L. Fitzgerald, *Congress and the Separation of Power* 35-39 (1986). For Article I claim, see Donald A. Dripps, "Delegation and Due Process," 1988 *Duke Law Journal* 657, 660-61. For Madison: "If nothing more were required, in exercising a legislative trust, than a general conveyance of authority—without laying down any precise rules by which the authority conveyed should be carried into effect—it would follow that the whole power of legislation might be transferred by the legislature from itself." 4 *The Debates in the Several State Conventions on the Adoption of the Federal Constitution* 560 (Jonathan Elliot ed., 2d ed. 1888).

3. For Madison draft, see Louis Fisher, *President and Congress: Power and Policy* 24-26 (1972); and *Creating the Bill of Rights: The Documentary Record from the First Federal Congress* 14 (Helen E. Veit et al. eds., 1991). For Sherman and Madison quotes, see id. at 196. For action in the House and Senate, see id. at 41, 47, 49; and Fisher, *President and Congress* at 25.

4. See, e.g., *Wayman v. Southard*, 23 U.S. (10 Wheat.) 1, 42 (1825); *Field v. Clark*, 143 U.S. 649, 692 (1892). Most recently, the Supreme Court in *Touby v.*

United States said, "From this language [in Article I] the Court has derived the nondelegation doctrine: that Congress may not constitutionally delegate its legislative power to another Branch of government." 111 S. Ct. 1752, 1755 (1991).

5. Hobbes quote is from Thomas Hobbes, *The Leviathan* 108 (Prometheus Books 1988) (emphasis in original). For *Fletcher v. Peck,* see 10 U.S. (6 Cranch) 87, 136 (1810); see also, e.g., *INS v. Chadha,* 462 U.S. 919, 967 (1983) (Powell, J., concurring). For *Gibbons v. Ogden,* see 22 U.S. (9 Wheat.) 1, 196 (1824).

6. E.g., John Rohr, *To Run a Constitution: The Legitimacy of the Administrative State* 16, 19-25 (1986); Fisher, *President and Congress* at 26-27. In a variation on this theme, Peter Strauss seeks to reconcile the text of the Constitution with delegation of legislative power to agencies on the basis that the Constitution speaks only about the powers of Congress, the president, and the Supreme Court and so leaves open the powers of subordinate officials. Peter L. Strauss, "The Place of Agencies in Government: Separation of Powers and the Fourth Branch," 84 *Columbia Law Review* 573 (1984). But the Constitution is specific in granting legislative powers to Congress and the president, working through the Article I process. Moreover, Strauss's proposed interpretation of the Constitution pays no heed to the procedural protections of liberty in Article I.

7. John Phillip Reid, *The Constitutional History of the American Revolution: The Authority to Tax* 185 (1987); Reid, *Constitutional History of the American Revolution,* ch. 1 (forthcoming).

8. *J.W. Hampton. Jr., & Co. v. United States,* 276 U.S. 394, 406, 409 (1928). The cases are divided on whether Congress must provide something more than an intelligible principle when criminal sanctions may be imposed. See *Touby,* 111 S. Ct. at 1756.

9. Only recently have opinions explicitly appealed to accountability as a fundamental purpose of the doctrine. See *Arizona v. California,* 371 U.S. 546, 626 (1963) (Harlan, J., dissenting in part). Previously, the Court implicitly invoked accountability concerns by reference to the separation of powers and its underlying rationale. See, e.g., *J.W. Hampton, Jr., & Co.,* 276 U.S. at 406.

The Court recasts the issue of protecting liberty in terms of preventing "judicial review from becoming merely an exercise at large by providing the courts with some measure against which to judge the official action that has been challenged." *Arizona v. California,* 373 U.S. at 626 (Harlan, J., dissenting in part). To serve this purpose, the statute must "sufficiently mark[] the field within which the Administrator is to act so that it may be known [by a reviewing court] whether he has kept within it in compliance with the legislative will." *Yakus v. United States,* 321 U.S. 414, 425 (1944).

10. The Court talks as if Congress must let others make the hard choices whether it delegates or makes the laws itself:

> [T]hat Congress accepts the administrative judgment as to the relative weights to be given to these [conflicting] factors in each case . . . instead of attempting the impossible by prescribing their relative weight in advance for all cases, is no more an abandonment of the legislative function than when Congress accepts and acts legislatively upon the advice of experts as

to social or economic conditions without reexamining for itself the data upon which that advice is based. *Opp Cotton Mills v. Administrator*, 312 U.S. 126, 145–46 (1941).

The Court says that Congress "accepts" administrative priorities, but in fact Congress avoids taking responsibility for them. The Court says that it is "impossible" for Congress to set the priorities, but Congress can set them by making the law. The Court says that, whether it delegates or enacts law, Congress simply accepts the advice of experts; but experts on controversial policy questions usually disagree, which forces the Congress that enacts law to make a choice. Moreover, Congress delegates not just the technical questions but also broad questions of policy. In sum, the Court fails to acknowledge that it has permitted Congress to duck fundamental policy choices.

11. See, e.g., Henry Paul Monaghan, "Stare Decisis and Constitutional Adjudication," 88 *Columbia Law Review* 723 (1988); Note, "Constitutional Stare Decisis," 103 *Harvard Law Review* 1344 (1990).

12. E.g., Robert H. Bork, *The Tempting of America: The Political Seduction of the Law* 157-58 (1990).

13. E.g., *Mistretta v. United States*, 488 U.S. 361, 373 (1989).

14. *Mistretta* did not explicitly rely upon *stare decisis*, but certainly sounded that theme.

15. Should the courts later decide that the statutes really did delegate, they would not necessarily be bound to uphold all statutes that do delegate. The earlier cases could be distinguished on the basis that they rested upon a misapprehension.

16. Quote is from *Moragne v. States Marine Lines*, 398 U.S. 375, 403 (1970) (Harlan, J.).

17. For public faith, see Monaghan, 88 *Columbia Law Review* at 752-53; Note, 103 *Harvard Law Review* at 1349; and *Planned Parenthood v. Casey*, 112 S. Ct. 2791, 2808 (1992).

18. Henry Julian Abraham, *Justices and Presidents* 198 (1974).

19. Monaghan, 88 *Columbia Law Review* at 749-52.

20. Bruce Ackerman, "The Storrs Lectures: Discovering the Constitution," 93 *Yale Law Journal* 1013, 1053-57, 1070-71 (1984); Ackerman, *We the People: Foundations* 47-50 (1991); Cass Sunstein, "Constitutionalism after the New Deal," 101 *Harvard Law Review* 421, 432 n.40, 447-48 (1987) (arguing that the New Deal amended the Constitution to allow delegation); Laurence H. Tribe, *American Constitutional Law* 213 (2d ed. 1988). Ackerman's argument has also been criticized. E.g., Lawrence G. Sager, "The Incorrigible Constitution," 65 *New York University Law Review* 893, 924-33 (1990); Ira C. Lupu, "Risky Business" (Book Review of Tribe, *American Constitutional Law* (2d ed. 1988)), 101 *Harvard Law Review* 1303, 1310-11 (1988)).

21. Ackerman, *We the People* at 49 (emphasis in original). Ackerman, 93 *Yale Law Journal* at 1054-55.

22. See William E. Leuchtenberg, "The Origins of Franklin D. Roosevelt's 'Court-Packing' Plan," 1966 *Supreme Court Review* 347, 356-57, 365-66, 373, 375-80. The quote is at 358.

23. "Roosevelt dismissed the amendment route as unacceptable for a number of reasons. In the first place, he thought an amendment would be difficult to frame." Id. at 384. Alleged ambiguities in the proposed Equal Rights Amendment provided ammunition to its critics. E.g., "ERA Strategy: Is There Life after Tsongas?" 35 *National Review*, July 8, 1983 at 794.

24. Quote is from Leuchtenberg, 1966 *Supreme Court Review* at 379. For public disapproval of the NRA, see id. at 362.

25. Id. at 384.

26. Id. at 385-86 (Raymond Clapper paraphrasing and quoting Stephen Early, February 8, 1937).

27. John Hart Ely, *Democracy and Distrust* 88-101 (1980).

28. U.S. Constitution XXIIth Amend. (prohibiting anyone from being elected president more than twice); XXIIIth Amend. (allowing the District of Columbia to vote for president); XXIVth Amend. (prohibiting poll taxes); XXVth Amend. (establishing procedures to replace an incapacitated president and to fill a vacancy in the office of Vice President); XXVIth Amend. (giving eighteen-year-olds the right to vote); XXVIIth Amend. (postponing congressional pay increases until after the next election of representatives).

29. "A Public Hearing on Congress," *American Enterprise*, Nov./Dec., 1992 at 82-92.

30. See Herbert J. Storing, *The Anti Federalist: Writings by the Opponents of the Constitution* 59-60 (1985); Richard B. Bernstein, "Hot-Wiring the Convention, 1787," *New York Times*, July 17, 1992, at A27.

11. Why the Courts Should Stop Delegation (and Nobody Else Can)

1. *Baker v. Carr*, 369 U.S. 186, 217 (1962); Alexander Bickel, *The Least Dangerous Branch: The Supreme Court at the Bar of Politics* (2d. ed. 1986).

2. Radio Address by President Roosevelt, March 9, 1937 (quoted in Gerald Gunther, *Constitutional Law* 123 (12th ed. 1991)).

3. E.g., Fritz W. Scharpf, "Judicial Review and the Political Question: A Functional Analysis," 75 *Yale Law Journal* 517 (1966).

4. John Hart Ely, *Democracy and Distrust* 102-03 (1980) (emphasis in original).

5. Id. at 87.

6. Id. at 131-34, 177.

7. See Jesse Choper, *Judicial Review and the National Political Process*, ch. 5 (1980). For cases, see, e.g., *Immigration and Naturalization Service v. Chadha*, 462 U.S. 919 (1983); *Bowsher v. Synar*, 478 U.S. 714 (1986); *Mistretta v. United States*, 488 U.S. 361 (1989). Quotes in id. at 372.

8. Choper, *Judicial Review* at ch. 5.

9. Lawrence C. Dodd and Richard L. Schott, *Congress and the Administrative State* 326-27 (1979) conclude that legislators' quests for personal power lead them to embrace legislative practices that undermine the institutional power of Conqress.

10. Because the power of Congress relative to that of the president has

ebbed and flowed in recent decades, one branch or the other has lacked the capacity to protect its turf effectively for long periods. See Thomas O. Sargentich, "The Contemporary Debate about Legislative-Executive Separation of Powers," 72 *Cornell Law Review* 430, 441-42 (1987) (citing J. Sundquist, *The Decline and Resurgence of Congress* (1981)). On turf battles failing to achieve the purposes of separation of powers: John Hart Ely makes the same point in the context of war powers. Ely, "Suppose Congress Wanted a War Powers Act That Worked," 88 *Columbia Law Review* 1379, 1411 (1988).

11. For a series of arguments that enforcing separation of powers does not undermine the Court's legitimacy, see John M. Farago, "Function Without Form: The Asymmetrical Hermeneutics of Jesse Choper" (Book Review), 15 *Valparaiso University Law Review* 605, 619-621 (1981).

12. Akhil Reed Amar, "The Bill of Rights as a Constitution," 100 *Yale Law Journal* 1131, 1133 (1991). "Choper nowhere signals his awareness of just how odd his ideas would have sounded to earlier generations." Id. at 1206.

13. Gordon S. Wood, *The Creation of the American Republic, 1776–1787*, at 608-10 (1969).

14. *Comments of John H. Crane on the 1990 Marketing Order*, Sept. 28, 1990 at 1-2.

15. *Comments of Oleah Wilson on 1990 Marketing Order*, Oct. 5, 1990 at 1.

16. Lawrence Gene Sager, "Fair Measure: The Legal Status of Underenforced Constitutional Norms," 91 *Harvard Law Review* 1212 (1978).

17. Jerry L. Mashaw argues: "Assuming that our current representatives in the legislature vote for laws that contain vague delegations of authority, we are presumably holding them accountable for that at the polls. How is it that we are not being represented?" Mashaw, "Prodelegation: Why Administrators Should Make Political Decisions," 1 *Journal of Law, Economics, and Organization* 81, 87 (1985).

18. "Contrary to popular belief, [fundamental issues concerning what will be required of industry] weren't settled when President Bush signed the Clean Air Act Amendments of 1990 last Nov. 15." Marianne Lavelle, "Talking about Air," *National Law Journal*, June 10, 1991 at 1. A NEXIS search for articles about the 1990 Clean Air Act retrieved over 500 newspaper articles. None of the articles addressed the question of who was actually going to make the rules, Congress or EPA.

19. 42 U.S.C. § 4332(2)(C) (1988). The provision is practically a dead-letter. Daniel R. Mandelker, *NEPA Law and Litigation* at § 8.27 (1984). Although the proposal for legislation lacks an environmental impact statement, the courts cannot stop Congress from enacting the proposal because Congress is not bound by prior statutes.

20. *Mistretta*, 488 U.S. at 372.

21. *Chadha*, 462 U.S. at 944. Many bill of rights cases state that concerns of practicality do not trump enforcement of the Constitution. *Schneider v. New Jersey*, 308 U.S. 147, 163 (1939) ("[P]ublic convenience ... does not justify an exertion of the police power which invades the free communication of information and opinion secured by the Constitution."); *Fuentes v. Shevin*, 407 U.S. 67, 90 n.22 (1972) ("Procedural due process is not intended to promote efficiency or

accommodate all possible interests . . . "); and *Frontiero v. Richardson*, 411 U.S. 677, 690 (1973) ("[T]here can be no doubt that 'administrative convenience' is not a shibboleth, the mere recitation of which dictates constitutionality.").

22. E.g., Nadine Strossen, "The Fourth Amendment in the Balance: Accurately Setting the Scales through the Least Intrusive Alternative Analysis," 63 *New York University Law Review* 1173 (1988); T. Alexander Aleinikoff, "Constitutional Law in the Age of Balancing," 96 *Yale Law Journal* 943 (1987).

23. Emphases supplied. The Court's current test of content-based infringements of protected speech, developed in *Brandenburg v. Ohio*, 395 U.S. 444 (1969), incorporates the "clear and present danger" test developed to distinguish advocacy from incitement in *Schenck v. United States*, 249 U.S. 47 (1919). See also Chapter 7.

24. See, e.g., *Hampton & Co.*, 276 U.S. at 406.

25. I am focusing on preventing future harms rather than repairing past ones because governmental immunities usually preclude recovery in damages for unconstitutional regulation. See Erwin Chemerinsky, *Federal Jurisdiction* 470-74 (1989).

26. Scalia, "A Note on the Benzene Case," 4 *Regulation*, July/August 1980, at 25, 27. To the extent that existing statutes are not immunized from delegation challenges, challenges to existing agency laws made under these statutes may be barred by statutory or equitable deadlines for filing petitions to review.

27. *Connor v. Williams*, 404 U.S. 549, 550-51 (1972).

28. For other cases allowing a period of transition, see, e.g., *Buckley v. Valeo*, 424 U.S. 1, 142-43 (1976); *Northern Pipeline Construction Co. v. Marathon Pipe Line Co.*, 458 U.S. 50, 88 (1982). Cases enforcing *Chadha's* ban on the legislative veto also illustrate court provision of a period of transition. Before Chadha, the president had used a statute that allowed him to reorganize government departments to reorganize the Equal Employment Opportunity Commission (EEOC). Because the statute contained a legislative-veto provision, employers subject to Commission orders sought to set them aside on the basis that the commission was illegally constituted. Of those courts that decided that the entire statute was invalid because Congress would not have enacted it without a legislative veto provision, a few set aside Commission orders. E.g., *EEOC v. Martin Industries, Inc.*, 581 F. Supp. 1029 (W.D. Ala.), appeal dismissed 469 U.S. 806 (1984). But most found a way to apply *Chadha* prospectively. Some decided not to apply *Chadha* retroactively to avoid unfairness to the employees who had sought EEOC relief. E.g., *EEOC v. Chrysler Corp.*, 595 F. Supp. 344 (E.D. Mich. 1984). One court held that EEOC should not be held powerless until Congress was given time to ratify its authority. *EEOC v. CBS*, 743 F.2d 969, 975-76 (2d Cir. 1984). In remanding the case to the district court, the court of appeals stayed its judgment for a period of four months, "to afford Congress an opportunity to take appropriate measures to validate the EEOC's authority over ADEA enforcement, or to otherwise clarify its requirements for enforcing that statute." 743 F.2d at 975. After Congress legislated in response, several courts held that EEOC's enforcement authority had been sufficiently ratified. E.g., *EEOC v. Westinghouse Electric Corp.*, 765 F.2d 389, 391 (3rd Cir. 1985).

29. I have attempted to summarize the principles of equity pertinent to deciding whether a court may stop short of immediately protecting a plaintiff: "The injunction should require the defendant to achieve the plaintiff's rightful position unless (a) different relief is consistent with the goals of the violated rule and (b) the case involves a factor justifying departure from the rule that was not reflected in its formulation." David Schoenbrod, "The Measure of an Injunction: A Principle To Replace Balancing the Equities and Tailoring the Remedy," 72 *Minnesota Law Review* 627, 664 (1988).

A related basis for providing a period of transition is the doctrine that courts may limit the retroactive application of new constitutional interpretations when people have reasonably relied upon the old interpretation, retroactive application would cause inequities, and barring retroactive application would not seriously jeopardize the purposes of the new constitutional interpretation. *Chevron Oil Co. v. Huson*, 404 U.S. 97, 106-07 (1971). In *James B. Beam Distilling Co. v. Georgia*, 111 S.Ct. 2439 (1991), and *Harper v. Virginia Department of Taxation*, 1993 WL 205718 (June 18, 1993), a sharply divided Court held that a new constitutional interpretation given retrospective effect in one case must be given retrospective effect in all others but left open the possibility that retrospective effect could be denied in all cases. For scholarly approval, see Richard H. Fallon, Jr. and Daniel J. Meltzer, "New Law, Non-Retroactivity, and Constitutional Remedies," 104 *Harvard Law Review* 1731, 1758-77 (1991).

30. For example, in *Weinberger v. Romero-Barcelo*, 456 U.S. 305 (1982), the Supreme Court gave the defendant, the Navy, time to apply for a permit rather than requiring it to comply immediately with a statute that forbids any pollution without a permit. The Navy had argued unsuccessfully that target practice which resulted in bombs dropping in the ocean was not pollution within the meaning of the statute, so that it did not need to apply for a permit. The Court reasoned that the statute did not prohibit pollution, just pollution without a permit. While the Court did not know whether the Navy ultimately would be given a permit, it emphasized that stopping the target practice forthwith would cause irreparable harm. The lower court, in contrast, had found that the target practice did no apparent harm to water quality, the ultimate objective of the statute. By analogy with this Supreme Court opinion, a rule promulgated under a statute that delegates unconstitutionally is not necessarily itself unconstitutional, except in the way it was issued.

31. See also Paul Gewirtz, "The Courts, Congress, and Executive Policymaking: Notes on Three Doctrines," 40 *Law and Contemporary Problems* 46, 65 (Summer 1976). (Interpreting statutes as not delegating legislative power is a "more modest and . . . preferable weapon in the service" of the constitutional principle against delegation than striking the statute down).

32. On preference for narrower grounds see *Ashwander v. Tennessee Valley Authority*, 297 U.S. 288, 345-47 (1936) (Brandeis, J., concurring).

33. *Industrial Union Department, AFL-CIO v. American Petroleum Institute*, 448 U.S. 607 (1980), is an example. See David Schoenbrod, "The Delegation Doctrine: Could the Court Give It Substance?" 83 *Michigan Law Review* 1223, 1271-72 (1985).

34. William Greider captures this shift in popular sentiment in *Who Will Tell the People?* 27–28, 407, 410 (1992). See also Morton Horowitz, *The Transformation of American Law, 1870–1960*, ch. 8 (1992).

35. See Chapter 2.

36. See, e.g., Gerald Gunther, *Constitutional Law* 432-84 (12th edition, 1991).

12. How the Courts Should Define Unconstitutional Delegation

1. *Mistretta v. United States*, 488 U.S. 361, 415 (1989) (Scalia, J., dissenting); see also Thomas O. Sargentich, "The Contemporary Debate about Legislative-Executive Separation of Powers," 72 *Cornell Law Review* 430, 456 (1987).

2. Compare *American Textile Manufacturers Institute v. Donovan*, 452 U.S. 490, 545-48 (1981) (Rehnquist, J., dissenting), and *Industrial Union Department, AFL-CIO v. American Petroleum Institute*, 448 U.S. 607, 671-88 (1980) (Rehnquist, J, concurring in the judgment) with *Smith v. Goguen*, 415 U.S. 566, 591-604 (1974) (Rehnquist, J., dissenting) and *Hampton v. Mow Sun Wong*, 426 U.S. 88, 122 (1976) (Rehnquist, J., dissenting).

3. Justices Marshall and Brennan have advocated a more vigorous application of the delegation doctrine to statutes "creating 'the danger of overbroad, unauthorized and arbitrary application of criminal sanctions in an area of [constitutionally] protected freedoms.'" *Federal Power Commission v. New England Power Co.*, 415 U.S. 345, 353 (1974) (Marshall, J., concurring) (quoting *United States v. Robel*, 389 U.S. 258, 272 (1967) (Brennan, J., concurring)). See also, e.g., *McGautha v. California*, 402 U.S. 183, 271-87 (1971) (Brennan, J., joined by Douglas and Marshall, JJ., dissenting) (deploring lack of standards for jury's decision to sentence prisoner to death as a violation of delegation doctrine).

They have, however, found few, if any, delegation problems in statutes regulating economic interests. E.g., *American Petroleum Institute*, 448 U.S. at 717-18 n.30 (Marshall, J., joined by Brennan, White, and Blackmun, JJ., dissenting); *National Cable Television Association v. United States*, 415 U.S. 336, 352-54 (1974) (Marshall, J., joined by Brennan, J., dissenting).

4. See, e.g., *Federal Energy Administration v. Algonquin SNG., Inc.*, 426 U.S. 548, 559-60 (1976) (quoting *American Power & Light Co. v. SEC*, 329 U.S. 90, 105 (1946)).

5. In *J.W. Hampton, Jr., & Co. v. United States*, 276 U.S. 394, 406 (1928), for example, the Court stated that "[i]n determining what [Congress] may do in seeking assistance from another branch, the extent and character of that assistance must be fixed according to *common sense and the inherent necessities of the governmental co-ordination.*" (Emphasis added.) Such reasoning is circular and unenlightening. See also, e.g., *American Petroleum Institute*, 448 U.S. at 676 (Rehnquist, J., concurring) (quoting "inherent necessities" language of *Hampton & Co.*).

6. On early decisions: *Wayman v. Southard*, 23 U.S. (10 Wheat.) 1 (1825). Subsequent delegation decisions failed to follow this opinion for reasons unrelated to its approach to delegation. Commentators have suggested, for exam-

ple, that its conception of federalism may have diminished its appeal. See, Note, "Rethinking the Nondelegation Doctrine," 62 *Boston University Law Review* 257, 270 (1982). On modern discussions: Judge J. Skelly Wright alludes to the possibility of basing a test of delegation on the distinction between legislative and other powers. Wright, "Beyond Discretionary Justice," 81 *Yale Law Journal* 575, 586 n.35 (1972). The Court's decisions relying, sometimes only in passing, on the "inherent powers" of the executive also hint at such an approach. See, e.g., *United States v. Curtiss-Wright Export Corp.*, 299 U.S. 304, 319-22 (1936); *Zemel v. Rusk*, 381 U.S. 1, 17 (1965).

7. See, e.g., 1 Kenneth Culp Davis, *Administrative Law* 150-51 (2d ed. 1978); Louis L. Jaffe, "An Essay on Delegation of Legislative Power" (pts. 1 and 2), 47 *Columbia Law Review* 359 and 561, 567 (1947).

8. Jaffe, 47 *Columbia Law Review* at 361. See also James O. Freedman, *Crisis and Legitimacy* 79 (1978).

9. *Webster's Third New International Dictionary* 1986 (revised ed. 1968). These characteristics of rules have basic appeal. See Leopold J. Pospisil, *Anthropology of Law* 78-81, 240-41 (1971). *Rule*, however, means different things to different people. Compare, e.g., Duncan Kennedy, "Legal Formality," 2 *Journal of Legal Studies* 351, 356 n.11 (1973) (rules as ironclad), with 1 Friedrich A. von Hayek, *Law, Legislation and Liberty* 17-19 (1973), and 2 Hayek, *Law, Legislation and Liberty* 158 n.4 (1976) (rules constantly developing but never fully developed).

The distinction between "rules" and "goals" is similar to Hart and Sacks' distinction between "rules and standards," on the one hand, and "practices and policies" on the other, except that their definition of "standard" may include "standards" that lack extrinsic meaning. Henry Melvin Hart and Albert M. Sacks, *The Legal Process: Basic Problems in the Making and Application of Law* 155-60 (tentative ed. 1958).

10. See Ronald Dworkin, "Is Law a System of Rules?" in *Essays in Legal Philosophy* 25, 52 (R. Summers ed. 1968); Hart and Sacks, *Legal Process* at 156, 1156-57, 1219, 1411, and 1415-16.

11. The distinction between law interpretation and lawmaking is different from the distinction between statutes that contain "law to apply" and statutes that do not. When a court finds that a statute contains no "law to apply," it will not review the agency action to determine whether it accords with the statute. See *Citizens to Preserve Overton Park v. Volpe*, 401 U.S. 402, 410 (1971). A court will find that a statute does contain "law to apply" as long as the statute indicates what factors or goals the agency shall consider. So, a statute that contains no "law," in my terms, can contain "law to apply."

12. 1 Hayek, *Law, Legislation and Liberty* at 83-84.

13. Ronald Dworkin, "Hard Cases," 88 *Harvard Law Review* 1057, 1058-60 (1975).

14. See sources cited in David Schoenbrod, "The Delegation Doctrine: Could the Court Give It Substance?" 83 *Michigan Law Review* 1223, 1256 n.184 (1985). As Ronald Dworkin argues, most judges and lawyers act as if they see a difference between interpretation and policymaking, and taking their opinions and

behavior at face value is plausible. Dworkin, *Law's Empire* 37-44 (1986). Although different judges may have different theories of interpretation and approach a given statute with different preconceptions (id. at 301, 304-15), they can agree that their role requires them to produce the best interpretation of the statute as enacted, not to create the best statute they can. Id. at 238, 337-38. The judge must honor the legislature's priorities (id. at 404, 451 n.11), and, in difficult cases, these priorities can be sought by scrutinizing how the legislation disposes of the easy cases. Id. at 339-40.

15. For another example, see the analysis of the Emergency Petroleum Allocation Act in *Consumers Union v. Sawhill*, 393 F. Supp. 639 (D.D.C.), aff'd. sub nom. *Consumers Union v. Zarb*, 523 F.2d 1404 (Temporary Emergency Court of Appeals 1975).

16. 5 U.S.C. § 706 (1988); *Chevron U.S.A. Inc. v. Natural Resources Defense Council, Inc.*, 467 U.S. 837 (1984).

17. See Hart and Sacks, *Legal Process* at 1302-47, 1368-80.

18. For early cases, see, e.g., *Smyth v. Ames*, 169 U.S. 466 (1898). "The most common method used to control aggregate revenue and to set maximum rates . . . begins with calculation of a firm's revenue requirements through application of the formula: $R = O + B(r)$, where R is the firm's allowed revenue requirements, O is the firm's operating expenses, B is the firm's rate base, and r is the firm's rate of return allowed on its rate base. Ernest Gellhorn and Richard J. Pierce, *Regulated Industries in a Nutshell* 97 (1982).

19. E.g., Stephen Breyer, "Analyzing Regulatory Failure: Mismatches, Less Restrictive Alternatives, and Reform," 92 *Harvard Law Review* 547, 563 (1979).

20. See Jaffe, 47 *Columbia Law Review* at 574.

21. *Smyth v. Ames*, 169 U.S. 466 (1898). On practices of states, see Louis Jaffe and Nathaniel L. Nathanson, *Administrative Law: Cases and Materials* 43 (1976) ("The controlling principle came to be known as the rule of *Smyth v. Ames* . . . ."). The definition of the value of the utilities' capital is found in 169 U.S. at 546-47. See David Schoenbrod, "Separation of Powers and the Powers That Be: The Constitutional Purposes of the Delegation Doctrine," 36 *American University Law Review* 355, 363-64 (1987), for discussion of the problems of defining the rate base.

22. *FPC v. Hope Natural Gas*, 320 U.S. 591, 602-03 (1944). See Gellhorn and Pierce, *Regulated Industries* at 112 (noting that 38 states use original-cost analysis exclusively).

23. See statutes discussed in *Bowles v. Willingham*, 321 U.S. 503 (1944); *Yakus v. United States*, 321 U.S. 414 (1944); *United States v. L. Cohen Grocery Co.*, 255 U.S. 81 (1921); *Lichter v. United States*, 334 U.S. 742 (1948). For court rulings, see, e.g., *Lichter*, 334 U.S. at 786; *Yakus*, 321 U.S. at 427. For an argument that these statutes provide no measurable standard, see Jaffe, 47 *Columbia Law Review* at 568-70.

24. *Yakus*, 321 U.S. at 423.

25. John L. FitzGerald, *Congress and the Separation of Powers* 35-43 (1986).

26. Laurence H. Tribe states the widely accepted view that the provisions of Article II, section 1 "that '[t]he executive Power shall be vested in a Presi-

dent' . . . cannot be read as mere shorthand" for the specific enumerations that follow. Tribe, *American Constitutional Law* 210 (2d ed. 1988). He points out that the president has conducted extensive military operations without declarations of war and has entered into agreements with other nations without Senate approvals. Whether these activities can be justified somehow under any of the Article II enumerated powers, established case law agrees with the view that executive powers go beyond those enumerated powers. See, e.g., *Curtiss-Wright Export Corp.*, 299 U.S. at 320; *Myers v. United States*, 272 U.S. 52, 118 (1926).

For criticism of this broad construction, see, e.g., John Hart Ely, *War and Responsibility: Constitutional Lessons of Vietnam and Its Aftermath* (1993).

27. E.g., Cass R. Sunstein, *After the Rights Revolution: Reconceiving the Regulatory State* 14-16 (1990).

28. U.S. Constitution art. II, § 1, cl. 1; § 2, cl. 1. See *Marbury v. Madison*, 5 U.S. (1 Cranch) 137 (1803).

29. See, e.g., *United States v. Midwest Oil Co.*, 236 U.S. 459, 474 (1915). Louis Jaffe writes, "Powers granted to manage government property could not be attacked as an abdication of the 'law-making' function." Jaffe, 47 *Columbia Law Review* at 376. Many state courts find that the delegation doctrine does not apply to the management of public funds on the theory that such management is "proprietary." See Stephen Koslow, "Standardless Administrative Adjudication," 22 *Administrative Law Review* 407, 417-18 (1970).

30. 415 U.S. 336, 343 (1974).

31. Since then, courts have held that Congress can delegate the power to tax. *Skinner v. Mid-America Pipeline Co.*, 490 U.S. 212 (1989).

32. 2 Hayek, *Law, Legislation and Liberty* at 35-38. Hayek declines to argue against delegation. Hayek, *The Constitution of Liberty* 211-12 (1960).

33. On family planning clinics, see *Rust v. Sullivan*, 111 S. Ct. 1759 (1991). On artists, see *Culture Wars: Documents from Recent Controversies in the Arts* 331–63 (Richard Boulton, ed. 1992). (Senator Helms has failed to get a ban on funding "obscene" art through the Article I process but has sometimes achieved the same result by pressuring the agency involved.) On regulatory use of government property, see Kathleen M. Sullivan, "Unconstitutional Conditions," 102 *Harvard Law Review* 1413 (1989).

34. For a discussion of the scope of that discretion, see David Schoenbrod, Angus Macbeth, David I. Levine, and David J. Jung, *Remedies: Public and Private* ch. 2 (1990).

35. The courts will generally honor statutes that expressly mandate specific remedies for specific statutory laws, so that the courts and Congress may be said to have concurrent power over remedies. E.g., *Hecht Co. v. Bowles*, 321 U.S. 321 (1944).

36. "Federal courts cannot reach out to award remedies when the Constitution or laws of the United States do not support a cause of action." *Franklin v. Gwinnett Public Schools*, 112 S. Ct. 1028, 1037 (1992).

37. For a more extended discussion, see David Schoenbrod, "The Measure of an Injunction: A Principle to Replace Balancing the Equities and Tailoring the

Remedy," 72 *Minnesota Law Review* 627 (1988). Political accountability is discussed id. at 658-63.

38. See, e.g., *Youngstown Sheet and Tube Co. v. Sawyer*, 343 U.S. 579 (1952).

39. Michael Wells and Walter Hellerstein, "The Governmental-Proprietary Distinction in Constitutional Law," 66 *Virginia Law Review* 1073 (1980). Wells and Hellerstein show that, while the distinction is used in many constitutional contexts (id. at 1073–74 n.9), it has caused confusion because courts often fail to recognize that it serves different purposes in these different contexts. They contend that courts will continue to use the distinction and can avoid confusion by specifying the purposes of the distinction in the context at hand. Id. at 1136. The purpose of the distinction in the delegation context is to apply the Constitution's procedural protections of liberty to exercises of government power which could threaten liberty.

40. See Jaffe, 47 *Columbia Law Review* at 577.

41. Richard B. Stewart, "The Reformation of American Administrative Law," 88 *Harvard Law Review* 1667, 1676-88, 1809-10 (1975).

42. Antonin Scalia, "A Note on the Benzene Case," 4 *Regulation* 25, 28 (July/Aug. 1980) (emphasis in original). Judge Carl McGowan wrote that such broad delegations lead to the danger of an "imperial" judiciary. McGowan, "Congress, Court, and Control of Delegated Power," 77 *Columbia Law Review* 1119, 1120 (1977).

13. America Is No Exception

1. Stephen Skowronek, *Building a New American State: The Expansion of National Administrative Capacities, 1877–1920,* at 3 (1982); Dorothy Ross, *The Origins of American Social Science* ch. 2 (1991).

2. Gordon S. Wood, *The Creation of the American Republic, 1776–1787,* at 409-13 (1969).

3. G.K. Chesterton, *What's Wrong with the World,* pt. I, ch. 5 (1910).

Index

Abortion counseling controversy, 15–16
Accountability: avoided through delegation, 8–9, 9–12, 14, 17, 55–56, 73, 88–94, 99, 157–58, 159; as goal of legislative process, 14, 27–29, 45, 99, 183, 183–84, 245n9; loss of, rationalized by criticizing democracy, 37, 133–34; loss of, rationalized by legislative oversight, 12, 14, 41, 99–105; loss of, rationalized by presidential oversight, 105–06; loss of, rationalized by election of legislators, 170–73. *See also* Hard choices; Responsibility shifting
Ackerman, Bruce, 160–64
Ackerman, Bruce, and William Hassler, 74–75, 123–25
Adams, John, 3, 27
Administrative Procedure Act, 51, 112–13, 121–22, 179
Agencies: dependent, 37, 83; independent, 32, 33, 37, 83. *See also* Expertise of agencies; Insulation of agencies.
Agricultural Adjustment Act (AAA), 37–38, 39, 49–50
Agricultural marketing orders, 4, 40, 49–50, 88, 140; unnecessary for orderly markets, 140–42; unnecessary to subsidize growers, 146–47
Agriculture, Department of. *See* Agricultural marketing orders; Navel orange marketing order
Alien Act of *1798*, 30
Antifederalists, 27, 164
Arizona v. California, 42–43
Arnold, R. Douglas, 89–90, 226–27n23, 231n21
Arrow, Kenneth, 131–32
Asbestos removal, 138–39

Balanced Budget Amendment proposal, 163
Barbar, Satorios, 206n13

"Big Green" referendum, 77
Block, John, 51, 52
Bodine, Ralph, 8
Boxer, Barbara, 7
Brennan, William, 211n62
Brig Aurora, Cargo of, v. United States, 30–31, 33
Broad delegation, 37–40, 43, 48, 49–57, 58, 60
Brookings Institution, 142
Burger, Warren, 44
Bush, George, 95, 230n50
Buttfield v. Stranahan, 208–09n27

Campaign contributions, 8, 19, 82, 94–95, 203n10
Cardozo, Benjamin, 39, 210n49
Carter, James, 70, 89
Casework: advantage to incumbents of, 85, 231n21; alternatives to, 86, 150–51, increasing opportunities for, as reason for delegation, 93–95, 96
Chadha v. Immigration and Naturalization Service, 44, 46, 102, 173
Chesterton, G. K., 196
Chevron U.S.A. Inc. v. Natural Resources Defense Council, 105
Choper, Jesse, 167–69
Citizens to Preserve Overton Park v. Volpe, 115–16
Clean Air Act, 58–81, amendments of *1965*, 59; amendments of *1967*, 59–60; amendments of *1970*; 48, 60–81, 123–24, 150, 183; amendments of *1977*, 71–72, 80, 123–25; amendments of *1990*, 72, 77, 80–81, 125; and delegation, 90–93, 95, 123–25, 136–37, 138, 144, 146, 147–51; and hard choices, 63–67, 73–74, 170–71; and airborne lead, 67, 70, 78; responsibility shifting in, 103–04, 110; statutory laws in, 17, 73, 121, 222–23n64
Coelho, Tony L., 8